The Wan

From the streets of Bristol to the Cambodian jungle.

GREG LYNN

Dedication

To everybody else who has strolled off the mainstream path and can't find their way back.

Contents

Authors' note

Everything that your about to read is a true-life account of what occurred (at least, to the best of my memory) Although, for the sake of greater clarity the order of events within chapters was changed slightly. I have used the real names of all the characters encountered with the exception of two people. With others, I decided it would be best if they were to remain nameless.

The biggest challenge lay in doing a total memory recall of the past decade. The conversations that I had with people would have to be described in the richest of detail as it's the dialogue that tells the story. So to jog my memory I went through multiple google street view images of where I was at the time. Firstly, the memory of the smell of a place would come which would first bring back the setting. That could be the rotting garbage of Mumbai or the thick sulphur like air of Belgrade. Then the daily occurrences would come flooding back followed by actions and audible dialogue. And having that pin-point accuracy of detail was essential. There wouldn't be much point in writing about it if that wasn't the case.

Inevitably, my account got compared to Jack Kerouac's 1957 title 'On the Road'. That would be an arrogant comparison to draw for myself. But what I have attempted to give you is a raw, energetic and entertaining unique tale. One of the less obvious themes of the book is about solving problems and overcoming difficulties. In this period of huge uncertainty, it's time that a little positivity was injected. By reading this I thank you for your investment with your time. (By far your most valuable commodity).

G J Lynn. Bristol, May 2020

Prologue
Amsterdam Christmas eve
2005

W hen you're young you think you're invincible, but this was an

unprecedented situation to be in and one that my 24-year-old brain was having difficulty in fathoming. There was me walking through the streets of Amsterdam on a cold Christmas Eve night and contemplating the fact that I would have to be sleeping rough that night; something I'd never done before nor had dreamed of previously. I'd recently been diagnosed with severe depression and subsequently ran away (quite literally) after a family feud. It had been a troublesome year. My once young, upwardly mobile life was over after filing for bankruptcy. Therefore, I'd had to move back into the family home. I'd journeyed by train to Prague first for god knows why, then headed back over to Holland, armed with the vague notion of finding work. Fat chance. It didn't take me long to realise that that wasn't going to happen. Within ten days, the money had run out.

I sought the assistance of a charity for tourists who had loaned me the money for a bus ticket back, but that wouldn't be leaving for a few days

1

what with it being over the Christmas period. There was nothing left to do but keep my head down and bide my time until then. Sleeping directly on the streets in the city centre was unquestionably a dangerous thing to do. A more sensible strategy seemed to be to head out of town and find a more rural setting – a woods or a small park obstructed from the main view, maybe.

But no. As I roamed, all there was to be seen was street after street of the pretty chocolate box terraced houses that ran parallel with the canals running through the centre. There was just *nowhere*. It was getting late. The temperature was sub-zero, and to cap it all snow was falling. Gradually, the surroundings morphed into suburbia. An aircraft up above was on its final approach. I must be near Schiphol airport, in the South West of the city.

Eventually, I found what I was looking for: a grassy area with a cluster of trees. That would keep the view obscured. With that, I dumped my worldly possessions down, made a ground layer out of clothes, then tied a sweater around my head to form a bandana. This act officially made me a vagrant. It was minus four, and I didn't have a sleeping bag. If I were to fall asleep, then I might not be waking up again. Now when it's cold like that you don't just shiver; you shake so hard that you think your bones are going to break. There was no use in self-pity; I only had myself to blame. In a situation like that, survival becomes a mental as much a physical battle.

What a soft life it had been previously: working in an office, always having money, dreams and ambition, but few responsibilities yet. Christmas before had always been a happy time, which I looked forward. The cold and harsh realities had been yet to hit, but life has a habit of biting you on the arse right when you don't want it.

The bleak landscape wasn't providing much inspiration. The dark night wasn't getting any lighter. This night seemed like it was never going to end. I continued to shake in a near-catatonic state.

Keep shaking. If you keep on shaking, that means you're still alive.

THE WANDERER

******

I opened my eyes to see that dawn had broken. No, this wasn't a nightmare. It was real. I can't have been sleeping for longer than an hour – but my hands had turned blue. A few dog walkers strolled past and frowned. Sometime later the noise of a car approached. Oh, fuck, it was the police.

"Explanation?" the officer asked, shaking his head while looking down at me.

I mumbled a truncated version of events.

"….Hmm….maybe you come down the station for some coffee with us."

His colleague even carried my suitcase to the car. How typically Dutch liberal-minded. We commenced the drive to the station. Once there, we sat down at the desk for the informal chat.

"Some members of the public called us. They were worried about you. How long had you been out there?"

"Just one night."

"And you were in a bad place to be sleeping. We get a lot of trouble with the Moroccans around there….and I'm not just saying that because they're Moroccan", he added thoughtfully.

"Next time you should sleep in the city centre. It's where we can keep an eye on people. Though I'm not recommending you do that, of course."

"Is it okay to get another coffee?" I asked while mulling this over.

"Of course, it's Holland!"

I helped myself to the third cup of the morning while popping in an ample amount of sugar — anything for calories.

"Hey, you want some Schnitzel? Come on; it's Christmas".

3

This wasn't the scene I'd expected: sat down with the officers having an impromptu pick-nick with them. Phone calls were made. It was arranged that I would be spending the next two days in the Salvation Army. They'd magically been able to find me a bed there and would also be giving me a lift over. I ended up going full circle, doing the 7 miles right back to the Damrak where this transient journey had begun. My first appointment was to be with the duty social worker. He eyed me in a friendly but authoritative manner.

"Sleeping rough in your own country is bad enough, but in another one? And when you don't know the area."

It was a statement that I was to do well to remember....

He asked me the gently probing questions. Why had I left the UK, and how did I end up in Holland? What were my plans now?

"Hmm...well it seems like you still have some spirit left. They don't" he said, pointing to the collection of street dwellers camped out in the lounge area, staring at nothing in particular.

"What sort of people do you get here?" I asked.

"All sorts. Drug addicts, alcoholics, the mentally ill, criminals. Some of them are just downright bad people. But we've also had those who used to be businessmen, teachers and doctors. I've even had one guy who used to be a psychiatrist. He can't even figure out himself", he shook his head.

"Well, Greg, I wish you a pleasant stay here. Let the staff know if you need anything and good luck on the return to your home country."

I adopted the strategy of keeping myself to myself. Straight away, I stuck out as somebody who wasn't used to being in such surroundings. For a start, I was a foreigner who was too fresh and evidently new to this business. In places like this that can make you a target. I certainly hadn't been expecting much in the way of dinner. Maybe some stew and a bit of bread. But no: we were served up with roast duck and all the trimmings and all the chocolate that you could shove down your throat. Honestly, your mum couldn't have done any better. It was a slightly surreal experience, sat down with the bums who had half their teeth missing but still had the good grace to wear Christmas hats.

By Boxing Day, I had mustered up a little conversation with them.

"Take some bread with you. You're going to be doing a lot of walking. Life on the street, it's tough you know", one of them briefed.

He was right. Over the years, I was to be doing *a lot* of walking, probably racking up thousands of miles in total. I retired to bed with those thoughts in mind. The staff had promised a 3 am wake up call for me to catch the 7 am bus out of Amstel coach station. It was to be another long walk over there. The staff gave me some bread to take with me.

What followed was an uneventful and lengthy journey to Victoria coach station. From there on saw me fiddling my way back to my hometown of Slough. I arrived in the dead of night and bunked down for a couple of days in a garage. More shivering in the cold on a hard, concrete floor. Now it was time to go and face the music. Then Thames Valley police took me off the missing person's list. I'd run away. That was 14 years ago. And guess what? I'm still running....

Introduction

And so life was. Your past dictates your

future. If you'd informed me earlier that I'd be living in a concrete shed underneath a flyover in Bristol in my late thirties, then I may have been a tad disappointed.

Holland turned out to be the first country that I'd be sleeping rough in. It was to trigger the start of a later 7-year cycle which would see me doing the same thing in a further ten different nations. Yes, you read that correctly. I know, that's ridiculous. Okay, I'm going to name them now in geographical order: Holland once again, Belgium, Germany, Austria, Hungary, Serbia, Italy, and Sicily, Spain (apparently, that one doesn't count; we've all done that) Thailand, Cambodia and Malaysia. You name it; I'd slept there. Wherever there seemed to be suitable shelter at the time, I'd grab a spot. A brief example being an underground cellar in Serbia, a derelict building in Kuala Lumpur and a slightly hairy two weeks spent in the Cambodian jungle (due in cobra mating season).

My personal foibles and a mix of social and economic factors led me to be in a less than favourable situation. When getting bored of being stuck in line at a Bristol soup run, I'd pack my rucksack, armed with only the bare necessities, a one-way ticket and just a few hundred pounds in spending money, in search of excitement and adventure, being gone for many months at a time. Wherever I lay, my head was to be my home. That could be underneath a bridge, in a forest or a derelict building. Like many people, I became entrenched in the cycle of homelessness, accepting it as a way of life. You see, after the initial shock, you get used to it very quickly. Sadly, this became the norm. With little chance of getting sufficiently housed, I thought it would be far more exciting if the *whole world* became my home.

Surprisingly, I wasn't alone, and I was to discover a distinct and curious breed of people who'll I'll term as being the 'international homeless'. This story isn't just about me. That would have been a very self-absorbed exercise. But it also includes the stories of the many people that I met along the way. I tell their story too.

I became reduced to living off my wits while I clocked up thousands of miles overland. After every trick in the book was used up, I re-wrote the book, filled with a bunch of new tricks. When we're are truly up against it can often be when we're at our most creative and resourceful and find out about things within us that we never even knew existed. Few of us ever get to achieve our full potential or find out what we're really made of until we get placed in the most extreme situations.

In the more productive times, I managed to (at least partly) learn two different languages and qualified as a TEFL teacher, though I was always against getting a job in this due to the industry's notoriously lousy reputation.

When arriving back in the UK, I became forced into the world of squatting commercial buildings. Yes, this is often done as a last resort and not through some lifestyle choice. If that's set off a load of negative connotations in your head, you'd be partly justified (but only slightly). In every society, there exists an underbelly. It's full of colourful characters and strange goings-on. Many people don't know that it exists. So, throughout this, I attempt to lift the lid.

Today, I write this inside what I'll pretentiously describe as my 'matured bachelor squat'. Nope, no wild parties with crustie dreadlocked girls going on here; I'll leave that for the younguns. There was no chance of getting housed in this area seeing as I'm 'not priority'. So, I occupied one of their disused buildings. Yes, they know I'm here (partly because I told them), but they don't seem to be in the slightest bit concerned.

A nice thick padlock separates me from the rest of the world. After moving in here on a cold January night, I first got the place insulated out in thick cardboard, then covered it in rugs and carpet, and then procured a king-size mattress from the street. I did that classic squat thing of covering the walls in blankets. In the Winter I would have the heater on full blast, then get myself energised in the morning by slurping through 3 cups of coffee. We've even got wi-fi here now. Some would say that I'm living the bohemian dream. Me? I'd say that you could bring a girl back, but she'd have to be pretty adventurous.

My day starts probably in the same way that yours does: by waking up and worrying about money. Then I get up and go off to work by working as a builder's labourer in the precarious gig economy. Though, I only managed to gross £10,000 this financial year. Unfortunately, not enough to dig me out of a hole. So, I became part of the new breed of *working-class* tramp.

On my days when I'm not working the first port of call is to a place adjacent where I go for a shower. It's also where I go to register to vote on an NFA basis to appear on the 'other electorates' list. You can't do it on-line like ordinary people. Thankfully, now I think this nomad is heading towards retirement. To quote a friend of mine, "*people like us die why we're 47, and by the time we hit 40, we're going to be dead inside already*". So, what does the future hold now? That's hard to say. Like anything, expect the unexpected.

But for now, let me take you back to where my life on the road began. Between us, we'll try to make sense of the unconventional and at times, insane journey. At the very least, it should give you a giggle.

Chapter 1

Black sheep of the world unite

Bristol 2012

Great Britain at the tail end of 2012 was a fairly grim place to be.

The financial crash of 2008 has sent shock waves across the globe and transmitted things into political turmoil. I, myself, hadn't been too bothered about the and so-called 'credit crunch' as I'd binged on that in my younger days when any muppet could walk into a bank and get a same day loan wired into their account. The general election two years previously had failed to come up with a decisive vote, meaning that we were left with a Conservative/Liberal Democrat coalition government that was met with widespread unpopularity.

Austerity had become the new buzz word which resulted in savage cuts right across the board – and in particular to housing. Political activism and civil unrest had been rife the previous year and seen the national riots commencing in North London and spreading right across the country. That led to the Occupy movement, which was my baptism of fire on arrival to Bristol the previous Autumn. Two months spent on College green in the city centre amidst the mud, the blood and the flying fingers. Socially this may have been a great event, bringing lots of different people together, though politically it failed. Many people viewed it as just a bunch of hippies sat around in a green space. It was hard to defend that. If you don't have a clear objective, then you are never going to reach your purpose.

Prior to all this, most of my 20's had been spent doing an awful lot of writing. Writing manuscript after manuscript, being stuck in my room with a bunch of debauched characters. Four books written but all rejected by the publishing houses. On top of that, I had a 'sort of' job writing for the dance music/club industry. They'd get me to interview DJ's and write articles in order to promote their nights. For this, I was paid £50 a piece, plus the associated perks of getting VIP guestlist to any club night that I wanted. Though it hardly warranted calling yourself a professional writer. I combined this with a series of numb-nut occupations such as postman and night security guard (I took full advantage of the jobs inactivity by penning a whole first draft on that security desk)

I'd permanently relocated out of the South-East, spending first a year by the sea in Bournemouth, then deciding to settle in Bristol. I'd never been to the city before arriving and didn't know a soul there. But a neighbour had advised that it would be an ideal place for me. It had been easy to make friends and forge links as everyone in the city seemed to know each other. There was a genuine sense of openness and community there, which I had never experienced before, growing up in a downbeat town where the locals were raw and harsh. It was an eye-opener seeing strangers actually talk to each other compared to being in cold, ruthless London.

THE WANDERER

I got housed in a bedsit in the St Pauls district. The area had managed to shake off its notorious reputation and was now vastly improved. Though it still had a bit of an edge to it. Since arriving, I'd only been able to pick up casual labour. When claiming £267 a month housing benefit, it seemed safer to stay on the dole to keep a roof over one's head than risk going into the precarious economy where you didn't know if you were going to be working from 1 week to the next. So, this was me relegated to the underclass - what the government referred to as 'the great scroungers of society'.

Things hadn't been going well over the past few months; I'd lost all sense of direction. My personal appearance had gone west, and people were understandably beginning to avoid my company. My old friend, the deep black pit of depression appeared and welcomed me back with open arms. I gratefully accepted and sank right back into it. Some days I wouldn't even bother to get out of bed. It had been an exceptionally wet year and seemed to rain almost every day.

Meanwhile, bed lice and rats had overtaken the house. Yes, it was that bad. A few years later the landlord was convicted by the magistrates and fined £38,000 for providing substandard accommodation and renting out properties without a license. Downstairs my neighbour was indulging in solvent abuse whilst living waste high in the litter. Listening to him giggling away to himself was making me feel mad by association.

This was a truly pathetic experience to be eking out, and I had to be doing something about it before I sank any further into the abysses. "Snap out of it, snap out of it!" part of my consciousness was firmly yelling at me. A few days prior, I had been casually discussing the employment situation with somebody at a free food place.

"You want to go to Germany, broth. There's loads of work out there", he said before shoving some bourbon biscuits into his mouth.

Germany? I'd never thought about that one.....

GREG LYNN

That trigger was enough for me to renew my passport and do a bit of research. Berlin seemed like the obvious target. I didn't know much about the place, but from scanning the guide books, it appeared amazing. News of my plans was met with queries about my sanity from various associates.

"But you don't speak any German."

"It's going to be Wintertime; you'll freeze to death".

"You'll just be even more fucked over there than you are here".

My neighbour in the house (the non-solvent abusing one) was more receptive.

"Listen, mate, stay here, and you're just going to rot. We're all slowly dying in this house".

"But what about money?"

"Oh, don't worry about money when you're travelling, because something always comes along. You wanna try hitchhiking; it's got me all over the place".

"Stay here, and I think you know how things are going to turn out, go travelling, and anything could happen."

"Anything could happen…" I quietly murmured.

That was the bit of encouragement that I needed.

The final spur came after getting back one day and receiving a call from the agency, informing me that I'd been binned after the first day off some nonsense factory job.

"Well, it is quite physical…." She said in an irksome, condescending tone.

The largest of the rats scuttled in to mark the occasion. It was the one I'd named Jimmy. I looked at Jimmy and Jimmy looked back at me with his big evil eyes as if to say

"Greg, what the fuck are you still doing in my house?"

"Okay, Jimmy. You win…"

It was only a short walk down to the bus station.

"I need a ticket departing for Berlin in two weeks. Your best price, please".

"Are you sure? It's a 23-hour journey", the guy at the desk asked, puzzled.

"Good!"

"Single or return?"

"Single", I answered defiantly.

"Okay, as you wish. We'll put you on the 09.00 National Express to London Victoria. Change there for the 14.00 Euroline service direct to Berlin. And please remember it is a long trip, sir".

Had I just said that? The words felt like they were coming from someone else.

"That will be £61.00, please. That's a special offer price".

The words hadn't come from someone else. He presented me with the ticket showing my name and the destination: Berlin. Within an instant, an entire phycological shift had occurred. That afternoon had seemed like being trapped in a dead-end existence forever. Now a whole myriad of possibilities opened up. Two weeks. There was no time to waste. I got on the phone and informed all relevant parties of my imminent departure. Nobody had thought I was serious. Now they were surprised.

"But you don't speak any German…."

"How long are you going to be away for?" was the most frequently asked question.

"A good while. Don't expect to see me back any time soon".

The previous listlessness disappeared. Now a rush of excitement and a sense of liberation greeted me in the morning as I rose. Money was the first priority. I'd managed to hustle a few hundred pounds together and felt more confident. But in reality, this was going to be on a dole cheque and a prayer. The last weekend was spent saying goodbye to family. There was many a shaking head and sombre tone.

"So, what was my plan then?"

There wasn't one. This venture was to be chartering unknown waters. Could there be a plan? Then there were practical matters like storing my stuff and buying things like rucksacks and boots. 350 Euros were deposited into a travel money account, leaving 100 Euros in cash to arrive on. The project gained a modicum of respectability.

Rather annoyingly, I was more popular than I thought. There were a good few people who wanted to meet up for a farewell drink, but this was digging into precious preparation time. After returning from the pub on Thursday night, there were only a couple of hours left to pack and a get a good night's sleep. That's one good thing about having nothing, you've got nothing to lose.

The morning of Friday 16th November was a cold and foggy one. I dragged my possessions down the stairs, whistling a song which drowned out the sound of the guy downstairs being violently sick. His insides were now totally rotten from all that inhaled lighter fluid. There was one last whiff off the stench of vomit, then the door of 6 Cairns Crescent was shut behind me for the last time. From now on the *road* was to be my home. For better or worse, richer or poorer, in sickness and in health. Armed with a 'devil may care' attitude, I set off.

"What's up, broth? You wanna a cab? ", a West Indian man called out. I shook my head.

The warmth of the bus station was inviting.

"Now, now Mr Lynn, you've got a long journey ahead of you. Let me take your bags for you, sir".

And I left Bristol courtesy of Michael, the camp coach driver with excellent customer service skills. I looked down at the bearpit underpass feeling a twinge of sadness. Don't know why; that place has been the ruin of many a poor boy. On our approach into London, something from a distance yanked my attention into focus. It was St Mary's church, the place where I was christened. It almost seemed like it was waiving a solemn goodbye to me.

There were a few hours to kill in a down at heel café above Victoria station where I sat, for some reason feeling like a character out of an Irvine Welsh novel. The bus that was to be my home for the next 17 hours looked old and uncomfortable. The passengers marched on disgruntled. After various passenger/coach staff heated arguments, the bus set off. At Folkstone, the formalities began when the French police came on board to do the document check.

"Merci, monsieur".

"Merci".

That was it. I'd officially left the country. There was a loud clanking as the bus drove on to Le shuttle. There was an eerier low noise as it seemed to take an age to reach the back. Mild panic set in. That's it; you've gone and done it now. What was I doing? This was madness of the highest order – leaving the country with only 450 Euros and no work prospects.

"*Just relax, we'll drive*!" the words on a screen in the train helpfully flickered. The only indication that we were deep below the English Channel was the fact that my ears popped due to the change in pressure. Another few loud clanks and the doors opened. The bus drove seamlessly onto the motorway and into inter-continental Europe as if by magic.

Night time fell, and we crawled through the Friday night traffic of Brussels.

"Before I leave, I've got to say that honestly, I've never been on a bus that's had such interesting passengers as this one", a lady commented before alighting, looking almost bewildered.

In place of the departing customers, a new group got on.

"Yo, man, you fancy some company?" an African American man inquired.

"Well, you're not quite the pretty French girl that was sitting next to me previously, but sure; be my guest".

    We struck up a travelling camaraderie and swapped US/UK comparisons. He was about halfway through his journeying, whereas I was starting mine.

"Have you booked a place to stay in Berlin yet?" he asked.

"No. I haven't planned that far ahead yet. I was thinking about Mitte as it's the most central".

"Hmm… I've heard great things about Kreuzberg. It's where all the cool people hang out. You know, like all the artists and musicians and stuff".

"Oh yeah? Sounds right up my street. Let's make Kreuzberg the target destination then".

"I can't wait to get to Berlin, man. I've heard so many cool things about this city. You know what I love about travelling you never quite know where you're going to end up. That's why I don't bother making plans", he enthused.

    But that was enough enthusiasm for me for one day. Everyone's mobile phones started pinging, indicating that they'd just switched over to another country's service provider: T-Mobile. We were now in the most powerful nation in Europe in ze Deutschland. I fell fast asleep.

    When I awoke, daylight was breaking, and there was the first dusting of snow. We pulled into a service station. Yup, the German cold was something harsh. I had a quick go at picking up the language by listening to what was being said. Morgen meant a morning greeting. Danke must mean thanks. Then I was to learn that even though you don't understand the language, you can tell what they're going on about as things follow the same routine as any other checkout. She was obviously asking me if I had a Clubcard.

"Nein", I smiled.

That was the first most rudimentary exchange, but it worked.

The journey came to a long and anticlimactic stop at the West Bahnhof. I followed the American to a telephone kiosk and handed him my guidebook for him to inquire about accommodation.

"She said that one is 16 Euro a night which seems kinda expensive".

That didn't seem too bad to me.

"But this one is 10 euro a night. Let's give this one a shot".

10 euro a night? That was less than £8! It looked like I'd come to the right city.

"Yup, they've got beds free. We gotta go to Görlitzer Bahnhof."

The first thing that struck me about Berlin was how unhurried and relaxed it was. Being the capital, I'd expected it to be all hustle and bustle like London is. Even the U-Bahn itself was uncrowded and ran smoothly all the way there. Soon we alighted in the district of Kreuzberg, and that came as a surprise too. From what I'd seen of Germany before it had been all modern, glitzy and sparkling clean. But this felt like a journey to back behind the iron curtain. The elevated U-Bahn tracks lined the whole length of the road. Trains rumbled along it every few minutes. The district had a very raw and gritty vibe to it, an almost moody feel.

We can't have been far from where the Berlin wall once stood. The entrance to the hostel wasn't obvious. It had a long walk up a staircase and had what the guide book described as a seedy feel. But inside there was a warm and homely vibe. Almost inevitably, the receptionist had dyed green hair and piercings. Bohemian was perhaps the best word to describe it. Compared to where I'd been living for the past year, this place was a 5-star hotel.

"Check-in is officially two o'clock, so you won't be able to access your room until then – but you're welcome to get a shower".

"That's fine. I think we'll go and hit the city. I saw a decent waffle place around the corner", the New Yorker stated. (I still hadn't learnt his name yet.) Besides, in backpacker hostels nobody ever remembers your name, it's all about your nationality. So, he just referred to me as "English".

We stopped first at a small Turkish restaurant. The sort of place I'd get a takeaway from on payday but would feature in most traveller's budget list. I guzzled down a small cup of super-strength Turkish black coffee while lunch was busy cooking itself on a skewer. The caffeine shot hit my stomach and took me straight back to alertness. After stopping by the waffle place, we went for a general scope around the area. All most every wall seemed to be covered in colourful graffiti. On a building above was a striking mural of two rats, one of them holding the other one upside down. A building to the right opened its doors for the first time, and a group of punks gathered round looking enthusiastically moody. Suddenly a thin man with long blonde hair, a super pale complexion and piercing blue eyes dashed up and began talking excitably in German.

"Do you speak English?" the New Yorker frowned.

"Oh, English, okay."

He began his preach, which made even less sense.

"I have the answer......I have the great spiritual answer that you have been looking for on your divine journey", he held out a card.

"For just the price of 2 euros, I can give you that answer", he pushed out the card in expectation.

"Sir, I'm sorry to say I've got no idea what you're talking about".

"Mental instability combined with trying to finance his smack habit", I remarked.

And with that, we trudged back off to headquarters.

My travelling companion retired to bed. But for me, sleep wasn't on order. Instead, I was busy e-mailing people, informing them that yes, I *had* made it over here and no, the small amount of money I'd acquired hadn't been blown on Southmead hookers instead.

A group of people had gathered by the stairwell entrance that served as the places smoking area, always where the cool kids hang out. Let's go and mingle.

"Hey man, where are you from?"

The line of questioning in a hostel always goes the same way:

"Where are you from?"

"England"

"Which city in England?"

"Bristol – though I was born near London".

Cue tenuous link to the place

"Oh wow, my second cousin fiancé lives there".

"How long have you been in Berlin?"

And so on.

"We're heading out to a bar in a second. Do you fancy joining us? An Israeli man about my age asked.

"Sure, why not".

I'd betted on an early night this evening to give myself the gentle warm-up for arrival. But it appeared this weekend had other plans in store. By now the New Yorker had earned himself the nickname of "Yoga man" (or Yogi) for short) since he was a yoga instructor.

"Oh no, he's touching his toes! Quick, get ready!" someone cried as we left the building.

We strolled out into the dark night and cold air. I was also accompanied by a young Brazilian Romeo and a French dude who seemed to get a little paranoid and upset about everything. The Israeli had been in the city a while, so gave me the rundown of the dos and don'ts.

"The number one most important thing is to not look like a tourist. Last night we were at a party and guess what? We were the only foreigners there. Everyone else was a local. It was great!"

"We need to get a beer each first. All these liquor stores you see here, they're called "spätkaufs", and best of all, they're usually open all night. That's what I love about Berlin; it's truly a 24-hour city", he enthused.

Apparently, a bottle of "Berliner" was the best one to go for as it displayed the city's emblem: a brown bear. I took a sip from the big brown bottle. It tasted cool and herbily. We popped into a kebab shop for nourishment. The meat actually contained real lamb.

"This bar here, I think", he said, pointing to a busy establishment that looked buzzing.

I offered to get the drinks in.

"Vier bier, bitte", I requested to the barman.

He stared back at me with the look of being insulted.

"It's okay; I speak English!"

Perhaps it was a little too early to try speaking in their native tongue. I returned to the group.

"So, you upped and left just like that?" they asked after I'd given my story.

"More or less. There didn't seem like there was much to be sticking around for".

There was a pause for a moment while they mulled this over.

"That's pretty much what I did as well when I was in Tel Aviv. I had a feeling......a feeling that things needed to be different somehow".

The others confessed to being in the same position.

"No way. My mother called me mad for leaving too!"

".... And all my friends called me mad when I told them."

".... And my friends too".

"But now we're here. And what do you think they're all doing? Probably still stuck in their boring lives", I declared.

That prediction called for a collective cheer and raising of glasses around the table.

We'd escaped.

I was then left to chat alone with the French kiddie as the other two got up and tried to impress some local ladies. He wasn't in such a jocular mood himself; he kept on reciting stories about his self-harming episodes. He then confirmed this by showing me the scars. All I could do was lend an understanding ear.

Fortunately, less than an hour later, it was decided that we should find out where the proper party was. We stepped outside, then headed down Warschauer Strasse, the road that led into a bridge, which took us over the river Spree.

"Can you feel that?" the Israeli murmured.

"What's that?" I asked.

"We're now crossing over from West to East. You can almost feel the drop-in pressure. Now we're heading into the old East Berlin", he added enigmatically.

We'd moved into the district of Friedrichshain, the other major party district, but with a slightly rawer feel.

"This is the thing about parties here; everything takes place inside. It won't be obvious when we're walking down the street; you've got to go and look for it", the Israeli advised again.

We stumbled across something that seemed like a mix between an underground club, a house party and a squat party. Dark Techno music thumped through the building and echoed across the high walls. An authentically punk-looking girl with long dark hair stood in the corner smoking a joint. There was hardly any lighting, just the odd flash of a strobe light. That was it; I'd found my venue. This was my party. The Israeli seemed fairly convinced too. But this was just a little too hardcore and out there for the younger two. They made their reservations clear, so it was agreed that we'd leave. (And why is it that your light-weight mates always win on a night out?)

"Okay, but please, I need to use the toilet first", said the Israeli.

He failed to find it; there wasn't an official one. If you wanted to go for a piss, then you went in a hedge in the back garden. This confirmed to me that it probably was a legitimate squat party. Lord only knows what would have happened if we'd stayed on there that night. Perhaps it wasn't my time yet.

Eventually, we settled on a slightly commercial club that was packed out.

A couple of blonde girls came up and asked me something. I had to confess that I didn't speak their language. I hated saying that as each time it lowered your place on the social pecking order; you weren't equal to the person in front of you.

"Umm….do you know where the toilets are?"

Shame. I'd hoped it was something more exciting than that.

The DJ put on a mix of Moloko's "*The time is now*", and the party stomped into full swing. The name of the tune seemed like a particularly poignant statement.

"*Give up yourself unto the moment. The time is now*".

"Wu-huh-hey! I raised a bottle at my companions.

"*Give up yourself unto the moment. The time is now*".

They returned the gesture and waived.

Had it really been only 48 hours ago that I'd been in a packed out soup kitchen in Bristol, full of tramps and no-hopers, winging that life had given them such a bad deal (or in other cases only been able to speak in their language of grunting and splurting) It hadn't felt like I'd left the country, but instead been exported to a different planet.

"*And the night is young….*"

And then it ticked over into the early hours of the morning.

The Israeli had managed to engage in a conversation with a local blonde lass that looked like she'd knock your block off if you looked at her the wrong way.

"I want to say that if people are going to come to my country, then they should learn my fucking language. I am not a Nazi, you understand".

I stated that I wholeheartedly agreed, then made a little half-hearted conversation just so I could say I'd been chatting to locals.

"Greg, I want your life! I have to get up and go to work in a bank on Monday morning, but you get to do what you want".

"Trust me, it's got its negs", I answered dryly.

"Sarah, it's been lovely meeting you and you are very beautiful, but we have to go now", the Israeli said, confirming the end of our night.

"Ja", she replied, looking unimpressed.

We walked back to the hostel.

"Sarah, she was a little crazy. Those guys that she was with, I think they were Nazis".

"What makes you say that?" I asked.

"She said that she was from the dark part of the city in the East. That must mean Hellersdorf and that place is full of Nazis", he commented.

We made our way up the staircase and reached the entrance, giggling like a bunch of naughty schoolboys that had stayed out way past their curfew. Just then, Yogaman entered the fray.

"Did you have a good night?" I asked.

"Oh man, we went to this club, I took MDMA for the first time", he answered with eyes wide open.

He smiled back at me then burst into a fit of giggles.

"So, here's the question English, do you want to go out again?"

The word 'yes' seemed to be the one that opened an opportunity.

"Yeah, okay – let's do it", I answered with a chuckle.

Back outside, it was almost full daylight.

"You know there's this place that I keep hearing about. It's a bar called Rote a Rose. I wanna go and check it out".

We walked up a diagonal road to get to the place. The flashing pink sign and trashy pop music being played indicated its presence. This venue was a bit out there even by Berlin standards. As we walked in, I swear over half the bar stopped silent, turned around and looked at us.

I offered to go to the bar. Yogaman was up for a G&T. Drinking beer at 7 am never seems right, so I opted for a vodka and Redbull. Come this time of the morning sleep deprivation and lowering energy levels make everything seem a bit surreal. Was this pub a charming place that was well and truly off the tourist map, or had I stumbled into the wrong place?

A man next to me asked me a question in German. He paused, then tried again in English.

"Whereabouts are you from", he asked in a Scottish accent.

"Oh my god, that's even worse", was his response after I'd answered.

A typically Scottish response. It turned out that he'd immigrated here from Edinburgh several years ago.

"You can feel the long, harsh German Winter coming. Don't underestimate it. I've known some years where it can get down to minus 20. The wind and snowdrifts are something else. Seriously, you can get piles of snow up to 6ft high. Everything freezes over".

Minus 20? Anybody caught out in that for more than a few hours would be turned into a human icicle, surely. I considered this for a few moments longer.

"What's the matter, son? You look all anxious".

"Nothing, just a long night, I guess".

Yogaman had been busy making friends the other side of the bar. Things seemed to climax with a few of Madonnas earliest and cheesiest hits being blasted out. (Do you still remember '*Holiday*' or '*Lucky Star*'?) The bar lady called time dramatically by pulling down the shutters to the bar. I guess that even 24-hour bars must close at some time. With that, I let things reach their natural ending and finally gave in to get some rest.

By Sunday evening, my companions, the Israeli and the Brazilian Romeo were still in high spirits, though the self-harming French kiddie was nowhere to be seen.

"You went down to Rote a Rote?" they exclaimed.

"Yeah, Yogaman dragged me off there".

"There's this other cool 24-hour bar that I know. No tourists, just locals. We're off there in a minute", the Israeli advised.

"You mind if I tag along?"

"Sure, last night was great!"

With it being Sunday evening there was no pressure to head off and see how long you could party. The weekend was heading for a gentle and chilled conclusion – like a baby being rocked to sleep.

"No. That's not it. Yes. This is the place where I was the other day."

The only other customer inside was a middle-aged German man propping up the bar. We ordered a large beer each. The barmaid, a stocky black woman, presented it to us with a bowl of snacks. After initially being quite surly, she became chatty.

"Guys, how much do you think I weigh?" she asked, the question came out of nowhere.

Do I give a polite answer or an accurate guess? There's no comfortable way of answering that question.

"About 60kgs", I replied.

The correct answer turned out to be 75kgs.

At that moment the classic '*Doors*' tune '*Riders of the Storm*' came on. The trippy beats, then the calm melodies filled the room. After chatting to the local guy for a bit, he informed that he ran his own engineering business.

"Ja, German economy always strong", he commented after the talk had turned to work.

I told him what I felt my work prospects were, being a little on the sceptical side and asked for his views on that.

"But I only speak about ten words of German" (That's how much I managed to pick up over the weekend)

"Ten words? No problem! I'm looking for a plasterer. Can you plaster?"

"No".

"Oh".

The others had an in-depth discussion with the barmaid. We were three-quarters of her custom, after all. We each began our rundown of how we'd left our respective countries and what had led us to patronise her bar that evening. In turn, she gave her tale of how she'd left Jamaica (though spoke English with an American accent).

We ended up having many further conversations between us about all sorts of topics, getting into all kinds of philosophical matters. (And no, that wasn't just because the alcohol was flowing freely) Sometimes the best conversations that you can have are with strangers. I guess because you're being more authentic that way and don't have preconceived ideas about each other.

"A lot of the Jamaican guys come over here to milk the system. They aren't interested in finding a job or learning the language. I used to be with a guy like that, but he didn't last long. That's what they do; they go for the typical blonde-haired and blue-eyed German girl. But you know what they say about blondes? They're dumb!"

A bit of a harsh statement that one. I'm not sure if I agree with it.

"I'm a very proud Jamaican; in fact, I will even go as far as to call myself a nationalist. But I'll say this to anyone first arriving here: if, after six months, you don't speak German and you don't have a job, then you must ask yourself what you're doing here", she said with conviction.

We chatted about this and that until she made a remark that stuck with me.

"You know, however hard they try some people are just never destined to be happy in life".

Yeah and I wonder if I'm one of them.

We thanked the good lady for her company.

"Oh no, the pleasure was all mine."

Once again, we took the short walk back to the hostel.

"I liked that Jamaican woman. Man, she was…. very……intelligent" the Israeli commented.

Once back, we sat down in the lounge, listening to the deep house music. The first weekend had implanted the seed of change within me. In the week that followed, I got myself busy getting to know the city and taking advantage of its excellent public transport system. There was never any shortage of company. Each night at our place of residence there would be fresh faces arriving and there was always someone worth chatting to. They came from just about every corner of the globe: Moldova, Colombia, Tahiti and of course your full sprinkling of Aussies.

We'd sit around in the lounge area at night, swapping travelling anecdotes.

"Oh right, in my country it works like this; in my country, we do it like that", communicating and educating each other was what it was all about.

The biggest thing that I learnt was no matter which nation you came from we were all pretty much the same. It being late November this kept the mainstream tourist away and left the more interesting folk. The demographics in the hostel could neatly be divided into three: the clubbing tourists that were here for the weekend, those that were looking to settle here and find work and the third arcane one, those that were here for something else, but hadn't quite figured that out yet.

You could sense the frustration of the "live-in crew". Although the accommodation was much cheaper compared with the rest of Europe, you normally had to upfront three months in advance. Plus finding a flat here was a highly competitive business. Being a foreigner relegated you to the bottom of the pecking order. That amount was too much of a chunk of money for many, and the whole time they were staying here meant it was digging into their precious savings. And try finding a job when your only address is Backpax, Kreuzberg. Understandably, they found the enthusiasm of the clubbing tourists a little tiresome, especially when they were trying to get on with their lives and take care of business. Bernardo, a Brazilian law student, best summed it up:

"Living in a hostel the whole time, you just feel like a tourist. You never get any privacy. I'm sick of hearing couples having sex! It is nice to be talking to people, but having so many people around you at once, it takes up so much of your energy", he said with quiet resignation whilst puffing away on a Marlborough.

I liked Bernardo. He was a cool and unassuming intellectual, but with a quiet authority. Another hurdle was going down the town hall and officially registering your presence. Again, you needed a proper address for this. Then going and recording for tax purposes (our equivalent of going for a NI interview) and they insisted that the conversation took place in German.

"You haven't been to Germany until you've had an interview with one of their government departments", a Swede shook his head.

"But Berlin is not the real Germany", I was reminded time and time again.

Later, Bernardo was in a more positive mood.

"We all came here because it wasn't working out for us in our respective countries. We were the black sheep there. So, we came to a place that's tailor-made for black sheep: Berlin. And we all found each other", he smiled.

The nights continued, as usual, going down to a bar or local restaurant where you could get the main course for less than 5 euro. Unusually for a capital city, Berlin was the cheapest city in the country, in fact, all Western Europe.

"But there is a lot of poverty here; over 10,000 people are living on the streets", a local informed.

Then the Winter hit, right on cue on 1st December. A full-on blizzard engulfed the city. At nights the mercury went down to minus 10. But on the plus side, it made the city look amazingly beautiful. Six inches of snow had settled that morning. I went for a walk around Templehof airfield. It was an old 1930's Nazi airbase that was now open for public roaming. With each step, the snow crunched beneath me. There was a real energy about the place which left me feeling calm after walking around there. It was the type of cold that felt good for you – crisp and sharp. I looked up at the clear blue sky feeling somehow cleansed.

The cold weather was making me stay in that weekend. There was just a few us left inside chatting to the receptionist. What a dull, boring night this was turning out to be. Why couldn't anything interesting happen?

"There's someone getting robbed outside!" An Australian with a giant perm cried as he dashed out from his room.

"Oh yeah, there it is", the receptionist said, gazing at the CCTV monitor.

Thank goodness for that; I love a bit of drama.

The Aussie and I hurtled down the stairs. It must have looked like the opening scenes to a 1970's cop show. Cue the cheesy music! As we neared the bottom, the Aussie jumped the final flight. His perm lifted into the air at the same time. I viewed it in slow motion and expected a caption to pop up.

We were greeted by the sight of two Turks giving a skinny wee lad a right good kicking whilst he was on the floor.

"They've got my phone!" he wailed.

"Give him his phone back!" the Aussie demanded.

The Turks looked at each other, then us and sheepishly scuttled off.

"Let's get after them!" the Aussie demanded again.

"No. They might be armed. Plus, it could be us that get arrested", I replied.

You don't take risks like that when you are in a foreign country.

"What is happening, man? Bjorn, the Swedish chef, asked as he came down.

"They've got my wallet with my cards in it. There's over two grand in my account."

Oh, yeah? Well, there's about 7 pence left in mine.

Thankfully at this point, the real police showed up and took over with typical German efficiency. The cops took a statement. The kiddie cancelled his cards. He'd sustained a few bruises but would live.

That had reminded me of my own finances. I clicked online and gave a payday loan company a story that had artistic license used   liberally — £200 in my account the next day. Well, surely, that was my reward for the good deed undertaken. By now, I had to start thinking realistically. Would I be getting a job here anytime soon?

No.

And a place to live?

Out of the question.

Would my fumbling German be good enough?

Doubt it.

One cold, hard fact; this was a proper winter that I didn't want to be caught up in. As much as I loved Berlin, it had appeared to become one giant bandwagon with everyone jumping on top of it and craving a slice of the pie when there were only a few crumbs left. I didn't want to be a rat left fighting over crumbs. So what then? The stories of others had inspired me. They'd told me whatever happened; I must keep on going. And that didn't mean you had to stick around the same place.

I got talking to a short, well-built Serbian man one night. We went down the usual "where are you from" line of questioning.

"But who's your team?" he demanded to know.

"Tottenham".

"Spurs? Oh good. They are very tough. They have the only firm that never ran from us. There was this one time down in Prague when their match got called off. So, we steamed in on them. Everyone else before had run away. But they stayed and fort-like men! Then afterwards we are all the best buddies; we have many beers together", he grinned.

It would appear that I just met one of Red Star's heavies.

"No. I was not one of the…. how you say…. top boys. I played very small role".

He told more stories about following his beloved Red Star Belgrade.

"We sang this song for 20 minutes", he said showing me the video of all the fans stood up and singing passionately inside the stadium. He then went on to explain the bitter rivalry between them and Partisan.

"Us Serbians, we were seen as the bad boys after the war", he said sadly.

32

I hung out with Ivan, the Serbian a little more. I liked him. He was a funny guy. He also had this very prim and proper way of dealing with everyone in the hostel.

"You know Greg; you should come to Serbia. I think you'll like it there".

Serbia. Now there was a thought. Other than hearing about it because of its breakup from the former Yugoslavia, I knew very little about the place.

"You will have a much better time in Belgrade than you will in Berlin. The girls in the club, when they go out, they wear almost nothing", he encouraged further.

That wasn't top of my list of priorities right now. Belgrade was a bit off the beaten track. I wanted to go out and discover something that was a bit fresh.

"Now if you'll excuse me, I must go and take care of my…… grey economy business", Ivan said politely.

I immediately went to go and look Serbia up on the map. Getting a flight there would be quite expensive. A cheaper option seemed to be getting a twenty euro ride down to Prague, then catching an overnight train to the Serbian capital. Ivan left the following morning, saying his impeccably polite goodbyes to everyone and giving me a knowing wink. I decided on setting off the next Saturday morning. The plan was to go down there for a short bit and be back by Christmas.

I was going to call it an early night, but couldn't sleep, so thought about mingling by the bar. A group of Danish girls had arrived the day prior and had just come back from a night out. So, I did what any other reasonable person would do: I picked the blondest and most attractive one, brought her a Carlsberg and got chatting. Her pupils were bolted and the size of saucers. She'd clearly had a good night.

The conversation began in the usual way. But then she started getting unnecessarily deep with things. She was only 21 but had an overly precocious way of talking, which I found quite annoying.

"What are you actually doing with your life?" she accused.

"Living it", I shrugged.

"No. No, you are not living it. You come across as very laid back. You must embrace life", she said, holding out her palms.

Oh, and did I mention she was a charity fundraiser. She continued on her psychoanalysing rant. I began to feel like a patient on her couch. She even dropped in the classic, *'it's all to do with the relationship with your mother'* line.

".… But wouldn't you like a more stable way of life?" she left that one hanging in the air.

I found it wholly inappropriate, especially as we'd only just met.

"You are living in a backpacker's hostel for Christ's sake".

That one upset Bernardo too.

".… And I think you are selling yourself too cheaply".

She paused for a moment, then came back looking deadly serious.

"You are afraid", she almost trembled the words.

"Afraid of what?"

"Afraid of settling down and that you will have three boring children. That you will grow old and get fat, and your wife will get fat", her mouth was open and aghast.

Thankfully she turned her attention back to her mates and soon after that they retired to bed, thus concluding the most bizarre of conversations.

I turned around to Bernardo.

"That Danish girl was getting right on my tits", I sighed in frustration.

"Yes. But did you see the size of *her* tits? They were massive!" Bernardo offered.

We both sat there, glumly nursing a bottle of Club-Mate.

"I've been getting annoyed too. That Moldovan couple last night, they wouldn't stop slurping", he groaned.

I checked out of the hostel at that point, promising to see them again in a couple of weeks.

"Have a good one in Belgrade", Bernardo wished me.

The previous conversation kept on playing over and over in my head. But you know what was most infuriating about it? I knew that she was at least half right….

Chapter 2

Tough guys don't bribe

T he effects of lack of sleep and over-stimulation were taking their toll. Jittery and agitated had been my mood all the way down to Prague cramped aboard the Euro city train. That made me get off at the wrong stop and wondering how far I was from Central Prague. It's always someone similar to you who offers a helping hand. A friendly Czech musician with a guitar strapped to his back advised me that I was several stops away from the city centre. In addition, he gave me the low down on the underground party scene in the East of the city. That might be worth investigating at some point. I arrived at the hostel late, then overslept which saw me waking up a full 3 hours late for check out. No amount of charming could placate the receptionist.

THE WANDERER

Prague was a different city since I'd been here last. The Czech ...,
was regarded as the most developed country in Eastern Europe, and the
capital was a significant tourist destination. Now it was all dressed up for
the world – clean, modern and trendy (perhaps a little too trendy for its own
good) But there were victims of this gentrification. All the junkies had left
for Berlin.

There was a further problem playing on my mind. Lack of cash. (It's
always a bad sign when the local tramps are asking you to share a bottle of
Vodka with them.)

It was a freezing cold morning in Prague bus station, and I was stuck.
Think man, think! Then a brain wave occurred. You see, in all the hustle
and bustle of leaving I'd never quite got around to informing the council of
my departure and for them to stop paying housing benefit. So scatty had I
become that one day I even went into their offices and requested that it was
paid directly into my own account instead of the Credit Union one. Today
was due day. Could it be that they were still paying it in there?

I couldn't check my balance abroad or withdraw cash as it was only a
basic account. So here was a way of finding out: go to the desk and attempt
to purchase a ticket with my debit card. If it worked, then that meant it was
there. If not, then I was out of luck. I ordered a bus ticket to Vienna as a
trial (the daily train to Belgrade had been missed, anyway). You wait for the
bleeps. Two short bleeps would indicate that it was declined. A single,
longer one showed it worked. I prayed for the magic bleep. "Bleeeep"
Purchase authorized.

I boarded the Vienna bound bus with the James Bond theme ringing in
my ears. There was even a young Russian girl who sat next to me for
company. This route led to a fair bit of hopping my way down to the
Balkans, but eventually, I found myself on a rickety old overnight train
bound for Belgrade. In the dead of night, it made its border stop. There was
a still silence for a minute, and then the doors sprang open.

"Passport control. Nobody move!" a slim woman with dyed red hair bellowed.

"No smoking in here", she remonstrated with a group of lads adjacent to me.

It felt like the train was being held up by bandits. Now we were leaving the comfort zone of the European Union and into something entirely different. A second formality stop was needed. My passport gained its first stamp. The officer looked at me quizzically then gently nodded his head up and down, as if to say: *so, you think you're tough guy, uh?*

There was no chance of sleeping for the rest of the journey. The early rising passengers were picked up, and it turned from being an international train into an early morning commuting one. Daylight broke, we embarked on the Serbian capital. A smell of Sulphur hung thick in the air. This wasn't a funky European country, but a cold, hard nation, make no mistake about it. Now time to be asking myself the proper questions as reality gradually caught up with me. For a start, that overly convoluted passage down had drained my finances. There were only 15 euros left to my name. Enough to buy some food and a packet of cigarettes, but that was about it

I went off exploring to go and see what the city was all about, you know - doing a bit of sightseeing. But there was no escaping the horrible realisation. With no means of support, I could no longer be called a tourist, or traveler, whatever the hell that meant. But simply a vagabond; persona non grata, not a real person. In Western Europe, that would have been fine and dandy. But in fucking Serbia and in December! It was like being in Russia. The cortisol rushed through my body, giving a feeling of being in my own personal Armageddon.

With no clear plan, I ended up wandering around in circles all day, trying to give the appearance of somebody who'd just arrived and were making their way to a hotel. Night fell and with it came the cold. Okay, enough mucking around. Admit where you are and take care of the practicalities - time to go and find somewhere to sleep. Instinct always tells me to head North and away from the city centre. It's a simple rule that I apply in such situations: out of town, out of bullshit. Once a few miles North, I finally found what I was looking for: a derelict house with a shed in the yard. That would do nicely.

I jumped through the window. Survival instinct in order to better myself immediately took over. The first job, trimming my possessions - the least you carry around with you, the better. In the first pile, tut that was no longer necessary and could be dumped. In the second, essential items needed for survival: thick Winter clothes, woolly hat and gloves, proper walking boots, torch and sleeping bag. A small amount of food that was high in protein and fat (two things that you need in Winter when you're doing a lot of physical activity). Toiletries; I'd have to figure out where to wash later. Though always put a bit of deodorant on. (Perhaps I'd be going out on the pull later.) Then lastly, wallet and travel documents to be kept on my person. My phone was now defunct. (These were the days before you could get cheap intl roaming.) As an afterthought a couple of pens and writing paper.

I changed into my long johns, then chain-smoked through half a packet of Camel. Nicotine could be a great comforter sometimes. That's the curious thing about nicotine: it acts as a stimulant when you need it to, but also a sedative when required. Finally spent, I curled up in a spot away from the window and snoozed off, not stirring for another two days.

****

T hat dog that had been barking for the past few hours was growing

annoying. Being tired of listening to it forced me to get up and face the world. I peered through the window. Strange, chickens were running around. Oh dear, that house I thought was abandoned was still in full use. I'd just spent the last couple of days living in someone else's shed. The

elderly gentleman, was out in the yard. Time to make a
:s. I leapt out with my rucksack over me, wearing army boots,
gloves anu ..ut. So, what would you do if you found out that some mad,
crazy English guy had been living in your shed? Demand to know what he
was doing, or stand there giving a toothless grin as if this happened every
day. He chose the latter. So out of respect, I flung him an army-style salute
and got on my merry way.

Soon after my first encounter with a local took place. Of all people a
Greek priest.

"Let me buy you something to eat", he offered after the conversation had
gone past small chat.

I followed him into the most basic of cafes. He treated me to bangers and
mashed potato with even a beer to go with it. The kindness of strangers - it
was to be the first of many episodes. We chatted about England and Serbia.
He seemed keen to know my views on the Royal family.

"I like your queen; she is a very good figure for your country", he smiled.

In the end, he insisted on praying for me. Oh dear, when someone starts
praying for you, you know you're in real trouble.

I carried on meeting a few more Serbs with the way that I'd learnt how.

"Where you from?" a bored street charity fundraiser asked in a square in the
city centre.

"England, UK."

"Ah, good" (They think you might be American.)

But who's your team?" (An even more critical question, it would seem.)

"Tott...en...ham"

"Tott..en..ham. Good! No Chelsea. No Manchester City. They money,
money, money".

"And who's your team?" I asked.

"Rrr…..Redstar!" he beamed proudly.

"Ah, Rrr…..Redstar!" I said while thumping the left side of my chest.

"No Partisan, puh…." I said, mocking spitting on the floor.

   And that is how you make friends in Belgrade. Things were still bad, but the initial panic was over. Serbia was indeed a hard country. But Belgrade was a relatively safe city for anybody who wasn't looking for trouble, though there were plenty of reminders from the civil war of the early '90s. The buildings still had lots of holes in them, no doubt from war damage. The Serbs had always been painted as the bad guys from that war which, understandably, made them bitter. They'd chosen to voice their dissatisfied views through graffiti messages on the walls and the odd artistic mural thrown in.

   Come night-time I decided to do a bit of additional site seeing in the district that contained the vast abandoned buildings. The area had a gritty and profoundly mysterious vibe to it, especially in Winter. Abandoned buildings fascinate me; where others see a wreck, I see potential. You could throw a massive party in one of those. Though there was no chance of gaining access as they were all protected by guard dogs. Belgrade was a very underrated city. Everyone checked out its neighbour, Croatia instead and went to its beaches and the festivals there. But if you asked me, this was where the fertile party territory was. There was definitely something here, something that was bubbling its way in the underground like a volcano waiting to erupt. It had called me down, and I'd gone to see what it was all about.

   Christmas came around again. Except it wasn't really as they don't celebrate it here until late January, what with it being predominantly Greek Orthodox. I'd sort refuge in the bus station.

"Get out!" a security guard shouted aggressively, kicking my rucksack.

"You were here last night. If I see you again, I call the police".

So much for trying to blend in just like another passenger. That was how 25th December began, just past the stroke of midnight. I wasn't worried. When you get moved on, they usually doing you a favour. I went down the 24-hour shop to spend the last few dinars on food and cigarettes (They were only about 60 pence a packet.) Then went wondering, not knowing what I was looking for. Just let the subconscious mind take over, and it will find a suitable answer.

What was that? A small hole in a mound by an underpass. Instinct told me to check it out. The gap revealed a rusted iron grid. I pulled it open and crawled through. It led to a small passageway that opened into an underground cellar. Perfect! A little dusty, but otherwise habitable. Then came the standard procedure of curling up in ones sleeping bag and smoking my lungs out: peace and a good night's sleep. I drifted in and out of consciousness, having the most bizarre of dreams.

Seven years later and history had repeated itself. I hadn't eaten properly in over a week. There was a slow grinding fear that was wearing me down. I'm not religious but felt like praying, to who I don't know.

After a couple of days spent in the Christmas holiday home, my back was getting a little cramped. Time to start thinking practically once again. I had to get back inside the safety zone of the EU, which would afford me certain rights. Staying in Serbia could prove to be a little hairy. Communication was a problem. On Christmas Eve I'd managed to get hold of an international phone card and had a very brief exchange with the family. Their lives had sounded so normal and civilised compared to mine. The library is usually a good bet in these situations. But etiquette here was different - internet access was strictly reserved for local students. I told the staff that I was just a curious tourist wishing to take a look around.

".... Okay, but very discreetly. Security here are very paranoid".

THE WANDERER

The golden moment came when some kiddie left his PC without logging off. I grabbed the chance. In the 3 minutes it took for the librarian to query what on Earth I was doing, I'd managed to send the old man a begging email asking for £50 to be credited to my travel money card. (The evil payday loan goblins were now trying to rinse my current account.)

A day later, it had arrived. Instinct told me it was a good idea to leave the sleeping bag behind. I dashed back to the station and made it in time for the overnight train to Budapest. It slowly creaked its way out. A couple of border cards were patrolling the carriages. They were on the lookout for any one sketchy who might be attempting a quick dash out of the country. Of course, they took one look at me….

I held up my passport in a kind of 'waving the white flag', motion. There was a pause while they looked me up and down.

"Why are you so filthy? You look like solider returning from Iraq; like you've been on an international crusade", he chuckled.

"I fell over, sir".

"Oohh…you tough guy, uh?"

I hadn't bargained on just how dusty the underground cellar was, or just how filthy it made me look.

"By the look of it, you never registered your arrival in Serbia. That is a misdemeanour here".

What on Earth was he going on about?

"So, you are going to have to get off with us at Novi Sad, spend a couple of days in jail, then face the court. You're looking at a 500 euro fine at least", he said somberly.

There had been nothing about this on the embassy's website, which I'd checked diligently. You can't bullshit a bullshitter, mate. These boys were on the blag.

"Hmmm…. how do we resolve this?"

"Ah, he wants to resolve it "

"Yeah, you know - like gentleman".

"Why, step into our office in first-class, sir"

We sat down on the much more comfortable seats.

"Now, for the very reasonable price of two hundred euro, we can lie to our boss; tell him you had too many beers in bar….and…. lost the form".

"Ah, for the pocket?"

"For the pocket", he winked.

"Alright, let me get that for you. Oh dear, doesn't look like I've got any cash. But the pocket takes Mastercard, right?"

You should have seen the look on their faces.

"Didn't think so. Sorry boys, looks like you're going to have to tell the governor the truth", that I was not informed of this procedure by your colleagues at passport control".

They even made me turn out my pockets to prove I had no cash. Sometimes being broke can save you.

"Okay, go back to your place whilst we figure what to do with you".

I trotted back to humble second class. A fellow passenger handed me a cigarette as a show of solidarity. I thought this through. There was no way they were going to drag me off at Novi Sad and use up time and resources over a fake crime. Novi Sad came and went. No sign of them. But no room for complacency just yet. The train chugged onwards, then stopped.

"You can smoke, we are still in Serbia", a lady informed.

Darn

Finally, came the sight of Hungarian immigration. They wanted to look through my rucksack. Thankfully, I'd disposed of the dirty old sleeping bag.

"Have you got any drugs in there?"

"No".

"Kalashnikov?"

"No".

"Why not?"

Steve McQueen had hopped back over the border.

Chapter 3

The coolest tramps in Budapest

Y ou may have noticed a pattern occurring by now: all of the cities

so far have begun with B. Someone told me once that the symbol of B stands for personal growth. I pondered that concept as I strolled down the Vaci Utca (the local good-time district). New Year's Eve was in a couple of days, so things were building up. I was going through my denial phase as if arriving in a new city would make everything magically better. *You've just come unstuck for a little while; you'll be back on your feet soon*, was what I'd told myself. In Germany, I'd only been another one of those '*yeah, Berlin. Isn't it amazing*', blah, blah, blah. By the time I got down to Serbia, the dynamic of this trip had changed. I'd been thrust into a raw and harsh experience where there was zero comfort zone. It goes back to obtaining the most primal basics: getting shelter, food and water. In that situation, you're forced to confront yourself and your issues in the most raw and authentic fashion.

I'd moped around for the next couple of days, getting to know the basic geography of the place and looking forward to the New Year celebrations just the same as anyone else would. Everyone gathered in the main square vörösmarty tér 90's house classics blasted through the cold night air. People let off fireworks out of beer bottles. It was all rather jolly. I stood there, bobbing my head up and down. The only difference being I foraged around for leftover food and alcohol as opposed to buying it there. And there was plenty of it to be had. 2012 ticked over into 2013 amid cheers and the cracking of fireworks. A woman next to me handed me a bottle of alcopop champagne as if to say, '*everyone deserves a New Year drink*' For her to do that I clearly looked down and dishevelled enough.

By the morning, I sat semi slumped on a bench, sipping from a large bottle of energy drink. It made me mentally hyper but stupefied at the same time while being physically drained. The local constabulary popped over for a friendly chat.

A couple of days into the New Year and things had turned decidedly colder. The past couple of nights had been spent in a woods located by the Danube with just an old blanket covering me. Doable if it's a couple of degrees above. But now the temperature was well into the minus. When it's like that, and you don't have the necessary equipment you have to start thinking about some form of shelter. I'd seen the many homeless people huddled together in the metro stations but hadn't fancied joining them.

The snow began to fall. What were the other options? There weren't any. I was to go and join their ranks. Once again, something unthinkable. Corvin-negyed was the nearest station. The illuminated metro sign looked almost threatening. I walked down the staircase like a convicted felon being led towards his noose, each step feeling particularly slow and heavy. I chose the quietest passageway and sat on my rucksack, not quite believing that this was real. The station was eerily quiet, but each echo sounded threatening and dangerous. Yeah, I don't mind admitting this: I was as scared as hell.

My breath turned to steam as I breathed in and out. Footsteps could be heard coming from around the corner. I tensed up. It was an old guy who'd clearly been living here for quite a while. He had a blanket draped around his shoulders. He looked me up and down then beckoned for me to come with him. I'd come to rely a lot on my natural instincts these days, and they were judging it to be safe enough.

He invited me over to his dwellings. It wasn't a bad set-up; he'd constructed a kind of cardboard house. His companions looked well fed.

"My friend, we have everything here, you come and join us", he offered and passed me a bag containing a large sausage and some bread.

"Köszönöm", I replied, the only Hungarian word I knew.

"How long have you been down here now?" I asked.

"For six years now", he said, looking wistful.

The old guy came back carrying thick sheets of cardboard and checked that none of it was damp. He carefully laid it out on the floor, then motioned for me to lay down on them. Hesitantly I did so. Then, to my utter amazement, the cold vanished. In fact, it was halfway comfortable. Something so mundane and yet it could save your life. That's the most basic and vital survival skill that I've ever learnt: whenever you're sleeping out in sub-zero temperatures, always find yourself nice thick dry cardboard. In any city, you'll quickly find it. Your own body is remarkably good at generating heat no matter how cold it is, just as long as you're consuming enough calories. You don't want to lose that heat, so the cardboard does a great job of reflecting it back. If you don't have any form of insulation material, then the heat will drain out of you fast – and you'll know about it. He placed a thick blanket over me. The local bums had taken me in just like the wolves took Mowgli in. It was enough to make me nod off into a sound sleep.

THE WANDERER

****

"Jó reggelt" a woman called.

She was opening the station kiosk, and I was in her way. 5 am, and the station was stirring into life. I wrapped myself in the blanket and sat upright. Not very dignified, but when you're trying to keep warm, you don't care anymore. Besides, in a foreign country that you don't have any connection to you have complete anonymity.

I watched the early morning passengers filter past, busy on their way to work. Then one of them, a conventional-looking middle-aged woman stopped, turned around and handed me a few coins with a smile - 150 Forint. It was enough to buy a coffee and a bread roll. I went over to the kiosk where I'd slept. It seemed only right and proper that I patronise it now. The small coffee gave me the jolt that catapulted me out of the station and back into the world - enough of being a metro rat.

I looked back at my companions from the night before. They seemed quite content to be there all day. Old school tramps who knew all the tricks, but I needed allies who were more progressive. After hitting the streets, I remembered what that guy in Amsterdam had said,'*You're going to do a lot of walking'*. And he was right. You see this bumming business isn't all about sitting on your arse. You gotta keep movin. When you can't afford public transport, that's all you do – often to kill time and keep your blood circulation going. But this day was all about foraging for food.

It not being long after NYE there were still quite a few tourists around. And where there are tourists, there's leftover food. (The Americans were by far the worst offenders.) So I went to the main spots where they hung out and would congregate. Sometimes they left entire meals out in silver foil cartons. There were plenty of cakes and bakery, sometimes a whole bag full. A male will burn off around 2,500 calories a day, but being continually in the cold with so much walking. that can rise to 4,000. Out on the streets, you learnt fast. I looked down at the bums without cardboard. Amateurs.

49

Day rolled into night once again. I walked down into the Blaha Lujza tér metro. It seemed to be at the centre of the bum action. There were at least 30 of them packed inside there. The main group was in one corner. The place was filthy with muddy footprints and rubbish scattered across the floor. It reminded me of Kings Cross underground station in the 1980s. Or had I just died and gone to hell? People were wailing and crying. Some of them were having a go at singing. It was dire. A man with dyed red hair caught my eye. There was something unusual about him. I surveyed the rest of the street dwellers in the station. None of them looked approachable. Then there was a tap on my shoulder.

"Hey, do you speak English?" It was the red-haired man. He was about the same age as me.

I nodded in the affirmative.

"Oh, great. I'm George, from the Czech Republic."

He stuck out his hand. His whole other sleeve flapped in thin air. Then I realised what was odd. He only had one arm. He noticed my reaction.

"I lost that while freight train hopping. It's how I get about".

George did the hardcore drifter stuff that you usually only saw in the movies. He gave a more detailed account of when he'd jumped onto the moving freight train, misjudged the distance and had his left arm severed clean off.

"How long have you been on the road?" he asked.

"6 weeks now".

"And you?"

"This time around, one year".

He explained that in a previous life he'd worked as a computer programmer in Prague, but got tired of the 9-5 grind and the stale office environment, so ran off with the travelling circus and got a job erecting tents

"That was a perfect job. It made you physically strong, and we were all like one big family hanging out afterwards".

Now with only one arm, his work prospects were heavily restricted, but he seemed to cope remarkably well.

"Here, you want some food? I have plenty", he said, digging out a bag full of sausage meat.

He seemed grateful for my company, but I still only took what deemed to be polite.

"It's good to have an English speaker to talk to. Most of the locals here don't speak English very well, so I've not had anybody to talk to for the past month", he confessed.

"Yeah, me neither", I added.

"Polite people don't talk to the likes of us", he laughed.

"What do you mean?"

"Well your hair is dirty and so are your jeans. Look at him over there; he's perfect", he said, pointing to a man hurrying past.

I was still a little put out by this comment.

"Where did you sleep last night?" I asked.

"In here, but I only managed about 5 minutes. This group of guys came down and threw a bottle at me. I thought I was about to be attacked. You must be careful. Eastern Europeans can sometimes be very aggressive. Hey, I have an idea, though".

He reached into his bag.

"This evening this Austrian guy gave me two city transport passes. The tram runs all night. We can sleep on that".

Just then there was the sound of glass smashing and loud, constant wailing.

"Not a bad plan; I think it's about time we got out of here".

We hit the tram that had the longest line. This was well and truly living on the road. Trees covered in Christmas lights lined the streets and added to the atmosphere. George handed me a drink that had a generous amount of vodka mixed into it. After slurping half of that, the world seemed like a better place. This is what I came out here for, never quite knowing where you were going to end up or who you were going to meet or what might happen.

George best summed it up.

"This way of life may be tough…. but you get experience, the experience that you'd never get by leading a regular life".

That was it: life experience. It's the one thing that you take with you when you die, no matter how much money you've earnt or what sort of status you've achieved. We laughed and joked the whole time. It felt like I was free, living a life without boundaries. When the tram came to the end of the line, we simply got off, went to the other end and waited for it to start up again. As you could imagine, the novelty of this 'free' type of living wore off fairly quickly. By the morning, I was still nodding in and out of a "half" sleep by the time the day's first commuters were on their way to work.

Now managing to find my feet somewhere in Hungary, I attempted to introduce a little structure into the day and give it a target. We managed to find a day centre where after a gentle bit of persuading, they agreed to let us have a shower each.

It's not that I didn't care about personal hygiene anymore; I just hadn't had access to the facilities. The warm water and soap running down my back felt refreshing. It had been three weeks since I'd last showered and the water was turning grey as it ran off me. Getting a shower; such a simple, fundamental thing. But living like this, it was a rare luxury.

From research gathered, it appeared that there were plenty of homeless support centres within Budapest. But for one they were severely overstretched. (The city had a substantial rough sleeping problem. You also had to undergo a TB screening) And a British guy turning up at one of them was going to summon up a lot of questions: who were you and what were you doing here?

You may also ask why I didn't just turn back at this point and return to England. But back to what? Back to talking to rats in a bedsit and sub existing on £55 a week? I don't think so. Plus, with the place vacated I would be heading straight back to the street in a cold January anyway. It would be admitting defeat all too soon. But that's enough of the self-pitying sob story. Now back to the party:

I'd arranged to meet George again at the Blaha Lujza that evening. He was sat in the corner having a sort of attempt at busking by way of blowing into a harmonica.

"My lips are too dry", he said, rubbing balm into them.

"I do not like Hungarians. Hardly any of them speak English. They have no brains; they are monkeys", he said scathingly.

"How long have you been here now?"

"This time around one month. Before I started in the summer homes in the countryside. This is a good trick: you come out of season when they are going to be empty. You try a few doors and eventually you'll find one that's unlocked. So, you just walk in. For six weeks, I had the house to myself. But then the owner turned up. He was like '*what are you doing in my house*?' Shame. I was having a sweet sleep in his bed at the time", he giggled.

George seemed to have made a few acquaintances here already. Unfortunately, to me, they appeared sketchy as hell. With nothing much more to be achieved in the networks most colourful metro station, we trotted off with them. In amongst our number was a girl called Suzanne. From what I could gather, she was a prostitute that fell into the 'tart with a heart' category. So, she wasn't a concern. What was more, perplexing was the relationship between her and the other males.

"Okay, I don't speak much Hungarian, but I think that they want us to stay with them", George advised.

A sinking feeling hit me. When you are in a vulnerable situation, there will always be people trying to take advantage of that fact. It felt like I was insidiously slipping into Budapest's dark underbelly without fully comprehending what I was getting myself into.

George noticed my trepidation.

"I think we should be okay. We have nothing, so they have nothing to rob from us".

(You've always got something worth something to somebody)

"I think they just like us", he said.

We turned the corner down a dark alley that led to a small block of flats. We entered the first one up the stairs. Patches of rising damp covered the walls, other than that it was quite cosy. Gingerly, George produced a bottle of red wine out of his bag.

"I'm going to offer them a drink each…. because…. alcohol is international language", he offered thoughtfully.

That seemed to go down pretty well. George raised the bottle with an open gesture, and the group gladly reciprocated. In no time, the bottle was empty, and the mood lightened. They chatted away to us in their native language. Of course, I couldn't understand a word they were saying.

"When someone is talking to you in a foreign language, and you don't know what they're saying just smile", George advised.

(It's advice that I've followed to this day, and it works.)

To my intense relief, the other guys got up and decided to go elsewhere. Now we were just left with Suzanne, 'the fine, hard-working lady'. She smiled and offered out a packet of biscuits. I gladly munched them up. Calories. Always needing calories. Then she pulled the other sofa over and explained that this was to be my bed for the night. (By now I was getting used to reading gestures and body language.)

"Aren't you going to take your shoes off? In my country it's good manners to take your shoes off when you're in someone else's house", George said almost scornfully after I'd laid down.

I was actually being considerate by not wanting to stink the place out with my smelly feet. By now I was just glad to be somewhere safe and warm. The TV in the corner was on full blast. I really don't rate Hungarian late-night TV. It mainly consisted of some sad old bloke wistfully talking into the camera for hours on end, as if he was giving some creepy confession.

Suzanna went into the kitchen.

George turned around and looked at me, then spoke in a low tone.

"You know, I don't think this is her apartment after all".

"What makes you say that?" I asked.

"Well for one she's had the TV on all night and the heating on full blast. No regular Hungarian person does this; they can't afford the electric bill. And secondly: look, she's searching through all the cupboards in the kitchen. She doesn't know where anything is. Now she's looking in the fridge to see what's in there because she doesn't know. Who doesn't know what's not in their kitchen?"

Whatever. I wish that old guy would shut up and stop moaning maudlin nonsense. I'm trying to get to sleep. Is euthanasia legal in this country? His voice got further and further away as I drifted off into the land of nod. But like with most nights, all too soon the sun rose not much later. Suzanne gave us about half an hour then spoke with greater firmness in her tone.

George nodded.

"Okay, we need to go now".

I thanked the hostess for her kind hospitality, then braced myself for the crisp morning.

"That definitely wasn't her apartment. She didn't have a key, and did you see how long it took her to figure out how to open the door? She was squatting it", George concluded as we walked down the street.

It made sense now. Suzanna had been a bit anxious about taking the place on her own, so she'd recruited a couple of streetwise drifters to help hold the place down. Except living in a residential property while the owners are away isn't squatting. It's more likely to be viewed as a dwelling burglary, which can result in a prison sentence. Oh well….

As it was still a cold morning, we returned to the underground network. This time around it was to be Keleti station. It was the stop that served the city's central train station. So, it was full of rush-hour commuters streaming in all four different directions, going about their healthy lives and getting ready for a day's work. Right in the middle of the chaos, a crowd had gathered. They were watching a group of American college kids perform a play. The guy who appeared to be the ring leader was busy narrating. It was definitely religiously-themed with a guilt element while it delivered a moral tale. It was like watching a Primary school Christmas play, quite cute, but cringe-worthy. It culminated in the lead character having a sudden death and falling to the floor. Things took a jollier turn when they burst into a song to round of matters.

"To the left, to the left, to the left, to the right, to the right, to the right", complete with movements.

Now looking thoroughly pleased with themselves, they applauded their performance and indulged in a group hug. After undertaking a post-performance briefing, the ring leader (a skinny wee lad) and a bearded fellow made a beeline for us

When and where ever you are homeless religious people are always trying to make an impression on you.

"Hello, where are you from?"

"UK"

"Czech Republic".

"Oh great. We're from California, USA. We've come over here to spread the good lords' message and offer hope to those who might be needing it. Tell me, where did you guys sleep last night?" he asked solemnly.

"With a hooker", I replied cheerfully.

"Oh…. was she… nice…...?

"Yeah, great fun".

"So, what are you guys doing in Budapest?"

"Because it's safer than in Serbia. They think I'm a soldier returning from Iraq over there", I replied.

"To spread international provocation", George beamed.

"Did you like our skit?"

"Yes. But I was having a little trouble in understanding what it was about",
I replied.

He went on to explain, but it made even less sense. They informed us
which organisation they belonged to. The bearded fellow began spilling out
his life story.

"I was abused as a kid and pretty screwed up, so I ran away from home. I
got in with the wrong crowd, started doing drugs and all sorts of things like
that", he sheepishly confessed.

"But then I found this organization *'Gods Hope Man Kind united'*. It was
like joining a family. They gave me hope and a feeling of being part of
something.

Right, he'd exposed his vulnerabilities. I was determined to take control
of this conversation and offer my own views.

"I think you'll find that's a fundamental human desire; to be part of
something bigger than ourselves, finding an identity and having a place", I
smiled.

"I'm very pleased that you found this in the form of religion. But don't you
think you should be finding that true meaning *inside* you self?" I smiled
once again after delivering the classic cliched nonsense.

They looked at me puzzled, then seemed to genuinely mull this over.
The ring leader tried to get things back on track.

"Do you have any addictions yourself?"

"Only caffeine and nicotine", was my current truthful answer.

"Right. Can I ask you another question?" he went on all serious.

"Who do you think Jesus was?"

"I believe that Jesus was the original schizophrenic before it got itself a bad
name", I replied in a sing-song tone.

I'd meant that as a wind-up, but they seemed genuinely intrigued by that answer.

"We'd like to say a prayer for you guys right now. Is there anything in particular that you want us to pray for?"

"Just tell the big man to give me a good weekend, dude".

"Sure, right".

He prepared himself for full-on preacher mode, screwed up his face in a real conscientious look and grabbed me firmly on the left shoulder. The other guy did the same on my right.

"Oh, please God, all-mighty forgive…., sorry what was your name again?"

"Greg".

"Please god almighty forgive Greg of the sins that have led him down this dark path in life. (*Steady on!*) Let him continue his journey to find meaning and purpose in life. Free him from his addictions and whatever it is that's holding him back. Please tell him that he's to *stop* looking at pictures of naked ladies the whole time. (*Cheeky bastard*). But please, please god, I ask you above anything else for him to have a great weekend".

He let out a gasp, seemingly exhausted by that performance.

"Nice", I thanked.

"Guys, it's been great talking to you. I wish you all the best of luck".

The bearded one got his wallet and produced 4,000 Forint in notes.

"Umm, here you go fellas. Buy your self-something nice. But don't go spending it on any of your addictions".

George and I exchanged glances.

"Hey, they saved us", George remarked after they'd gone.

"They were good kids, man. It's just a shame about all the religious mumbo jumbo", I commented. Then marched off to the kiosk without hesitation.

I purchased a packet of Camel and two cans of bad-boy energy drink.

****

"......Stop referring to her as '*the hooker*'. She's a real person and has a name. Her name is Suzannah", George remonstrated.

It was Friday night down the Blaha Lujza and things were livening up. Suzannah scuttled past on her way to work and could only manage a waive. I guess it was going to be one of her busiest nights of the week.

"Cops.... cops", George nudged me in anticipation. We both reached for our ID.

Two burly officers were checking out the group opposite us. That's what they did here in Eastern Europe. They went around purposely patrolling and asking every single street bum for their ID (It didn't matter if they were causing trouble or not). Then ran a PNC check on them. By now I was getting stopped and asked about three times a day. It was their way of exerting control and keeping tabs on people who otherwise lived off the radar.

"Hey, maybe they are having a special competition today. Look, any minute now a fanfare sound is gonna come blaring from that cops' radio. Do....duh, duh...der", he mimed.

"Congratulations. You are the hundred-thousandth bum we've stopped. You get a special prize; a tin of dog food each for you and your K-9!"

Now it was our turn.

"Show us your documents!" the bigger one demanded.

I handed mine over without fuss or emotion. Sometimes the police were looking for a reaction. So, every time I acted more stoic. They looked at Georges Czech issued ID card as if to say "*oh, we've got one of those again*", but frowned in puzzlement at my British passport. They rubbed a thumb over the royal crest and were surprised to find it real.

"Gregory, why you know stay in hotel?"

"Because, I want to experience *Hungarian* way of living, sir".

He read my details into his radio.

"Gregory…. Jams…. Lynn. Gypsy nora.

That always used that phrase. What did it mean?

"You've checked him twice today already", the dispatcher responded, sounding exasperated.

"*What* are you doing in Hungary?" the big one asked George.

He stood up earnestly.

"Please, sir; I am travelling to Bosnia because I want to join the *army*, sir", he said, flaying his empty sleeve.

"Do you have any drugs?" the cop asked, bemused.

"No. Sorry", George responded wistfully.

We sniggered once they'd left.

"You know, I'm not up for cotching in the metro station tonight. It being Friday I think it's a bad idea. What say we seek some safer accommodation", I offered.

"Yeah, I agree".

We decided to head out of the city centre and into the Southern suburbs. We stared up at the tower blocks.

"This is what I've done before. You press the button on the door a few times and eventually, somebody lets you in. Then you go right to the top of the block and sleep on a staircase there", said George.

"Why's that?" I asked.

"Because at the top nobody will take the stairs down. They'll all take the elevator, so you should be left in peace."

We tried one of the blocks and pressed on the buzzer a couple of times, but after getting suspicious looks from passers-by, I wasn't too keen on the idea. So, we headed back into town. We passed by an area of more downscale housing.

"These apartments are easy to get into", George claimed.

"All you have to do is stick the holding end of a spoon in them, jiggle it around a little bit, then turn it 90 degrees. They don't make very secure locks in Hungary. I'm going to try this one".

He marched over to a red door and stuck the spoon into the lock. To my surprise, within 5 seconds, it was open. George waved at me to come over, and we both entered. We located ourselves at the back, underneath a staircase on the ground floor. (It was only three story's high) As it was past midnight, most of the residents should have been in bed by now. I wrapped a blanket around me and lay down on the smooth floor. Once again, I was glad to be under a roof and in the warmth.

"You know, those American kids this morning, they were looking at you as if you were some kind of Messiah. They were clinging on to every word you were saying", George laughed.

"Really?"

"I heard them. They were saying: "Listen to the English guy. I think he knows what he's talking about".

"I personally think they were young and highly suggestible", I sighed, then turned over to sleep.

One of the residents gave us our 7 am a wake-up call. It was the usual routine of suddenly waking up, gathering your possessions, then getting out of the door. I could now get through the whole thing in under 90 seconds.

Keleti was to be our morning base. The punters were in a generous mood this morning. They kept on giving us food donations. Before 10 am, I had a bag full of bread, bakery and meat. One girl even handed me an entire packet of cigarettes. Folk always seemed to be in a good mood on Saturday morning. Maybe because there was no work and they were off to do a day's shopping or go and see the family.

George piped up.

"Hey, I've been busy people watching. It's better than watching TV".

He mimicked, pressing a remote control.

"On channel 5, we have a guy having a blazing row with his girlfriend. Now she's slapping him around the face. Funny."

He did the remote-control thing again.

"On channel six, a man is trying to open his umbrella. It's springing out entirely the other way and breaking. On channel one, a man is walking through with his dog. Now the dog is going to see that bird and chase after it. There you go. Now he's sending the owner running across the station. "

Besides people watching we had another source of amusement, and that was people coming up to us and wanting to have a chat. We'd get all manner of folk. Often, they were just friendly, but sometimes they could be downright crazy. We'd moved to a different metro station that was out of the centre and much quieter.

"Hey, It's Saturday night tonight, and you know what that means?" George asked.

"What?"

"Party people! 'Cause party people, they think that people like you and me are cool!" he claimed optimistically.

We sat down on a bit of cardboard each. Fortunately for George, the first person to come up to him was an attractive, blonde yoga instructor. She was having an in-depth chat with him, though wasn't paying me a blind bit of notice. Right now, she was going on about him finding 'his authentic self' .

"When you reach the age of around 35, that's when you discover who you truly are. It's like you become a different person", she preached.

"You are an intelligent person. In fact, you're cleverer than most of the people who walk through this station. I can see it in your eyes", she told him.

"No. He is the clever one, this English guy here; he is a very intelligent man", he pointed at me.

She's still not paying me any notice.

The next one to come along and be sociable definitely fell into the crazy category. She was a middle-aged lady who was pleasant enough. She asked the usual round of questions. "Where were we from? How long had we been living on the streets? What had led us to be in this metro station on this cold winter night?" blah, blah, blah.

"Oh, you are very poor. I'm going to go down the deli and get you something. What would you like?"

"Olives and cheese....and maybe some red wine", George requested optimistically.

"I can get you the olives and cheese, but I'm not going to buy you any alcohol", she replied firmly.

Half an hour later she returned with a bag full of deli goodies: bread, olives, cheese and a small bit of cake as an afterthought.

"That's very kind of you", I said while making myself up a sandwich.

She stopped and looked at me intently.

"Your eyes, there is something in your eyes", she looked at me with fright.

"What? Is there a problem with them?" (They occasionally go bloodshot for some reason.)

"I was going to let you come and stay around my house this evening, but now I'm not so sure. There is something in your eyes that is really frightening me".

Oh, come on, you're hurting my feelings now, love.

"Your eyes…." And with that, she scuttled away without a goodbye.

"What the hell was all that about?"

"I think she fancies you, man. She is definitely a little crazy, I think", George laughed.

With that, I retired to bed. I'd figured this location was just about safe enough. Not long after that, I awoke to the sound of a female voice.

"Is he still alive?"

I opened my eyes to see a female crotch directly in my line of view. I couldn't be bothered to get up, so replied to that.

"No. Talk to this", she said, pointing to her face.

"Not this".

She was with a group of friends. They were coming back from a night out and were in jolly spirits.

"This is Elizabeth. She wants to take us down the pub", said George.

I stood up and shook myself awake; Elizabeth had clearly had a couple. As they were a few minutes deep into their conversation, I couldn't pick up its thread. But he'd probably been laying on a sob story which she wasn't buying.

"Do you know what I think? I think this is all about you guys seeing how anarchist you can be. I don't need to work. I don't need to abide by society's rules. Blah, blah, blah".

Well yeah, of course.

"Anyway, I don't mind taking you out for a drink, but I cannot let you stay in my house tonight".

We made it quite clear that it was fine, and we didn't expect her to.

"I need to go to the ATM first. Would one of you come with me?"

Naturally, I offered. The roads outside were icy; I took care not to slip.

"You have to protect me", Elizabeth murmured quietly.

Except was I really up for defending others when I could barely protect myself? Burning through so many calories a day was making me skinny. There was hardly any body fat left on me, which meant I felt the cold a lot more. In contrast, Elizabeth was quite voluptuous, in her early twenties and with dark hair. We met up with the others and walked the short distance to a bar down the road. It was a cool, funky place. The spiral staircase took us down to a cellar bar, and Elizabeth brought us a pint each.

"How old are you?" was the first question she asked me.

"Thirty one".

I guess by my age I should be living in suburbia somewhere, staying in and watching Coronation Street and looking forward to mowing the grass on Sunday morning…. or something……

"I get bored easily, that's my problem. Staying in some boring, dead-end job and only just about managing to scrape by and pay the rent. It's a life of mediocrity that I almost fear", I explain.

Elizabeth didn't seem convinced, so I continued.

"I guess you could say that I was addicted to excitement and taking risks. We've all got to inject a compelling drama into our lives. Otherwise, it feels flat", I elaborated further.

It wasn't long before I was on my 2nd pint, then third. This was a Saturday treat that I hadn't expected. Being brought a bag of bakery produce when you were hungry was one thing, but being taken down the pub by a girl a fair bit younger than you was another.

"I work for BT in a big corporate office. It's a boring job, but it pays me to live. Why don't you teach English? You are a native speaker, and there are plenty of people here who want to learn".

"But it's his accent. Half the time I can't make out what he's saying", George chipped in.

"But I can understand him fine".

That's because by now, I was learning to use my foreigner voice with the accent moderated.

Elizabeth was a chatty girl. She seemed full of energy and even made a point of walking us back to the metro station.

"Greg, get yourself out of those rags. Go and get a job teaching English and have a proper life", Elizabeth said as she parted company with us.

Oh yeah; if only it were that simple.

I lay in all through the next day. It was Sunday so there wasn't much going on and it seemed more sensible to put down and conserve energy. But come the early evening, something was telling me to get up and face the world again. Sometimes if you're feeling bored and lost the best thing to do is go for a walk, get the blood circulation going and let the ideas flow into your head.

I took a stroll down the Vá ci Utca. Don't know why. It was the last place that I wanted to be. Garish neon signs lit up the sleazy long narrow street. Something was winking at me from the floor. It wasn't a 50 euro note, was it? It was as well! A rush of dopamine hit my brain. One of those moments went you can't quite believe your luck. I marched straight over to the Bureau de change and handed it over, half expecting the clerk to declare it as fake. He placed it under the UV scanner then handed me back a fistful of Forint. It seems ridiculous now, but at that moment, it truly felt like I'd be able to turn things around.

There was a cheap and cheerful restaurant opposite. I went in there and ordered a 12-inch pepperoni feast. So lovely to be sitting down in the warmth and comfort having a meal like a normal person. The Wombats Hostel was at the end of the street. Good old Wombats; they've seen me right all across Europe. A wave of paranoia hit me as I approached. Would they let me in? I must be looking pretty rough by now.

"Yo, what's happening, man?" the security guard greeted me as I entered. Him trying to sound cool; that's a sign of acceptance. I paid for a night in a four-bedroom dorm, then went and ordered the largest and strongest beer at the bar.

"It's been a tough week", I said to the bar lady, taking the first gulp.

"Oh yeah, what have you been up to?"

"Oh, you know, this and that".

I stared at the posters on the wall. One was actively discouraging people from feeding the homeless.

'These people are cared for. Such neglect would never happen in Hungary. Give to your favourite charity instead'.

Bullshit.

I retired to the dormitory room but couldn't sleep. For a start, there were other people in there. Could they be trusted? That last statement may sound incredibly paranoid, but you have to remember I spend life looking over my shoulder and looking out for potential threats. When sleeping, I was particularly wary of who and what was around me. Then there was the heat. By now, I'd become used to sleeping in sub-zero temperatures every night. Lying in a bed in a heated room felt like being stuck in the Sahara Desert. Though getting access to a shower was a blessed relief.

I picked up on a conversation from a group of American tourists.

"Oh my gosh. Have you seen what we've gotta do to get to the airport? We gotta like get the metro to Kőbánya-Kispest then take a bus all the way there. Oh, jee wizz, man; this is like the hardest thing I've done ever", he winged.

Pull yourself together, son.

Being stuck in here with a load of tourists felt boring and sterile. I wanted to get back out on the streets again and experience adventure. It was where real life took place. The frustration got too much, and I checked out early.

One thing was for sure, though; it had been a great weekend!

I met George back at Keleti metro that evening.

"Hey, where have you been? I was getting worried. I thought you had been arrested. The cops can lock you up for spitting on the streets here you know".

"Nothing to worry about, mate. I just got lucky. Here, you know that new flute you wanted?"

"I handed him over 1500 Forint".

"For me? Wow! Thanks."

"It's for a new flute, mind", I cautioned.

The cops came marching over again, as if to welcome me back.

"Show us your documents!" they demanded.

"And what are you doing in Hungary?"

There was now a story that I'd devised: there were some problems on my bank account (some fraudulent activity or something) which meant that I couldn't access funds. So, this is how I'd come a cropper. Some money was to be sent over from the UK, but it would take a couple of days. Once received I'd be on my merry way. Always make it explicit that you don't intend to stick around and are going to be moving on at the earliest opportunity.

But for now, it was back to the age-old problem of where to sleep tonight.

"Hey, I have an idea!" George said enthusiastically as ever.

"Keleti Hall, it's never locked. Come on; I'll show you".

Keleti Hall was a block of flats that were part of the main station. As he'd stated the front door was unlocked. We galloped up to the top landing, so we were above all the residential flats. But then directly ahead of us was another door. Curiosity got the better of us, so we decided to try it. It was unlocked and led to a vast attic We stumbled in to investigate. Bats were flying around. (You must be careful; bats can carry rabies.)

"Could do with a little more light, but other than that I reckon this takes care of our needs quite well", I commented.

"It's perfect!" George enthused.

Then a sound came from right beneath us. We both stared down at the floorboards.

"We are sorry to announce that the 21.00 Rail jet service from Vienna West Bahnhof is delayed by approximately 19 minutes".

The train station was directly below us. We were squatting the attic of one of Eastern Europe's main stations. The equivalent of doing the same thing at London Euston or Victoria. Only a couple of weeks ago I'd arrived here on the platform and looked up at the ceiling. Never had I imagined that I'd be vacating the inside of the roof. A rush of euphoria filled me. We put our possessions and blankets down, then made a home for the night.

"You know, when I was a kid, I always got a thrill out of finding hidden places where the adults wouldn't find me. I guess some things you never grow out of, huh?"

Again, George hadn't understood a word of what I said.

But of course, our good fortune didn't last. The following day they'd locked the door to the attic. Fortunately, I'd learnt this lesson already: when you're in a place of precarious lodging, anything that you don't want to lose, take with you. Though I broke another one of my golden rules that day: don't get caught out in the wet. Or in this instance, the snow. Moisture and cold is never a good combination. I'd come down with a bad chill. But out here a bad chill can turn into pneumonia if you're not careful. I lay down with my blanket over me at Corvin negyed metro.

"Greg, aren't you going to get up? It's 3 o'clock in the afternoon", George pondered.

"Errh......give me another 5 minutes, man", I gurgled.

"But you've been lying in all day. What difference are 5 minutes going to make?"

The truth was I wasn't getting up for anybody. It felt like I'd been pole axed.

"I don't feel well", I said in my best wingy tone, like a kid trying to get off school for the day.

"Oh", George replied, then very thoughtfully placed an empty Styrofoam cup by my side, but the cup didn't get any fuller.

"What's the matter with people? Won't they give money to a sick man?" George protested.

Well, would you give money to a corpse?

My lack of finesse that day brought the attention of the local constabulary. Except for this time, they were a little more sympathetic. A policeman came over to ask if I was alright. I gurgled a response and was shivering savagely.

"Do you need medical attention?"

I shook my head, not wanting to kick up a fuss.

I sat up then one of Georges dodgy acquaintances came along looking concerned. He gripped my hand and rubbed it. Clearly, he wasn't a bad guy after all; just somebody who spent too much time on the wrong side of the tracks. The next thing I knew two paramedics had arrived. This wasn't what I wanted. All I needed was to curl up somewhere warm and in private. I explained that there was nothing terribly wrong with me and I didn't need to go to the hospital. A doctor's response to my symptoms would be, '*go home and get plenty of rest*'.

"Can you stand up", the paramedic asked.

I did so.

"So why did you call us?"

"I didn't call you; I didn't want you to be here!" I snapped.

He looked perplexed as to what to do. The police were adamant that I wouldn't be staying here.

"Okay, come with us", he eventually said.

We boarded the ambulance. They whizzed me off and took me to the entrance of a night shelter. They briefly explained things to the guy at the door, then wrote out a piece of medical paperwork, which was to be my entry ticket here. The paramedic acted like a mother dumping her newborn child at the entrance to a hospital because she doesn't know what else to do with him.

The person at reception explained that as I was a non-national, I was entitled to a stay of 3 nights only. Well, that was fine by me. The place was vastly overstretched. There must have been close to 300 people in residence. A third of them were sleeping on mats on the floor. Every type of bed had been put to use, hospital beds and even baby cots. It was a surreal sight watching grown men curl up to sleep in them. This place seemed to serve as one-third prison, one-third homeless centre and one-third funny farm. Many of them looked like they'd come here to die. They were no longer able to survive out on the street, so spent their days in here waiting for nothing in particular. I heard the sound of an American voice.

"Hi, I'm Frank", he introduced himself as one of the other inmates.

He'd been living in Hungary for several years now, due to having family connections here, so could speak the language fluently, but had been living in here for the past couple of years. Therefore he could act as my translator and guide. There were certain do's and don't in this place, official and otherwise. So, he was the one to show me the ropes. He showed me to my bed, which was a top bunk above his. His comrades were sitting down in the corner. One of them pulled out a bag full of provisions.

"Hey, you want some bread? It's not the freshest but give it a try".

I took a couple of slices. It was indeed stale around the crusts, but just about edible. A large bloke kept on staring down at my boots.

"Business?" he kept on saying and pointing, wanting to swap his for mine. (At least I hope that's what he meant.)

"Dinner gets served at 9 pm. We gotta queue right by there. But make sure you get in the queue early, cause there's a lotta people here", said Frank.

I took his advice. At nine there was a scramble to get to the front and I still only managed about 50th in the line, and it took half an hour to get to the front. Dinner was a cup of tea with a tube of liver pate and two slices of bread. I took place on the top bunk, gazing down at Frank and his comrades. They were playing cards together. Every so often, Frank would remonstrate with one of them for trying to cheat. It was like watching a prison movie.

"Are you doing good there, buddy?" Frank kept on asking, sticking his head up inquiringly.

I was doing just great. All I needed was to be left alone and get rested in order to shake off this, whatever it was. I merely nodded.

With 300 punters in the building, the noise of coughing and whatever else was incessant. Come dawn the huffle and cufuffle began. For some reason, we all got kicked out at 05.30. It was still pitch-black outside and bitterly cold. I mooched around the city, then tried to remember the way back. There was little scope for achieving anything. After midday, we were allowed back inside the lobby area. One of Franks mates had managed to get hold of a bottle of wine, so we sneaked off the back with it to surreptitiously have a drink. Just like George said, alcohol is an international language.

Come three o clock in the afternoon we all had to take place in our beds and get registered; otherwise, we'd lose our spot. Then that was it, the doors were locked, and the only thing to look forward to was a liver pate and bread dinner. Some people had been in there years. With a system like this little wonder that folk just sat there and slowly died. How were you supposed to get a job or doing anything constructive? I've always been highly critical of the hostel/homeless shelter system, but that's a rant for another day. Let's just say you can see why so many people prefer to stay out of them. (Though don't get me wrong, on this occasion I was grateful for the support.) There was nothing else to do except keep my head down and get through this imposed 3-day sentence. The big guy was looking at my boots again.

"Business?"

I looked out of the bar windows. Finally, Monday, the day of release came around.

That evening I found George in the spot where I'd been carted off three days earlier. He'd been cleaned up and was in fresh clothes, though seemed in a subdued mood. His explanation that some crazy woman had put him up for a little bit.

"I've been thinking about where to go next. I've been hearing good things about Palermo", he pondered.

Palermo. I'd never even heard of the place.

"It's the capital of Sicily".

Sicily. I didn't know much about it apart from the Godfather episodes, but it seemed so exotic and mysterious. It was one of the most Southern parts of the EU. But the trouble was it was over 1300 miles getting there by land transport. At the moment, we only had enough for a can of beer between us.

"I know some people down there who could help us out. Maybe we could get jobs as security men at the casinos, working for Mafia", he pondered once again.

I'm sure they were nice boys really and had probably signed up to the 'Investors in people' scheme in their own little way.

"How will each of us get down there, George?"

"I don't know. But we will find a way like we always do. I think I'm going to make Slovenia my first point of call after this. It's somewhere I know, and they have some beautiful forests there".

The station was emptying of its passengers. You could hear the sound of the last train whizzing out down the tunnel. It was quite chilly; my breath steamed as I exhaled.

"I spent one-year camping in that forest in Slovenia", George began to talk again.

"Being there in amongst the trees. Plants have consciousness; they're living things, of course, they do. And that means they can communicate, just not in the same way that we do".

The metal shutters slammed shut to the station entrance and landed with a loud clang on the floor.

"Trees have been living for hundreds of years, so they have far more knowledge and wisdom than we do. I slept by the same tree for one year. You have to be with it a while before it's your friend".

It had turned eerily quiet in the station. The staff had gone, and the mad old guy in the corner dozed off to sleep. You could hear echoes and the faint sound of wind coming through the air vents, but that was it.

"After a while, the tree began talking to me; I don't mean physically as we do, but I could feel what he was transmitting. And do you know what he said to me?"

"What?"

"He told me that I must quit being a parasite in life and that I should make beautiful things instead."

I glanced over at George. It seemed as if he was locked in a trance.

"……. He told me that I should make *beautiful* things".

As he repeated, I wondered what career advice a tree would give me….

We decided to return to Keleti hall again. We could probably get away with sleeping on the top landing above the flats. It was nice and warm up there. You could hear footsteps and voices from below. We waited until the last door slammed shut before we dumped our bags down. George pulled out a bottle of red wine, then did his usual trick of splashing some on the floor.

"To bless my friends who are now in the ground", he finally explained.

A few hours later I was woken up by the sound of scuffling. George was getting his belongings together.

"I see you in Palermo", he whispered.

I gave a nod in return.

As luck would have it the rent cheque was due in the morning. I considered the long trip down to Sicily. Heading South meant getting out of the cold and that was fine by me. Getting a flight down there at last minute would cost two to three hundred euros. Besides, there were a couple of things that needed my attention first, such as buying new clothes, taking care of personal hygiene and loading up on food. The journey was going to have to be conducted in a series of hops. How do you achieve a big goal? Break it down into a series of achievable steps. Getting a bus ticket to Vienna wouldn't cost that much. Being centrally located, it was an ideal transit point. From there I'd be able to get into Italy, then keep working my way down until I reached the bottom and cross over to Sicily. Simple.

The journey of 1,327 miles begins with a single step and that first step was to Budapest intl bus station to purchase the ticket. 21 euro. Not bad. But the Euroline service to Vienna wasn't leaving for another 7 hours. That was fine. After Serbia, I'd learnt a lesson. Don't go crossing the border into another country looking like a scuzzy fucker.

I turned the corner and plonked my arse down on a leather barber chair. The barber hardly spoke any English, so I was going to have to communicate via alternative methods.

"Sweeney Todd", I said pointing at my face, seeing as every barber on the planet will know this story.

"Ah, Sweeney Todd", he answered with recognition, then picked up the cut-throat razor.

I pointed to my hair, indicating that needed trimming as well then did the various hand gestures. (The spikey hedgehog and 3 for a grade.) It went without saying that it needed washing first. A month's growth of mane got clipped off, then he lathered the foam on and put the cut-throat somewhere near my jugular.

"Your beard very strong", he remarked.

The hot towels went on in order to make the hairs stand out from my face and he gave it another two goings over with the cutthroat. My facial skin had taken a hard battering over the past month from all that cold air and sleeping in dubious places. But here was proper facial surgery going on, giving me a proper face to show to the world.

"You are getting full service", he said taking care of my eyebrows, then nostril hair. There was a sting as alcohol disinfectant was applied, then came the smell of lime face balm. After a final dusting of powder, he stood back to admire his handy work.

"A new man", he concluded.

The face staring back at me in the mirror looked somehow respectable. I was to be leaving the city that had been my home for a month on good terms. It had undoubtedly thrown up its challenges but had taken good care of me. I boarded the 19.00 Eurolines service to Vienna – Erdburg. The slamming shut of the luggage doors gave me a satisfying feeling. Task completed. I'd made it out alive. The start of what seemed like an impossible challenge had begun. The end destination was a long way off. But as I was to discover, the journey was to be far more important than the destination.

THE WANDERER

Chapter 4

Cold feet in Vienna

Another city to walk through in the cold and snow. 120 Euros was never going to stretch that far. I didn't like Austria or Vienna that much. Sure, it was grand and full of historical monuments, but it felt a little *too* grand and had a very sterile feel to it. I'd spent the last night in a backpacker's hostel and caned the 5 euro all you could eat breakfast. After kicking out time I'd headed to Vienna's excellent central library, but soon got bored of looking at historical artwork. But at Wien West Bahnhof (the central train station) I'd done my best to blend in as 'just another passenger'. Periodically, I'd get up to look at the departure boards with impatience, then sat upright on the benches occasionally nodding off then remembering to rotate position.

But come midnight that game was over when they locked the doors. It was down to minus 5 with the thick frozen snow, and I didn't have a sleeping bag. (I didn't like transferring sleeping apparatus between countries.) On occasions like this, it's best to get up on your feet and keep moving, if anything to keep your blood circulation going. It's incredible how much this warms you up and gives you a mental distraction from the cold. And remember, cold can kill if you're not careful.

I headed towards the river. Maybe I could get underneath a bridge, find some cardboard and make a blanket out of something. It's best to avoid alcohol in these situations as it lowers your body temperature. So, I tatted a bottle of Vodka and orange off the floor just to be a prick, because getting mildly drunk can be slightly good for your soul.

After drinking it all, this road to nowhere seemed a tad more bearable. It was 2 am, and I'd strayed into a dodgy part of town.

"Excuse me, do you know where I can get a tram from?"

The question had come from an attractive dark-haired woman with beautiful green eyes. Two things were strange about this: one she'd asked me outright in English (why ask a foreigner?) and two; she was local. Any local would know that the trams had stopped running by now.

"Ja, Zentrum", practicing my fumbling German.

"No. No. I don't think there is", she smiled.

We chatted briefly. It was one of those random conversations that you have with strangers on the street.

"Do you fancy coming for a drink?" she offered after introducing herself as Selina.

"I'd love to. But funds are a little tight at the moment".

"It's okay; I can get you a drink".

Result.

I followed her to a late-night bar, and we got a large beer each. I gave her the bare bones of what I'd been up to the last couple of months: Berlin – Serbia - Budapest and now here. Naturally, the rough parts of the story got omitted.

"Sure, yeah; I'm just passing through Vienna on my way to Italy. It should be a little warmer there", I added casually.

"But how do you get around? What do you do for money?"

"Oh, you know, I get by".

Selina was a tall and stocky girl. Tough, but vulnerable looking at the same time. She was more candid with her own story. She'd not long been out of prison for armed robbery.

"I put a knife to a taxi driver throat and said: "give me all your fucking money", she said sheepishly like a naughty school girl fessing up to not doing her homework.

I was finding this quite sexy; you know. I like um a little dangerous. Besides, don't ever worry if someone does this to you. It's tough to kill someone this way – your jugular is exceptionally well protected.

"He only had a few hundred euros on him. Fortunately, I had a good lawyer. It cost me four thousand euro, so I got away with a 4-month sentence".

The excess alcohol, highly charged scene and her rather exciting disposition were making this lady seem considerably attractive. I slurred something nonsensical.

"You have a beautiful face", she smiled.

I really should have tipped that barber.

Our bodies entangled, and we got down to the passionate, smoochy business. Though this was a little too fresh for the landlords liking and he told us to pack it in. So, we continued with the getting to know you chit-chat. She lived in a small village up on the Austrian/Czech border and kept on going on about her abusive ex-partner. I listened patiently then she made me the offer of staying at hers for the weekend. Well, that was accommodation issues taken care of quite swiftly. She settled the tab. We linked arms and left the bemused landlord to it.

I was glad to have female company for a change. We headed towards one of the cities train stations. There was something that Selina needed to attend to urgently. By now, I was half guessing what it was. She found an empty phone booth in the station, pulled her jeans down, then injected into her thigh.

"Should I have walked away at this point? Typically, I'll go out of my way to avoid the company of heroin users. I want to say I'm a nice guy who has a soft spot for needy women, but the truth was I was tagging along for entirely selfish reasons. Although, it seemed irresponsible to leave someone like that.

She chose to enjoy her gauge in the station café. She muttered something non-nonsensical, then slumped her head down on the table. I held her hand the entire time. The sharp winter sun was rising over Vienna and life was kicking into the metropolises. For over half an hour, not a word was spoken between us. She was quietly mumbling to herself. The manageress came over, and the pair had the sort of bitchy exchange that only females can.

Selina walked out of there defiantly.

"My mother should be in by now. I can take you to meet my family, but first, we need to do some grocery shopping".

Well, at least I was achieving my aim of meeting the locals. We stopped by at the local Penny Mart, then walked down to the first district to a block of neat townhouse apartments.

"My mother will be glad to meet you because now she has somebody to talk in English. But first I need to warn you about the dog. He's not very good with strangers".

When she opened the door, there was a great big German shepherd at the who started growling at me. Her brother said something in German to warn him off.

"This is my youngest brother. I have another two. He's a perfectionist; that's why he won't talk in English with you, because he's scared of getting it wrong.".

He seemed like a cheerful chap. He was clearly the one she got on with – her teammate in the family. Then an older woman came in, complaining loudly. She spoke with a gravely East Coast American accent.

"I had to go to three different grocery stores, and they still didn't have what I wanted".

She stopped, then looked at me. An awkward silence followed. She reminded me of the "Momma" character out of the film "The Goonies". Selina made the initial introductions. Momma rolled her eyes as if to say, "oh, she's done this again". I did my best to stand there innocuously in the background, being polite and non-intrusive, yet still providing good company and being personable. This approach appeared to work. Slowly momma warmed to me and came quite chatty as she cooked lunch. She was hard as nails, no doubt about it, but essentially a decent woman. She was from Philadelphia, USA. I'd been to the North-East corridor of the states a couple of times, so we found some common ground. And the fish was delicious. By now, momma was trying to be hospitable as a matter of principle. The strong coffee had woken me up. The mood had lightened, and rapport got established.

Then talk resumed of Selina returning to her hometown. It was a three-hour train ride away. I was meant to be having some UK money arriving in my travel money account that day at midday. But what about if it didn't? As you're probably aware by now, financing this trip was a highly precarious business. I should have played it cautious and backed out, but momentum was taking over. Momma was pretty keen to get her daughter dispatched.

"You gotta kick her ass; otherwise she'll never get moving", she notified me.

"You know your train leaves at 14.00 You gotta get two trams and a metro to get there. If you don't hurry, you're not going to make it".

Unfortunately, momma thought it best if she accompanied us up there. We took the journey there by public transport, without tickets. Periodically Selina reassured me by winking and fixing a kiss on the lips. She figured she just about had enough time to sink into the underground network and score off a dealer. In the meantime, I checked the ATM. No dice. Fuck.

There'd been an admin cock-up at the post office. At that moment Selina returned looking reassured. This was the same train station we had been in this morning. To the untrained eye, it appeared a mundane setting. But after being exposed to the underbelly, I could see dubious business occurring everywhere.

"Okay, you can buy your tickets there. They are 24 euros each. If you're quick, you can make it".

I sheepishly explained my predicament. Momma sighed like a burst formula one tyre.

"You mean we came all this way for nothing?"

Selina appeared non-plussed with this.

The journey back was awkward. I had some appeasing to do and fumbled my apologies.

"Shit happens", momma shrugged.

"My darling, you must be very honest and open with me – for I have been honest with you", Selina said as if she was talking to a small child. Well, that's blown it.

"So, you are broke. It's okay; we can still have some fun in Vienna this weekend. And my mother, she likes you. But you must be straight forward with us" then gave me a reassuring kiss on the lips.

We got back to Mom's, and Selina preoccupied herself.

"I have something here".

It was two wraps. One heroin, the other cocaine – the makings of a "speedball" – the concoction that killed Kurt Cobain. She cooked up.

"Not for me, thanks". I said gently but firmly.

"Are you sure?"

"Positive".

"Okay, but if you change your mind, just open your mouth."

The needle went into her flesh. It being Austria, I'm guessing the coke was pretty shit (as it was all across Europe at the time), But the smack was probably quite potent. A jolt hit her body; she vomited into a paper bag that she thoughtfully had ready. That was the cocaine taking effect, but then the smack took over and won. Again, this sent her into a stupor, and she lay semi-conscious on the sofa, not uttering a word.

Momma came in and looked wistfully down at her daughter.

"A junkie", she sighed.

"I've tried everything. You know I almost had a heart attack last year", she shook her head.

"We've taken her to rehab, but nothing has worked".

I, of course, had my sympathies with momma. What could she do?

I sat there by Selina for the next hour or so. I'd love to say it was like watching sleeping beauty, but really, I was only doing it to ensure that Selina didn't choke on her vomit.

Eventually, she sat up and was ready to start talking.

"That's the spot where he killed himself", she said, pointing to a spot in the dining room.

"Who did?"

"My brother. It was around this time 16 years ago. I was just 14 at the time, and he was 17. I didn't know what to do or say to him. What can you do when someone close to you says they're going to do something like that? I mean I couldn't stop him, so I decided the best thing to do was for him to have somebody he loved by his side and for him to be happy in the final moments of his life".

"He killed himself in *that* corner right there", she reiterated, pointing emphatically to the corner.

"But my family. They blamed me for it. They asked, why didn't you try to stop him? They held me responsible for it and still do, I think".

"So, my mother, she kicked me out", Selina said, screwing her face up sorrowfully.

"I was just 14, and it was in the middle of Winter!"

It all made sense now. She'd become a scapegoat for the traumatic and highly complex family event at a time when she was too young to comprehend it all entirely. You've always got to have someone to blame, to take the rap. So, they'd picked the most natural target when they couldn't understand what was going on themselves. Confusion can often turn to anger. She'd been banished to the harsh wilderness as a young teenager as if that would solve it all. No wonder she'd developed a smack habit.

This is a trait that's universally shared by all homeless people I've ever met: they come from more complex family backgrounds. (Yes, I appreciate that family life is always complicated.) I don't want to use the term "bad" as this would signify blame, and that's the wrong thing to do. In many cases, they've been forced to accept a burden of guilt. Or live a lie that has been dysfunctionally running through the family tree like a spike of poison.

None of us was born tramps. (Not my phrase).

After finishing her piece, Selina sort refuge in her old bedroom.

"You wanna watch a movie? We've got just about everything", momma proposed.

"Comedy sounds like a good idea", I suggested. (Obviously, I wasn't going to recommend '*Trainspotting*')

The Brit flick '*Ship on a rock*' was put on by her younger brother who joined us. It was a jolly movie about the pioneering and underground radio station movement of the 1960's – '*Radio Caroline*' and all that. It came complete with a swinging soundtrack.

"Now if Selina had just stuck to doing Acid, I'd have been happy", momma commented.

We collectively agreed that we were all off clubbing that evening. Selina emerged from the shower looking far healthier now she was cleaned up, made up and changed. We ended up in a bar that was frequented by bikers. That classic Rick James number came on.

"*She's a very kinky girl, the type you don't take home to mother….*

She's a freak, super freak, this girl is kinda freaky, yow".

How poignant; that song could have been written for Selina. Check out the original video. The dancer in it with long, dark hair looked and acted exactly like her. It's a great tune.

By this time Selina had lost interest in me and got cosy with some other guy. But that was fine by me. Her other brother, Peter, took me by his side.

"Look, Greg, If I were you, I'd forget about Selina. Don't get me wrong; I love my sister, but she's a cruel bitch and a stupid slut".

"Peter, I think you're right".

"Okay, let's get out of here".

He dragged me off down to a drum and bass night. We partied away till 4 am, but by that time I was spent. Outside, he treated me to a doner kebab.

"I'm a little bit angry with my sister", he said while we stood munching the alleged meat.

"She shouldn't have dragged you into all this when you're just a tourist here on holiday". (Holiday? Is that what you call it? My actions were quite justifiably attracting this sort of caper.)

"You can come and stay on my couch tonight if you want", he offered.

It was the classic persecutor, victim, rescuer cycle.

He led me to his flat and showed me the sofa. Then left a loaf of bread and a handful of cigarettes on the table. Whatever happened, the family had undoubtedly been hospitable.

"I've got to get up for work in the morning, so I'll see you around".

My head could finally stop spinning as I lay down. Peter left in a hurry a few hours later.

"Vielen Dank", I muttered.

I lay in until the early afternoon and left half the cigarettes by way of politeness. A quick and quiet departure was required. It was time to face the streets again.

The next few days past by thankfully uneventfully while I waited for the cock-up at the post office to resolve itself. A routine got established. The Central library served as day time headquarters, sat with the other tramps, reading English newspapers. We discreetly nodded to each other in solidarity. To other people, they may have appeared to be regular punters, but I knew who they were. They always carried around a bag with a small bulge in the middle as if it was part of their anatomy. The slight bump indicated a sleeping bag. I felt like a sad, lonely old man sitting here all day. It was a very passive battle for survival, but anything to stay out of the harsh, icy cold.

Come the evening I switched to the West Bahnhof, once again pretending to be "just another passenger" awaiting their train. By night I hit the metro station for sleeping. Karl Platz station seemed to be the main bum hangout. Though things weren't quite as cultured as Budapest, outside the temperature hit a new low of minus 7, so I was grateful to be lying down on thick cardboard. Sleeping here at night was reluctantly tolerated by the city's transport police. They knew they'd be dealing with a load of dead bodies on the street if they didn't.

At midnight they came around for the usual document request. The standard story given. "Just passing through officers, honest". Now it was safe to lie down and relax. I took this opportunity to formulate a plan for the next stage of the journey. Northern Italy was the target. Florence seemed like a good bet. At 6 am, the cops helpfully came around with their wake-up call.

"Morgen! Is time to wake up now, my little twinkle toes".

The following morning his colleague wasn't quite so pleasant. A sharp kick to the sole of my boot awoke me.

"Get on your feet, asshole!"

Spare time was spent foraging for food and other necessities, as usual going to the main tourist and party hangouts at certain times. I developed a keen interest in opera concert times. By the end of the week, there was an account credit of 80 Euros. I marched straight down to Erdberg bus station.

"Florence bus has left already; we've only got one going to Verona", the ticket counter informed.

THE WANDERER

Not as far South as I'd liked but sounded lovely. After coffee and cigarettes, there was just enough left for the ticket. I'd be arriving with 70 cents to my name - a new personal best.

The bus wasn't scheduled to leave until 21.00. A long wait. The only amusement in the cramped waiting area came from watching the Winter Olympics on mute. Arnie kept on flashing up. I'd noticed that a lot of Austrians were into their bodybuilding and martial arts. Some were blatantly caning steroids. They looked like pumped up Michelin men.

Come nine the waiting area closed, and we were forced to wait outside, No sign of the bus. If there were an award for Europe's worst international bus station, then this one would win it hands down. We were waiting on the tarmac in minus 4 - no departure boards or info. No shelter. Not even a fucking roof. The only staff member on duty was the gateman. There was no telling when the bus was going to turn up – if ever.

My fellow passenger waiting was a young Serbian lad.

"I'm so cold. It's my feet that are the worst", he complained.

I grabbed a sheet of cardboard for him.

"You need to stand on this. The cold is going to be shooting right through your body. Roll your sweater up over your head. Don't lose heat. Now you need to keep your blood circulation going. Curl your ankles up and down. Now keep on pressing your fingers up and down onto your palms", I demonstrated.

But there was still no escaping the cold. It was as if the country was giving me one final challenge before escaping. Not for the first time in Vienna, I'd got cold feet.

"When the bus driver come, I'm going to fuck his mother!" my Serbian friend declared.

Coach after coach came and went, but not ours.

"Is it this one? It has to be this one", the Serb said, staring ahead.

Its headlights seemed to beam brighter than the others. At last! Four hours late – it had been caught up in a snowdrift in Slovenia.

"Verona", I handed the driver the ticket and jumped straight on. But the Serb was choosing to argue.

"I'm going to fu…."

"Get on! It's lovely and warm in here", I yelled.

The joyful sound of the luggage doors slamming once again as if to say, well done, you made it out. The bus was to be my hotel for the night. I leant over, and within minutes I was asleep.

The warmth of Italy was coming......

Chapter 5

The long way down

So much for it being warm. The snow was still on the ground.

Verona was a beautiful city – the land of Romeo and Juliet. Then what was that in the distance on this bright and sunny morning? It was the Alps! An awe-inspiring sight.

I spent the first day of arrival, getting to know the city. It wasn't that big. Straight away I bumped into an abandoned building and earmarked it for a return that evening. You can always spot an abandoned building by the amount of graffiti that's on the walls. I came back at night then quickly checked that no cops were passing by - all clear. I jumped through a hole in the wall and took out my torch. Hmm, in need of a little modernisation, me thinks. It was a massive building on three floors. Looking by the paint spray markings on the walls, it appeared that it was about to be demolished.

I took a walk upstairs checking first that the stairs were still intact. Obviously, in a building like this Asbestos is a cause for concern, especially around the doors. My (limited) understanding is that it's only dangerous when it's airborne. You need to be exposed to it for years before it does you any damage. Thankfully the top floor was in better condition. The rooms even had carpets. The roof didn't look like it was going to cave in anytime soon, though it might leak a bit. There was another reason for coming up here; in these circumstance's height is always your friend. The main concern was junkies wandering in and using it as a shooting gallery. The thing is a junkie will generally want to come down, do his business, have a happy gauge out, then leave. It's doubtful that they're going to bother climbing stairs and do a bit of urban exploring. And yes, I'd already checked the place for sharps. It wasn't the Hilton, but most importantly, it was a roof that sheltered me from the rain and was relatively safe.

Two members of my family sent me £50 every month. I will mention at this point that no one ever makes it on their own despite what they might say. The next one was due in 10 days. This place would have to serve as a home until then, and then it would be time for a further hop South.

Surprisingly, Verona didn't make much of a fuss about Valentines Day. That's the day that I left on and discovered the delights of riding the Treno Regionale. Sixty Euros got withdrawn on the travel money card. It was enough for one good day: a proper meal in a café and a coffee while I motivated myself for the next mission. Florence was to be the next hop I could afford. Not very far, but still progress.

"Buongiorno. Un-solo biglietto per Firenze Centrale, per favour, Treno Regionale", I said at the train station.

"Treno Regionale?" he said in surprise.

"Si"

The reason why they were puzzled over that request is that the Treno Regoanale was the local stopping train that called at every little village through Tuscany. Though it only cost 12 Euro. The InterCity train or Eurostar Italia would have cost far more. A four-hour trip, but that didn't matter - plenty more time to watch the mountain scenery unfolding.

Darkness fell by the time we had arrived in Florence. The first person to greet me was one of the Roma aggressively jangling her paper cup right in my face. She held up a bit of cardboard which I think read, *'homeless and broke'*.

"Niente soldi", I replied.

She pointed to the ice cream in my hand as if to say, well if you can afford that. *That* hit a raw nerve.

"Vaffanculo!" I snapped.

Everyone hates the Roma.

Florence, as you can imagine, was a massively touristy place. Americans and Chinese were by far the most prominent visitors to the area. Well, that was great news for someone like me for reasons already stated. (I seriously overdosed on Belgium waffles.) While all this may have been great for the city's tourist board, it was causing resentment among the locals. Everything in the city centre was enormously expensive. That meant they couldn't afford to eat in any of the restaurants or drink in the bars. It kept the price of accommodation high, and they were pushed further and further out.

Most of the profit went to the wealthy Russians who owned the hotels. Sure, this may have provided plenty of jobs in the hotel and catering business. But that would entail them working their arse off for the minimum wage, paying them just enough to survive, hardly living the dream.

Armed with this sympathy and empathy, I got busy befriending the locals. The Italians seemed to like me, and I liked them. By now, I was getting the hang of this international homeless lark. My total monthly income equalled about £400 or 500 Euros at the time. £100 from family support, £135 from the rent cheque and the rest just seemed to come into my hands. It was hard to describe this phenomenon as it was so random. But I'd just be walking down the street one day, minding my own business and clutching my belongings like the respectable hobo that I am and suddenly a punter would hand me a 5 euro note. There would be the briefest of non-verbal communication. I'd reply with a "grazie mille signor/signora", and they'd be on their way. It must have meant that I appeared pretty screwed to them, though on the plus side inspired enough hope for them to sponsor me.

My sleeping quarters were underneath a bridge by a dried-out canal just outside the city centre. I got back there around nine every night then lay down in my sleeping bag. You can often find perfectly good ones lying on the street, which no one else appeared to be using. Sleeping all night with my clothes on meant that my skin was dehydrated. Personal hygiene had become an issue. Back in England, there were always places where you could go and get a shower. But abroad it was much more difficult. Each morning I'd get a wash in the accessible toilets of McDonald's. Hands and face first because that's what people see. Then pay particular attention to the places that sweat the most. (I'll leave that to your imagination.) Even the act of throwing water over one's face was a morale booster.

There was one thing I did every morning without fail, and that was brushing my teeth. Not having a shower or shave for a while was easily rectifiable. But poor dental hygiene would be a different story. You can tell a lot about a person and what type of life they've led by their teeth – what kind of condition they are in. After all, it's what you'll be looking at when they talk to you. Someone under the age of 30 with terrible teeth usually indicates a drug addiction (heroin/crack/amphetamine), and that tells you just about everything. By the way, to this day, I still have one of my milk teeth left. Go figure.

It was the following morning when the next random encounter occurred. The weather was cold and gloomy. I was out on the street with not much to do. But then a young, attractive girl almost danced up to me. She seemed full of the joys of the world.

"You wanna beer?", she smiled. We stood in one of the Piazza's sipping from a brown bottle each. She chatted to me in broken English, while I did my best in fumbling Italian. She introduced herself as Julia from Milano, 23 years old. She came across as quite middle class and educated, though had led something of a colourful life.

"Let me take you to the best sandwich shop in the whole of Firenze!"

She led me down a maze of side streets off the main drag in the city centre.

"No tourists come to this place, only locals. It's the only one in the city that we can afford to eat at".

The proprietor chatted to us enthusiastically. Julia translated for me.

"He say you are from England. London is his favourite city in the whole world".

We sat down at the table as I munched from the salami and green olive sandwich. It was spicier and richer than anything you'd usually find in an Italian restaurant.

"This is what *real* coffee tastes like", Julia said, passing over the pot.

"I have been to your country before, and I'm sorry, but over there it's more like flavoured coffee water".

Julia gave me a little more background info as we chatted. She was an art student. Her father had been a fighter pilot in the Italian Air Force, and her brother was a sports journalist. But then she got down to the real nitty-gritty.

"When I was living on the streets here, we were all so close. Every night one of us would get leftover pizza that the restaurants left outside and whatever we had, we shared between us. We were like a family".

It was at this point she fessed up to having developed a smack habit at that time, and she was now in the latter stages of recovery. Though it can't have been that bad; her teeth were in good condition. And she looked too healthy. By now you should have seen a pattern emerging: attractive junkie girls sure like taking me out for a drink.

"But this is the most important thing I've learnt of all: when you live on the street you get your saviours".

Again, it was something that I was to do well to remember. So, this was Julia returning her good bit of fortune. She walked me back to the place where she'd found me and made a point of buying me a packet of cigarettes. I offered her one out of the pack, and we had a smoke together. She gave me a firm hug with a childlike girly squeal, then disappeared just as quickly as she'd come into my life.

So, there you have it: even nice young girls from respectable middles class families can end up being on the street.

That meeting left me in high spirits for the rest of the day. It was the fact that someone had chosen to give you the time of day, then show affection, warmth and encouragement.

The next payday was due (another 60 Euros) and with that the next-hop South. Same procedure: a trip to the supermarket for essentials, then on the Treno Regionale down to the capital this time. As the train chugged down and made its endless stops, I considered that I was well over the journeys half waypoint. But the amount of time it was taking was concerning. It was early March. I should have been in Palermo by now.

The train was almost empty as we disembarked at Roma Termini late on Thursday night. Rome was a major international city, and the set-up would be quite different here. More cosmopolitan; it would be easier to blend in with the hustle and bustle of things. With the support of a big city, they' rd be the more significant opportunity. Although, you're at your most vulnerable upon arriving in a new place, especially when you're living in such precarious circumstances as I do. The usual routine dictated that I stopped to puff on a cigarette outside the station, then immediately vacated the area. Hyper-alertness overtook me as I trotted out of there.

Here was something I'd seen in every major city so far: The outside of the central train station is a place that you never want to hang around. It acted as a magnet for every unsavoury type who was looking to pick on the vulnerable. In Italy, they were a draw for the many homeless people (the proper wreck head types) as they came with long concourses with a smooth, flat surface making it ideal for sleeping. But train stations are where journeys start and end. By doing this, perhaps they were hoping to get away.

Once I'd walked into the city itself, the anxiety drifted away to a feeling of calm familiarity. Rome reminded me a lot of London. The road layout was the same as well as a lot of the architecture. Then I suddenly remembered why: London was, of course, originally a Roman settlement: Londinium.

Where to sleep in a city you haven't been to before when it's late at night? Head for the river, as a major international city will always have a river running through it. This is what the city will have been built on, so it will be easy to find. You can also navigate your way around the place using that as a point of reference. You follow it, so you're some way out of town. Remember, out of town, out of bullshit. Very obviously, a river is always going to have bridges which shelter you from the elements. You find a nice quiet one, pitch up your sleeping bag and that's your home for the night.

To my relief, it was no longer cold. Rome may not have been that far from Tuscany, but the climate was very different. In Florence, up in the mountains, it had been cold and wet with the harsh wind. Here, by the Mediterranean Sea, it was distinctly warmer with a soothing climate.

The next two days took up the in-depth city walk around. The better you know your surrounding territory, the better chance you have of surviving in it. First, what were the main tourist spots and how many fat Americans were hanging around there (food and water). Plus, where were the main commuter hubs, where office workers sat down on their lunch breaks? (the same). Where was the party district, especially at the weekend? (alcohol and tobacco). What were the local parks and green spaces like, where I could set up daily headquarters now that the weather was better? Where were the sketchy areas and places to be avoided? What were the cops like with the other transients? How safe was the city in general? Remember, I am far more likely to come into harm than a regular punter. How clean was it? (Increased risk of infection.) Where were the places you could go and adhere to personal hygiene? You get the picture. After that, I'd pop into a posh hotel and asked them nicely if they'd give me a free city map. Then I could get my head around the local geography.

The first two days in a new place are always the worst and the most energy-sapping as you don't know shit from shovel. Your sleeping quarters won't be up to much either. Then I happened to pass the Piazza Della Repubblica. In the centre was a beautiful fountain and it was lined with grand buildings propped up by pillars and came with marble-floored walkways. That's all most people would perceive. But then I noticed something else: it was where the more upmarket tramps appeared to hang out. Up the road was the Termini (central train station) and there was to be no going there.

Tentatively, I went and joined their number. I kept a few yards distance from the main group and set up a base. A few minutes after lying down, a figure approached.

"Good evening. My name is Angelo, and I am sleeping just down there with my friends. Please let me know if you need anything. Some blankets perhaps? You'll find the good cardboard by the restaurant bins around the corner", he sounded more like a concierge. A few moments later, he appeared with several blankets.

"Come and join us", he offered.

THE WANDERER

In the corner, a group of them were sat diligently snapping off the ends of dog end cigarettes foraged from the ashtrays of upmarket hotels. (The posher the hotel, the longer the dog ends are likely to be.) One of them looked like Joe Pesci and was about the same size, so I referred to him as 'the little guy'. They offered me a glass of cheap red wine, which I gratefully accepted.

Angelo was a stocky chap aged in his early forties.

"How long have you been on the road?" I asked

"For seven years now. I have been to many places: Milano, Turion, Bologna".

He went on to explain further that he worked on and off as a brick-layer in the industrial cities of Northern Italy he'd just mentioned. I assumed that in more prosperous times, he lived elsewhere and right now he was in his 'off' stage. He was originally born in Italy, but when still young his parents chose to emigrate to Australia in the wave of Italian immigration in the 1970s. So, he'd been brought up viewing Australia as his home country (hence why he spoke good English). But it had been tough for the family, being perceived as lesser foreigners. Sometime later the family had been forced back to Italy. He'd come back speaking with a funny accent to a land he didn't identify with that now also viewed him as a foreigner. Not truly belonging anywhere and not being entirely accepted would have caused a lack of self-identity. You could see where his unsettled roots had been planted.

"Life on the street, it's very tough", he said gravely.

"Nice to meet you, but if you'll excuse me, I'm off to make up my bed now", he finished.

I lay down on my bed of cardboard and blankets. Then looked out at Rome, one of the most beautiful cities in the world, wind down for the night. You never quite knew where you were gonna end up next on this trip.

The next morning, we had to be up and out by 07.30. The cleaner came along to wake us up.

"Buongiorno, signor".

He made a point of being chatty and affable as we packed up.

"Here is where we leave our carboard for the rubbish men to collect. We must always leave the place tidy, as long as we do so and don't cause any problems, I think it will be alright for us to sleep here", Angelo advised. (Do you see what I mean about hanging out with the more conscientious tramps?)

"Up by the Termini, they are always drinking and fighting. They will steal anything from you, even your boots", he added.

The last time I walked past there, the place was reeking of piss.

I set off to co-ordinate my day. Every city has its strong points and things that it's good for. In Rome, one of those was finding clothes. For no apparent reason, people often left bundles of perfectly good clothes sat on top of a wall. The first thing you did was run it through the 'shit or soap' powder test. You smelt the garments, and if the smell was fresh and clean as opposed to an odour of somebody soiling themselves, then you knew you were on to a winner. Then you checked them over to ensure they were undamaged. Oh, and while you're at it, you might as well check the pockets - there could be a fiver in there, you know. This morning I found myself a nice pair of jeans and a stylish blacktop. Now I looked a tad more respectable.

That day I made another important discovery, I wasn't unique. For there were a distinct tribe of people whom I'll term as the 'international homeless' and many of them congregated in Rome. I'm not sure what it was, but we recognised each other straight away.

For whatever reason, they'd become homeless. Some had left care homes at the age of 16 and had nowhere permanent to go. They'd never known what a proper home was. So after being permanently rootless, they hit the road, bouncing from country to country across borderless Europe. The European Union freedom of movement act allowed them to do so and under the Schengen agreement, they didn't even have to go through passport checks; all they needed was to carry their ID cards.

If there's one good thing about having nothing, it's that you can pick up your bag and leave whenever the mood takes you. It was easy enough to scrape together the bus fare. A day busking could take care of that. So off they went to their destination of choice and then performed the usual tricks. Most of them could speak reasonably good English – that was the major ticket. They could also muster a splattering of German, French or Spanish. That was enough. Plus it never took too long to pick up the local dialect. Leading the nomadic lifestyle could be very dependant on the weather; in Winter they might head to sunnier climbs such as Spain or Italy.

In Europe, you had a bit of everything: the cosmopolitan cities full of commerce and rich culture, the forests, the mountains. Southern France was the best place for free food. Switzerland the most generous nation when it came to panhandling, and if you wanted a decent squat, then you got yourself down to Barcelona. You would hear them swapping notes:

"You cotched in Karl Platz metro? I cotched in Karl Platz too!"

"Napoli? Nah, that's shit, broth. If you want yourself a nice bit of free food then head down to Toulouse; they do a cracking Sunday roast every fortnight".

Some of them had been doing it their entire lives. It had become their way of life, whether they liked it or not.

I returned later that evening to the Piazza Della Repubblica.

"Tomorrow we go for a shower", said Angelo.

GREG LYNN

"There is a place you can go to every Thursday. But you must be in the queue by 06.30. Otherwise, you might not get a spot. They only serve the first 40 or so, and there will be many people there".

After making up my bed of fresh cardboard and blankets, I sat with the others and chatted over a glass of cheap red wine and recycled tobacco. We discussed how our days had gone then entered into an in-depth discussion about the fate of the Euro.

"It would have worked fine if you just had countries like Holland, Belgium and France who are all financially on the same level together. The problem is when the poorer countries such as Portugal and Greece joined", a young Danish guy mused.

"The Euro is finished. It is Germany who invented it and let me tell you something: they hate the Euro", another one commented.

Not long after returning to bed, I was awoken by the sound of music. But was I still asleep and this was a dream? There were a group of people in costume, and they were energetically dancing to Indian bhangra music only yards in front of us. A guy in the corner was orchestrating it all as he blasted out the music from portable speakers and banged in time on the drums. They seemed utterly oblivious to our presence as we looked on speechless and bemused. It was incessant. They were thoroughly enjoying themselves. No, this wasn't me dreaming; it was definitely for real.

We rose early the next morning after a night of not so good sleep.

"I wanted to tell them to shut up and go away! They were dancing in our living room", Angelo ranted.

"But then they might have called the police and they would have taken their side", he shook his head.

We started the walk to the centre where the showers were and passed by the parade of upmarket hotels. The obligatory dog-ending from the ashtrays took place

"You see that man there?" Angelo said, pointing towards the hotel doorman.

"He is a piece of shit – a piece of shit in your arse!"

"The other day I asked him for a cigarette, and he looked at me like this".

He screwed up his face into a pompous expression.

"Why? Because I am poor man and he works for the rich man. Rich man, poor man. It doesn't matter. We are all equal in the eyes of god".

We got to a courtyard. It wasn't even 06.30, and as predicted, there was a long line already. Someone came out with small numbered paper squares. She hurriedly passed them down the line. I was number 23.

"How do you say 23 in Italian?" I asked Angelo.

"Ventitré", he replied, then gave me some coaching on pronunciation.

The doors opened. A guy with a grey beard came out. He held that typical religious authority. Then the chaotic scramble began. They called out the numbers and let four in at a time. It all happened in a language I barely understood but had to get to grips with fast.

"Ventitré?"

"Si", I said, holding the number up. We were ushered into a changing room and then business began. A fair few people were foreigners: West African illegals or Sri Lankens. It felt like being shoved into a cattle market. Was this worth it? As I got changed, a lady offered me fresh clothes. I politely declined, though grabbed some fresh fruit that was on offer on the way out. I emerged cleaner, but with slightly less dignity.

These weren't the only homeless services on offer. Back at base camp every night around ten-ish a charity would come around dispatching food parcels. It consisted of bread, pasta, a bit of cake and a drink. Quality would vary depending on which organisation was giving it out. Angelo took a particular dislike to the Salvation Army.

"There's no oil in this goddam pasta. It's too dry. We are like pigs to them, and they are the ones throwing us the food, thinking that they are so high and mighty".

On a clear and crisp Friday night, it was the turn of another organisation.

"Okay, the Red Cross are coming. Tell them that you need socks. Get as much off them as you can", said Angelo.

I requested the socks, and they also handed out several pairs of boxer shorts. Feeling generous, they offered a cup of hot chocolate and a bag of biscuits.

Once again, Angelo was in a bitching mood.

"What's up broth?" I asked, munching my biscuits.

"They are supposed to give us things to keep us warm. I asked them for blankets, but they wouldn't give me any. They get given this money, which they are supposed to spend on us, but they keep it for themselves", he declared.

The 'Little Guy' was nowhere to be seen. He and Angelo had fallen out.

"My friend is short, that's what's wrong with him. You know what my father always told me? Never trust the man with red hair, the one who has been born disfigured or the short man. They have all been punished by God for being bad people", he announced.

A little harsh if you ask me.

"Anyway, on the street, it's better that you are on your own. Sure, it's nice to be with your friends, but you must walk your own path when you are walking the street life", he sighed wistfully.

Fortunately, by the next morning, he was in a more cheerful mood as he woke me up.

"It's a time to get up. It's a lovely sunny morning and do you know why? Because today is your birthday!"

Indeed, it was. I'd made it to 32 years old.

Here, I have a present for you. He pulled over a blue holdall bag. (Its appearance would instantly mark me out as homeless.)

"Ah, safe broth", I mumbled, awakening from my slumber.

"And don't forget to ring your momma."

(We share the same birthday.)

I'd received £100/120 Euros in birthday money from back home. Though annoyingly had to wait until 11 am before I could access it. Then it was time to treat myself to a birthday meal. I had a hamburger for Hamburg (a place that I wished to visit one day) and a Tiramisu for Sicily, washed down with a large Moretti. I purchased an ice-cream from a stall by the Fontana Di Trevi. Italian ice cream is the best I've ever tasted. It is something special.

I sat munching it by the wishing well. Two security guards were standing there permanently to ensure that nobody went fishing for all the loose change that had been frown to the bottom. It being my birthday I made two wishes and chucked the coins into the water.

I passed by the Colosseum. It looked a little overrated to me: just a cracked building. The Pope had recently been in town, so there was a big fuss around the Vatican. But the sight of the Monumento a Vittorio Emanuelle was absolutely stunning as always, illuminated in the dark night sky.

I stopped by at the supermarket. It was my turn to buy the cheap red wine for the lads. They were waiting for me upon my return. But now here was the 'Little Guy'! Him and Angelo had reconciled. God knows what they'd fallen out over. The 'Little Guy' gave me a peck on each cheek – the way that close friends greet each other in Italy. I reciprocated. Well, when in Rome.

"I'm going to give him another chance", said Angelo.

I sat down and offered out cigarettes, then poured out the wine. It was a mild night, so we went into the Piazza itself and stood by the fountains. I looked at the scenery around me. It was stunning. The Romans, they were arguably the most successful and prominent civilisation in the history of humankind. It was only after visiting the Italian capital I'd realised how strongly their legacy lived on and played such an essential part in our day to day lives now. All the fundamental things that society relies on - medicine, law, the roads, engineering, construction, they'd either pioneered or revolutionised. They were the real rebels of the day. They were people who decided to defy convention and do things their own way. That's what ultimately generates progress.

Everyone raised their glasses in the air.

"Ti-saluto!"

It was a cheer in my birthday honour. They did it again just for good measure.

"Ti-saluto!"

With the emotion and the setting, it sent a bolt of energy running right through my body. I raised the glass once again.

"Veritas vos liberabit!" I roared: the truth will set us free.

We returned to quarters. By now, I was feeling slightly tipsy.

"My friend was talking to me today about going to Holland. Apparently, there is plenty of work in construction", Angelo considered.

"Do it, man", I replied.

"Yes. But it's the matter of getting the ticket there".

I could have given him a few tips on this but chose not to.

"I know one thing. If I stay in Italy, then I will never get off the street. Italy, it's one of the most beautiful countries in the world. But its politics, the government, the system. We are trapped down here".

"Karma will see you right", I replied.

"Yes, well I think I have a little bit of the bad karma. I've done things in my life which I'm not proud of. I've gone to prison. That's bad. Too much Cocaine. It's bad".

He'd led a colourful life which had manifested itself into him being the archetypal 'rough diamond.'

"But hey, I think we will find our way in the end", he concluded.

Without saying anything else, we went to collect our cardboard and blankets then dumped them down on the smooth marble floor with quiet resignation. All of us trying to improve our lot but not quite sure how. It was a strange, sad, poetic moment. Pavarotti might as well of turned up and performed 'Nessun Dorma' for us at this point. Due in my time there, a few people had wanted to take pictures of us for some project. They must have felt we looked uniquely beautiful.

The next morning, I packed up the blankets and cardboard for the last time, then disappeared off to the Termini without saying a word of where I was going. There must have been a few people by now who wondered what had happened to me. Once again, the Treno Regionale chugged South. Destination, Napoli.

I looked out the window as we dashed through the villages of Campania. Straight away, I could tell that Southern Italy was a different ball game. First, there had been opulent and sophisticated Verona, mountainous Tuscany and cosmopolitan Rome. Now things looked wilder, rural and far poorer. Before when I'd informed the Italians that I'd be passing through Naples at some point, they'd replied with a "Napoli? Mafioso!", then made the cut-throat gesture. So far, the place hadn't got good references at all. People had warned me to stay away from there or pass through it as quickly as possible. But that had made me more curious to see what was going down there.

We disembarked at Napoli Centrale. It was warmer, and the sun was stronger down here. I walked through the streets leading out of the station. West African immigrants were trying to sell all manner of tat from the market stalls. I'd been told if you brought an I-phone off them, then it would most likely be full of sand.

Firstly, Napoli served as a stopover for the many cruise liners that passed through the Mediterranean. My first thoughts on the place? It was indeed rough as hell. There was to be no sleeping anywhere near the city centre. The tramps appeared to be of very low quality - the sort that had trouble controlling the contents of their stomach (and bowels). People were screeching around on motorcycles. Crossing the road was dangerous if you weren't careful. It was one of the ugliest cities that I've ever been to and had the laziest garbage collectors known to man. There was rubbish piled high on every street. But yet, it had something. There was leftover food everywhere. Straightaway I picked up a bag full of cake.

Choices here. The ferry going directly to Palermo cost 60 euros, and that would be mission accomplished. I just about had that much left. Or did I spend a night in a backpacker's hostel here and get a much-needed shower or continue the journey down the foot of Italy? The comfortable option won.

One night in the backpackers turned into two on account of the fact I had the whole dormitory room to myself. But another 40 euros gone. That left no more money for venturing further South. I was to be in Naples until the end of the month. Not a massive disaster. But this was taking far too long. I was annoyed with myself for not just jumping on the ferry to Sicily.

Things went back to the same routine. This was the first coastal city that I'd been to. Coasts are suitable because you'll always find loads of little hideaway places. On the downside, serious naughty business can take place on the shoreline. There's something about being at the end of the line means that you often have dubious people hanging around. Plus, major port cities often have big drug business going on there.

I made my way down to the marina and slept on a disused boat. I wasn't the only one. The place was awash with stray cats. Time passed by uneventfully. Life had become more manageable since travelling/living in Italy after the high drama of Eastern Europe in Winter. Every morning I'd bump the local train to Napoli Gianturco and listen to the locals as they spoke. I'd been trying to learn as much Italian as possible. It was a lovely language to learn and not tricky. Though, as is often the case with languages, the pronunciation would take some getting used to. As the Italians were quite an expressionist lot, it was much easier to link up what they were saying with their actions. By now, I could start to speak Italian in full sentences.

Every day I questioned what was the point of this mission anyway? What was there going to be for me in Palermo? Why not turn back now? Then one day, I happened to meet a Sicilian lawyer who was busy getting drunk in a bar. He brought me a coffee. There was one thing you could say about Napoli; they made a fantastic coffee. He'd split up from his girlfriend and was in the process of getting back together with her but seemed a little anxious about the reconciliation meeting.

".... My penis just.... isn't......ready.... yet", he lamented after slurping down a cocktail.

The conversation turned to lighter matters when he was talking about his island nation. He drew me a diagram on a napkin.

"Messina is where you'll arrive. It's the main port town. There's not much there. Whistle straight through. Then go down to Catania. Be careful there. There are many gangs of boys going around looking for trouble. But you will like the girls; they are all sluts. After that, continue to Siracusa. Then go around the island to Ragusa. Finally, you will end up in the capital,

Palermo. Be careful there also. It's quite rough. Oh…. you…. must…go!
You cannot visit Italy and not go to Sicily", he concluded.

That's it – he'd sold it to me now.

On the way back I found a whole bag full of Pizza, then a load of cake to
go with it and bread that was still fresh. I was fattening up again. Getting
food in Naples wasn't a problem as there was so much left lying around and
the quality was pretty good.

It was the first Saturday of April before I could leave. I requested the
railway ticket down to Regio De Calabria, the southernmost town of Italy
where I could pick up the ferry into Sicily.

"Trenni Rigonali not possible", he shook his head at the counter.

It's not possible? Well, that was like a red flag to a bull! The InterCity
train was too expensive. Time for a little creativity here. We were on a
proper gipsy mission. The furthest I could get to on the cheap Treno
Regionale was a place called Sapri. It was here that I had time to stock up
on bread, olives and salami. They did terrific olives down here. The other
mistake was in thinking that Naples was near the bottom of Italy. The 'foot'
of Italy is longer than you think. Maps can be seriously deceitful. And
travelling by train adds on to the journey distance as the line must twist
everywhere. The total journey distance was over 250 miles, almost like
going from London to Newcastle. Italy is a bit like one of your teeth once
it's extracted: you realise how long it is. Night set in on the Southern Italian
coast. It had been a day of steady progress. The region of Basilicata and
Calabria reminded me of Cornwall: being stuck out there, away from the
rest of the country, its ruralness, rugged coastline and a certain mystique.

It didn't take long to find an abandoned building. I climbed through a
gap, went through the usual procedure of turning on the torch and keeping a
watch out for weaknesses on the floor. Then looked for material to make a
bed out of. I found two iron frames and placed them at either side, then laid
a wooden top on it to serve as a base. (Always try and keep your self off the

floor, you never know what could be scuttling around.) I placed a sheet of thick polystyrene on the board to serve as a mattress. Then a layer of thick polythene on that and used another one as a blanket. It wasn't ideal, but better than being on a dusty floor.

In the morning, some random guy came wandering in. He didn't look like a junkie; perhaps he was with the building. He seemed pleasant and didn't appear phased by my presence. I cheerfully uttered a "bonjorno", then a, "don't mind me, I'm just passing through. What a lovely derelict building you have here. Thank you *so* much for letting me stay in it. Grazia millle, arrivia aderci", he looked back puzzled.

I scoped out the train station and the possibility of getting down to Regio de Calabria with no money left. I wasn't down with ripping off the national train operator of my host country. But this was a one-off. It was only two stops on the intercity train with a journey time of around 90 minutes. It was coming all the way from Bologna. The last leg of a very long journey. They'd have done the ticket checks after the major cities and probably wouldn't bother doing one on the final stage.

The train pulled into the station. *Just get on it!* a voice inside my head screamed. Ramifications could be dealt with later. I stood in the vestibules and spent the entire time looking out of the window, trying to appear anonymous and pretending that I wasn't there. As predicted, the conductor was nearing the end of a long shift and didn't look like he could be bothered anymore. But this was still nervy. *Keep looking at the sea. Just keep looking at the sea!* something inside me said. The Mediterranean Sea was a bright, blue colour. We whizzed past it at 100mph. I stared out at the ripples in the water and the waves crashing against the coast. It was as if the sea was supporting me somehow....

One last stop.

Finally, we pulled into the terminating end.

"*Nothing* stops me", I muttered nonchalantly, then headed into town.

If nothing else works, then a raw determination will always pull you through. There, just a few miles away in the distance, was Sicily. I could see it. Ten weeks ago, on a freezing cold night in Budapest, it had seemed like a near-impossible target, but now it was within reaching distance.

Trios of wise guys dressed in dark suits roamed through the town. I went off in search of sleeping quarters. There was a small hut by the marina. It even had a mattress inside. I sat down and placed Angelo's 'tramp bag' on the floor and tried to figure out how I was going to make the short trip across the water.

The generosity of strangers lent a hand, and by the next afternoon, there were three euros in my pocket. Enough for the ferry. It speeded out of the marina, sending out a ripple of white foam. Mission almost complete. Once again, it felt like I was taking part in a James Bond movie as the boat roared its way along the sea and 20 minutes later I was casually trotting down the gantry and into the port of Messina. Sicily had a distinctly different feel to it and may as well have been in a different country. Think the difference between England and Wales.

I sat down on a bench and allowed myself a satisfied smile. Then, out of nowhere, a lady in her thirties smiled and handed me a 20 euro note.

"Grazie mile, seniorer", I said, not quite believing my luck.

"Prego", she smiled and disappeared back into the street.

It was as if her action meant to say, *well done; you made it down here'.* I'd come to the right place.

Chapter 6

Steve McQueen rides again

The generous donation was spent wisely. I dropped by at the supermarket for the usual emergency provisions consisting of bread, olives, chocolate and yoghurt. That would set me up nicely for the journey down to Catania, the 2nd city of Sicily. I wanted to go where the action was. Palermo could wait for a bit.

I could immediately tell that it was a lively place and something of a party city. Gangs of local youths hung outside the entrance of the train station. They tried to strike up a conversation. I gave them a humorous retort and ignored them. I gave the pavement a quick glance. If you ever want to work out how rich or poor a city is, then check out the length of the discarded dog end cigarettes. If there's at least a centimetre left on them, then the place is quite wealthy. If they're smoked right down to the butt, then it's a poor town. Catania fitted into the latter category. I stopped by at the local deli to judge the mannerism of the locals as they went about their daily business. (Remember, the more you understand about how the place functions and what the crack is, the more chance you have of surviving or even prospering there.) The locals were a very downbeat crowd. They had a no-nonsense approach way of interacting with each other (not the same as unfriendliness). Behind the tourist scenes it was a gritty working-class town.

I walked down the main drag. Safe locations to sleep looked a little thin on the ground. The troop of local bums were huddled together by McDonald's. They seemed reasonable enough. Sod it. I was tired, so I grabbed some cardboard and pitched up a few metres down from them. I pulled out a can of deodorant and placed it within easy reach. If anyone tried it on, then I'd spray them in the eyes and kick them in the groin (but only if they were male). Some people carry knives in this situation. This isn't a good idea as you are putting yourself at further risk. If you're going to carry a weapon, then beware of the consequences. If you don't strike first and they manage to get it off you, then you're really in trouble. Besides, you can't get done for carrying an offensive weapon if it's just an aerosol can.

The next morning, I awoke with a cramped feeling and went to explore the city further. It had a growing tourism scene plus an alternative one and a budding music industry. There were elephant statues everywhere. That's what appeared on the city's emblem. It was to do when the Romans brought them over from Africa. It wasn't so long ago that I was battling against the cold, but now the heat was getting to be a problem. The suns rays were stronger. It was a piercing heat. Then I remembered that we weren't too far off the coast of Africa.

I nodded in solidarity with the other bums as we wandered past each other, going about our daily business.

"Ti-Saluto", we murmured to each other discreetly.

Things were harsher and more precarious for people here. This was a place that had no proper benefit system to act as a safety net. If things suddenly went wrong, it was all too easy to fall foul and end up living on the rough side. So in this nation, there was more public sympathy for the homeless. Here you were viewed more as an unfortunate by-product of society.

In one of the piazzas, a French busker approached me.

"Hi, I've seen you around, so I just wanted to say I salute you properly".

In one hand he was clutching a violin and in the other a plastic bottle that contained a brown liquid.

"Here, have a swig on this. This is a good strong beer for you".

I took a full swig. It was, indeed, a strong lager.

"How long have you been on the road?" I asked, casually.

He smiled first, then hesitated.

"For 23 years now", he murmured, not quite believing his answer.

23 years? Probably most of his adult life. How on earth had that happened?

"I am from the South of France originally. I travel around and make a little money by busking every day".

(The amount was probably dependent upon his alcohol intake for the day.)

"You like Catania? It's a good place".

"Yes, but I'm heading to Palermo next", I answered.

"Anyway, I just wanted to say that you are not alone here, my friend. There are plenty of us out here just like you. And we are all brothers on the streets", he concluded, then gave me a firm handshake and we went our separate ways.

Each night I'd be moving a yard closer to the main cluster of rough sleepers so that they could get used to my face. I didn't just want to walk straight in as they appeared to be a clique. By now, I was on their periphery. One by one, they did their introductions. They were a cheerful bunch.

"Welcome to the family", one of their number declared, then shared their food out with me and passed over the obligatory bottle of vino wine.

The volunteers came around and dished out the free food, even handing out a couple of cigarettes each. That was a first. They told me about the free food places that you could go to due in the day though I wasn't interested in joining that cycle, especially as tomorrow was the rent cheque day.

The next morning as soon as funds had arrived, I dusted myself down, then headed straight for the local barbers. I hadn't shaved since Budapest; now there was a thick beard on my face which was getting annoying. But for the price of a few euros, it was clipped off, and I could see my facial skin once again.

The last leg.

It involved another long train ride right across Sicily. It took several hours and went deep into the countryside. It went past thick forest which had a deep green colour. I changed at Enna, a place that was famous for its volcano, which pumped out ash over the whole island. As we approached the ultimate destination, there was an odd anti-climax feeling within me. Here was a sudden realisation: I'd climbed to the top of the mountain, only to realise that I'd become stranded on top of it. *Now* what?

Palermo was an attractive city, no doubt about it, but it came with an intense, edgy feel. You could virtually smell the scent of organised crime within the air; after all, this was the home of the Mafioso. I treated myself to a Grande Moretti in a local bar, then based up by the marina. What to do when you're stuck up on top of a mountain? Sit back and enjoy the view, I guess.

An area down the road served as the local red-light district. On any given night there'd be at least 20 girls touting for business along the palm tree-lined street. Many of them were West African or from further away places such as Uzbekistan. People came from all over the island and beyond to indulge in their naughty business. The vehicles would slowly creep up. Each girl would lean in and quote a price for her services. Out here on the street you always saw a different side to the city; the one that doesn't get talked about in the tourist brochures or the lonely planet guide. You learnt that this side of the metropolis throbbed along to its own set of rules. I felt that by viewing things this way, you saw the best and worst sides to a place.

I'd been plodding along for a week or so, doing my usual getting to know the city business. One thing that you'll hear people talk about a lot is how tough homelessness is. There's no denying it can be – sometimes even life-threatening. Though, that will all depend on several different factors, such as whether it's Winter or Summer (a vast difference) your disposition at the time, how connected you are to the place and what kind of support network you've got.

But here's the flip side: once you've got the knack of things life becomes ridiculously easy. There's no landlord to deal with, no fretting about the gas bill, no boss to answer to and no girlfriend in your ear going rah, rah, rah. It frees you from ordinary life's stresses and strains. But here's the unexpected downside. 90% of the time, it's soul-crushingly dull. And that's the real killer. You spend a lot of the time simply wandering around, trying to look busy for the world – not just an offcut of society. The whole time knowing that you're pissing your life away.

As I've said before, there's the sheer amount of walking. Six to ten miles a day is not an exaggeration. That takes its toll on your feet. Your socks can end up rock hard after being saturated with stale sweat. Always make sure that you get as many pairs of socks than you can lay your hands on. Don't get you're your feet wet, otherwise your skin softens, and they'll blister far easier. You know you are in trouble when they start to throb. Sometimes my feet have hurt so much the pain had been agonising. I've had to force myself to the required destination. A decent pair of walking boots are essential. I swear by Karrimors; they're made for street walking. Going hungry for a few days or not getting a good nights sleep you can live with, but when your feet have gone, you've had it.

I now take a size bigger as my feet have lost their arch through all the many years of street walking. Though, on the plus side, it's done wonders for my cardiovascular system. My resting pulse rate rarely goes above 60 and let's not get too morbid. The outdoor life can also be a lot of fun. Seriously, do you think I had girls drag me down the pub and pay the bar tab before all this? Trust me; it didn't happen. When you're out on the road, there is always something around the corner.

That Saturday evening, I had been mooching around the Piazza Franco Restivo. It seemed like a vibrant place to be. A guy came up to me with his 'donation cup' and politely and humbly asked in Italian if I had a few cents to spare. I smiled then let him catch a glimpse of the sleeping bag poking out of my holdall. He returned a knowing grin and gave a half-apology. He pulled out two bottles of Bavaria beer from his pocket and cracked one open for me. I placed his accent as Austrian. We went and sat by the steps. My new companion pulled out a packet of Marlboro and introduced himself as Alex from Gratz, Austria.

"You makes around in Palermo? It's a good place".

"How long have you been down here, Alex?"

He hesitated for a moment.

"For one year now".

By way of making conversation, I briefly told him about my time in Vienna.

"Wow, you makes around in Wien? It's a shitty place. And the cops there are arseholes".

He cracked open another bottle of Bavaria and again offered me one.

"Where are you staying at the moment?" he asked.

"By the Marina", I replied without really giving much away. Alex seemed to be done with the Piazza Franco Restivo at this point. I followed him down through the maze of side streets. We sat down at the table of an all-night café. This appeared to be where all the buskers and local hustlers hung out after a hard day of doing whatever it is they were doing. People living from day to day, doing whatever they could to survive, be that busking, panhandling or selling dodgy goods out on the street.

Alex chatted away to a plump Italian woman, whom most of the time seemed pretty melancholy.

"She says you have a nice face", he translated.

Well, that was something at least.

She went over to the other side of the road and engaged in a heated dispute with a local. Alex looked on transfixed. This guy seemed to have a reasonably respectable drink problem.

"Oh man, will you look at that. That's a real woman for you".

"What does she do in Palermo? I asked.

He turned back to face me.

"She makes *around*", he winked.

I can only guess what he meant.

"She's your dream woman, man. Look at those hips. At that arse. At those breasts. *Ruby* red lips", he almost sang at the end.

The alcohol consumed was making my brain fuzzy, anxious and confused at the same time. Just as in Budapest it seemed like I was slipping into Palermo's dark, but colourful underbelly without fully comprehending what I was getting myself into. There was an electric energy to Palermo, which made it seem like you were in a viper's nest.

I was glad when Alex decided to call it a night out on the streets. Almost by default, I walked back with him. We arrived at a block behind the via Della Libertia. The walls that lined it were suitably graffed up. I went and sat on the double mattress that appeared to be vacant.

"Hey, the old man brought back some food, you want some?"

He passed me a couple of silver foil trays that contained ravioli and pasta with sauce, plus some bread to go with it. Probably leftovers from a restaurant. It was pretty tasty stuff. Alex and I chatted for a while longer. He passed me yet another bottle of Bavaria and a cigarette.

"You have to remember that you are in Sicily now, my friend. Mafioso", he made the cutthroat gesture that everyone used to describe them.

"But you are tough guy. I can see it in your eyes".

"It's a good place, but if you cause problem, they cut your balls off, man. And your dick. Then......they open your arse. You lose your dick, and your life is over", he added gravely.

I eventually nodded off to bed on the nice, thick mattress. It was a warm night, so the cold was no longer an issue. A long lie-in was called for the next morning, and that became my base. Over the next couple of weeks, I settled into a routine. It was a blessed relief, not having to think about the destination target constantly. I could hang out here for a little while. What was I doing here? I don't know, just biding my time.

I got to know the local buskers and accompanied them in the evening. There was quite a party scene that took place deep in the forests of the island. Mafioso were happy for it to go ahead as that meant more drugs profit for them.

Alex and I chatted every night. He informed that many homeless Austrians travelled down to Sicily, especially in the Winter. You could see why: plenty of warm sunshine and no getting kicked awake in the morning.

"In Austria, if you're living on the street, then the government give you 800 Euros a month", he informed.

800 Euros was a fair bit down here. You could certainly see what the appeal was. The old guy who occupied the spot with us brought back food every night, mainly pizza that was still hot and bread to go with it. He clearly relished this role as provider. Food was never a problem as it always came. Plus that morning the pair of them had found a load of decent clothes. They kindly let me in on the spoils. My nightly chats with Alex continued. We were there tucked away down the dark alley in the dead of night, sat on our mattresses against the graffiti backdrop. It reminded me of a film about two blokes being stuck in a foreign jail together. Perhaps it was this feeling of incarceration that led us to talk about the opposite sex.

"I like Sicilian girls; there is something unique about them. They've got really dark hair and coal brown eyes. Or those women with the flame-red hair. I've never seen that before, except in Palermo", I pondered.

Alex tied his long blond hair into a ponytail and put on his trademark dark sunglasses that he always wore, even at night.

"Yes. But you must be careful with Sicilian girl. Remember my friend, you are in Sicily now, not England; things work differently here", Alex never seemed to tire of saying.

"You cannot just get with a girl, have your fun with her then leave her as you could in London, Berlin or Vienna. Let's say that if you got her pregnant. You couldn't just run off and leave. In Palermo, everyone knows everyone else, and everyone knows someone working in the Mafioso. Her father will say, "who is this guy?" Then he searches you, and then he founds you. He put a gun to your head", he did the gun clocking noise and action again.

"And he say: you marry my daughter, or you die". They cut your balls off here, man", he semi slurred.

The next Saturday, we were in the same Piazza as where I'd met with him, and he was up to his panhandling tricks again. You had to hand it to Alex; he certainly had a charismatic style.

"Here, now you try", he said, passing me the cup.

No way. Asking strangers on the street outright for money just wasn't something that I had in me, no matter what your circumstances or how hard up you were. And I was a foreigner from an affluent country. How would that go down?

"You are British. That's okay. They don't have a problem with them. It's the Roma that they don't like", Alex reassured.

"Come on. Makes a little money. Yes. Why not?"

"Because it's rude. That's why" I protested.

He wasn't giving in and even told me what to say in Italian. But he hadn't realised how stubborn I could be.

"Come on. You are tough guy, man. Greg from England, my friend, my brother – great *warrior* of the street".

Eventually, he realised that I wasn't going to give in and finally relented.

"You are too proud, man….and too young", he sighed. That was a cheek; he was only a year older than me.

But sometimes your dignity is all you've got left. He spent part of the night's proceeds on a local bottle of wine and in a drunken state became transfixed by the picture of a woman on the label. She looked like a 1950's film star.

"Oh man, will you look at that. That's a real woman for you", he slurred.

We made our way back to base camp.

"What was your job in Austria? I asked him.

"I was a plumber. I hated it", he remarked.

"Did you have a girlfriend back there?"

"No. I had nothing."

"But what about your family?"

"They…. don't exist", he said after a long pause.

That disclosure said it all. Alex was clearly running from something. Just like we all were. That's why he'd gotten himself as far South as he could, then got himself stuck on an island where there was no further left to run. I reflected further for a moment.

"How old are you know?" he asked me.

"32"

"And you don't have kids? You're not married?"

I shook my head.

"Didn't you have girlfriend in England?"

"No. Just like you, I had nothing".

Now it was his turn to analyse me.

"You makes around all over Europe and live like a vagabond. What are you looking for exactly? I shrugged my shoulders.

"You need a wife man", he let that sink in for effect.

"Yes. You *really* need a wife", he added emphatically, looking at me with a pair of sharp blue eyes.

But for now, I had more immediate concerns. My skin was painfully dry, not being helped by the heat. It was especially bad on my thighs. I lent back underneath the blankets spread my legs and gave them a good old scratch. Ah, that was lovely. Now scratch them some more. Vigorously this time. My thighs began to shake and tremble a bit. Oh, the relief. No more itching.

"Ah…. ah…. argh", I let out a contented sigh. Blissful.

******

The Italian woman sleeping with us had been in a disagreeable mood with me all day. She was a funny lass. Herself and Alex were engaged in a heated exchange, and she stormed off. I could never quite get what the relationship between them was.

"Umm…. she is quite angry with me", Alex remarked sheepishly.

"She is quite angry with you, also".

"*Me*? What have *I* done?" I protested puzzled.

"Last night. When you makes around with your dick".

"What? No. I was scratching. My skin is dry".

"You were having *really* good time with your dick, man", Alex chuckled.

"I wasn't masturbating! I was scratching my thighs. Like this, see", I got up and gave an in-depth demonstration. But Alex was having none of it. He was in hysterics.

"It's okay, man". He said after finally calming down.

"I said to her, why shouldn't he make around with his dick – he *has* one".

There was a pause.

"Make around with me for a second. Let me show you something".

He led me to the other side where a load of old bums were passed out on carboard.

"You see these lot here", he said, pointing to the passed-out bodies.

"Pathetic, wasted, *finished*", he said while pointing to each one in turn, then lifted the cardboard that was covering one of them and scoffed as if to say, do you see what I mean.

"This is just their problem, man. They have no.... dicks. Your dick function. You *have* a rifle", he made the clocking sound complete with gestures.

And that was to be our final night in that particular spot. The next day the police came and cleared us out. We were no longer allowed to sleep there. It was an odd feeling. You were homeless, but now on top of that – you'd been made homeless. This presented me with a problem. Sleeping out on my own in a city like Palermo would virtually guarantee a good kicking at some point. As a foreigner in an unfamiliar location, I stuck out. I had to get off the street and find a place where I'd be out of public viewing.

I went down to the marina again and kept half an eye open. It didn't take long; look for a gap in the building. And like a rat I crawled in. Then clambered about over various broken items and eventually found a flat spot in which to lay my sleeping bag. I wouldn't rate this place on trip advisor; it was like being trapped in a dark dungeon and dusty as hell.

But now you'll see why I took this course of action. The following Friday, I was up to the usual foraging for provisions business when four local teenagers approached me. Out on the street, you developed a kind of 6th sense for when trouble was approaching. I remembered what the Sicilian lawyer had said: "*be careful in Palermo also, there are many gangs of boys going around looking for trouble*". They came up to me pretending to be all cheerful and jovial in the same way as somebody about to con you comes up to you with a broad smile. They spoke to me in a few sentences of mixed Italian/English, which I briefly responded. There was a pause. Then they shoved me to the floor. One of them launched a kick.

Think quick!

They were looking for a reaction. Either for me to run scarred (then they'll chase) or for me to strike back in anger. There were four of them and only one of me. They may be punani's, but I was never going to win in a fight. Instead, they were to get neither. I sprang up and faced the leader; cause, if he crumpled then so, will the rest.

"Why did you do that? *What* is the problem?" I snapped assertively.

What I *did* have over them were age and experience. I continued to look at them with contempt. And what did they do? To my utter amazement, they all ran off. I was almost tempted to run after them.

"Yeah, that's it little boys – run back off to momma and suck her tities!" I yelled.

The next time I may not be so lucky, back to the dungeon. The place sucked hard. But that night, I was counting my blessings. Some days it was quite tempting to lie in 'bed' all day and not face the world. But if you do that, then nothing is going to happen to you, and you'll stay where you are. So get up and face the world I did.

"Ciao!" A young and beautiful Sicilian girl called as I walked down the via Sampolo. It was the girl who worked down my local coffee shop, hurrying by as she was on her way to work.

"Ciao!" I replied.

A sign of local acceptance. Exchanges like that can make you feel a whole lot better.

That evening I hung out with one of the buskers down the Piazza Esedra Matteotti. He was singing Elvis's '*Blue suede shoes*' in Italian and doing an excellent job of it. Suddenly, I began to feel a shortness of breath and nausea, so got up and walked further into the piazza. But then it got to the point where I could hardly breathe. What was going on here? Dizziness followed due to not getting enough oxygen. My steps turned into staggers. Then the world turned upside down. My head hit the concrete floor first.

Ouch!

Everything went silently quiet for a moment. It was almost pleasantly peaceful. I lay motionless on the floor panting for all I was worth. Getting back up was out of the question; that would involve consuming more oxygen. A few more moments passed.

"Va tutto bene?" a voice suddenly asked.

It was a security guard who probably assumed I was drunk. He didn't get an answer.

"Acqua?" (water)

"Si, grazie"

"……. ambulanza?",

"Si"

This time I *did* need one. They fetched a chair and helped me onto it, then passed me a glass of water. I gratefully sipped from it as water is good for just about anything. The ambulance was quick to arrive. The paramedics asked the standard round of questions then requested my passport to prove that I was a real person.

"Were drink or drugs involved?"

I answered, honestly.

"No. They weren't".

"I think we need to take you to the hospital", he answered matter of factly.

I climbed in, and they warranted it severe enough to put the blue lights and siren on. They treated me to another bottle of water and a bit of cake upon arrival. Questions from the nurses, blood pressure checked, blood sugar levels and body chemistry investigated. As I'd sustained a head injury, a CT scan would be needed. It was a large hospital. Given how chaotic Sicily could be, it was surprisingly efficient. I lay down strapped in, being slid into the chamber. If you've ever had a CT scan before then, you'll know how claustrophobic it is and mildly unnerving as the machine scans your brain. But what was more concerning was that I didn't have my EHIC card on me. This could cost thousands. A few moments later, the radiographer came back with the results.

"Everything is fine", he reassured.

They strapped me up to an intravenous drip, which seemed to work wonders. I felt so much better. The doctor came in to do his examination.

"......And do you have any problems in the head?"

Was this a question or an accusation? Sane people don't get up to this sort of malarkey, surely?

"I don't......*think* so", I answered tentatively.

"Ah...ok", he smiled.

"Now lie down. Be quiet. Shut up!", he barked, then ran a stethoscope over my upper half.

I continued to be quiet as he sat down at the desk typing.

"Okay......you can go home now", he said and handed me the paperwork.

Now get out of here quick before Vicki in admin lands you with a five -euro bill, I quietly yelled to myself.

"Grazie mille, arriva aderci"

"Prego, arriva aderci".

THE WANDERER

I quickly made for the exit. But where was I? A good few miles from the
city centre. Hmm. That was simple enough. Just walk through the streets
until you hit the main road because nine times out of 10 that's either coming
or going to the city centre. You walk up to it, and if the surroundings seem
to be getting denser, then you know you are on the right track. Sticking to
the main road at night is also a safer option. Once in town, I hit the main
drag and navigated my way from there. There was even time to hit the
restaurant skips on the way back. So I lent in. Ah, my ribs! It was gone 3
am by the home I returned to the dungeon. But now it was time for some
proper thinking and tough questions to be answered.

I'd found out only years later that my trip to A and E was the result of a
severe asthma attack. I must have developed it while spending all that time
on the street and breathing in exhaust fumes. Inhaling in all the dust while
living in the dungeon had triggered it, so it wasn't an excellent idea to be
staying here any longer. I was officially in trouble.

These were warning signs that had to be headed. A return to a place of
safety was called for immediately, and that probably meant returning to the
UK. But that was a long way away, and there were 20 euros left in my
wallet. So how was I to make it back? Simple; the same way as I got down
here – one bit at a time. Take the first step, get in motion, then momentum
takes over.

That's the philosophical way of putting it. Now the proper plan. I had
enough for the train fare back to Messina. It had been a lucky place for me.
From there getting back into mainland Italy wouldn't be that difficult, then I
could claw the way back up to Rome just like how a cat climbs up a tree.
Maybe hitch-hiking was worth a go. From there, I'd be in a major
international city that had plenty of access to the UK. I naively believed that
maybe the British consulate in Rome could help me do this.

So the next morning, I packed up my bags once again. But first I went
back to the Piazza to find the security. Security guards are usually a drifter's
arch-enemy, but I wanted to thank him for helping me that night.

Fortunately, he was there, and I passed on the gratitude. When on the road, you remember your favours. Then who should I bump into on the way to the station but Alex. He'd continued to sleep out on the street since we got moved on. I didn't need to tell him how dangerous this was in Palermo.

"Yes. You sleep with one eye open", he answered.

I kind of half told him about how I thought it was best to leave and return to my native land, then showed him the hospital paperwork. He looked at me and shrugged, as if to say, do what you think is best.

I boarded the train to Messina, but for some unknown reason thought it best to get off at Cefalù and spend a couple of nights there first. It was located around halfway across the island and was quite a touristy place with a proper seafront that had sandy beaches. It was a warm evening. The sky was clear. I stared out at the Mediterranean Sea. The destination target was 1,730 miles away. How was that ever going to be possible? The setting sun glistened against the water, and the waves crashed calmly onto the shore. I stared out at the sea and the distant horizon as if somehow this was going to provide me with an answer. The previous anxiety felt gradually got washed away and in its place was a calm feeling. Of course, the fishes didn't start chatting to me, but the setting opened another part of my consciousness, which said, keep your feet moving, focus on the target to the point of obsession and eventually you'll get a bit of luck. Well, that was good enough for me.

Time to go and find a place to sleep. Some people reckon that sleeping on the beach sounds romantic. It isn't; it's a stupid idea. For a start, you're wide open to the elements. Even in a sub-tropical environment, it can be surprisingly windy. So, you're not adequately sheltered. Also, just about anybody wandering past can see you. At night, you'll always get dodgy characters lurking around (plenty of naughty business occurs on the coast). The chances of you being robbed, attacked or coerced into doing something are high. Oh yeah, and at night the sound of the waves crashing is bloody noisy, which will keep you awake all night. Not to mention that you'll get sand in every crevice.

Cefalù was an upmarket town. (You could tell by the number of golf courses around.) So finding a place to rest in the town itself wasn't going to happen. Instead, I headed inland and up the steep, spirally road to the forest. Nice, thick, dense forests. Excellent. Now find a nice bit of flat terrain. But a word about sleeping in the forests. I've done this lots. And yes, I get insulted whenever people call me a hippy for it. Forests look like lovely places, and they are beautiful places. But they can also be dangerous if you're not careful. In the dark, it's also quite easy to trip over a branch and break a leg. Even British forests can be seriously wild places, the New Forest in particular. Midges and insects are a real concern. As always have something to lie down on. And be wary of falling branches. Staying in a forest due in a gale could be fatal as a falling tree comes with a massive crash.

Now I was out of my sight and could bed down for the night. They couldn't find me here......but who were *they*......?

The time spent in Cefalù left me invigorated. It was a kind of holiday. It's a lovely town which I'd thoroughly recommend. By midday Saturday I'd arrived back in the port of Messina. I always reckon it's best to enter a new place on a Saturday. This would have to be my new base until I figured out a proper plan. As expected, Messina Centrale was the main bum hangout. I kept a distance from the insane lot that screamed and yelled the most insanities then lay down cardboard for the night, using my bag as a pillow. Essential items kept on me, boots tucked inside the sleeping bag and a can of deodorant at the ready.

Messina was a happy medium town. Not poor, but not stuck up rich. Not too busy, yet still vibrant enough. The locals were laid back and friendly, and the weather was a perfect 20-24 degrees and sunny every day. It was late May. The following Sunday, I took a stroll. Then what was that by that building? A long line of bums queuing in an orderly line outside and looking expectant. That must mean a free food place. Wherever you are in the world and require free food, just look for the line of bums queue. I made sure to converse in Italian with the staff. That would get fewer questions asked. Generally, at these places the food sucks and the surroundings are chaotic, but this one served up a cracking Sunday roast. It was the best meal that I'd had in ages. The staff gave me a load of milk and fruit to take with me.

And over the coming days, people kept on giving me stuff. For example, I'd wake up one day, and there'd be a bottle of milk left to my side, or a guy would give me a new pair of boots as my old ones were falling apart. Or a group of young people would give me a load of fresh clothes. Again, people would stop by for a chat. Sometimes it felt like I was taking part in a bizarre social experiment without my knowledge and any minute now Derren Brown was going to come around the corner saying, "for the past six months, I've been *programming* Greg, and the results have been.... surprising".

On a more rational level, what I've often found is this. If you're in a tight jam but are open and honest about your situation and show a concerted effort to improve your lot, then people will always be willing to come around and help you no matter where you are. What I'll say is this: don't ask people for stuff, make them want to give it to you instead.

It was Friday night by the station, and that meant we had to sing for our supper tonight. A religious lot would come around with some cheap pasta and tea. Before they dispatched that, they'd make us huddle in a corner and sing '*hallelujah*'. Well hallafuckinglujah! The reward just wasn't worth the effort. That would be the last time I'd be participating in Friday night hallelujah humiliation sessions.

I looked down at the ceramic floor, then thought for a moment how this abnormal situation now seemed reasonable. Sleeping rough outside a train station in a foreign country where I didn't have rights to anything didn't seem like such a big deal anymore. It no longer concerned me. I'd been on the road for six months, getting about far more than I thought possible. The worst that could happen probably had already. Being homeless, yeah call it travelling, a bohemian nomad, whatever, had turned into a lifestyle. Wherever I lay my head was my home. And it didn't concern me. *That* was the concerning thing.

As stated already living like this wasn't that difficult. It was much easier than getting up in the morning, boarding a packed-out train to work, then taking abuse from your Korean office on the phone and worrying about how you were going to pay your bills. And that is why people continue to live like that. Taking the path of least resistance is a very human trait.

Then suddenly, things began to look up. For a start, I got a much-needed shower down at a day centre. All that sweat and grime was washed off. It was long overdue. While there, I got offered a three-night stay in a shelter. It seemed like the logical step to take. The guy asked me to meet him back there at 4 pm the following day. The next morning, I had a cup of coffee in the Bar Italia, and I have to say that it was probably the *best* cup of coffee I've ever tasted. It put me in an optimistic mood. The wheels were starting to turn in my favour.

The clock was nearing 4 pm. I was about to make for the appointment, but then strangely, something told me not too. I questioned this intuition which was advising me to continue out on the street, writing my journal. People seemed to like this. They'd stop and ask me what I was writing. I guess they were surprised I could read and write.

A man approached who was maybe a few years older than me. He spoke first in Italian. By now, I could hold necessary fumbling conversations.

"Par Inglese?"

"Si"

"Di dove sei?" I asked.

"Australia"

"Di dove sei?"

"Inghilterra"

He stopped and looked up.

"No way, mate!" came back the unmistakable Aussie accent. Wherever you are in the world, you'll always meet an Aussie.

"So, what brought you to Messina?"

It was the inevitable first question. I decided upon a direct response.

"I left England one day because I wasn't happy. I had an idea about going to Germany looking for work but instead ended up going on the road and having adventures. I certainly got a few of them in".

"I bet you have", he replied.

"How far have you travelled so far?"

I stopped to figure this out in my head roughly.

"I reckon I've clocked up about 6,000 kilometres so far".

"Jesus Christ".

"I've seen you out and about here recently and to be honest, I was getting a bit worried about you.

"Why's that?"

"Because you don't quite look like you deserve to be out on the street. But you seemed happy enough, so I thought maybe I should leave you to it".

"Yeah, well – it is what it is, I guess. And what do you do here in Messina?"

"I'm a marine architect. Work brought me here from Melbourne a few months ago".

"So what's your plan now?"

"I've been thinking about knocking it on the head and returning to the UK. My next move is to make it to Rome, then go begging to the British consulate for repatriation".

"Well, I'll buy your ticket to Rome", he said enthusiastically.

"Really?" I answered, astonished.

"But how do I go about paying you back?"

"You don't have to, mate; just promise that you'll do something nice for somebody else one day".

"Alright. I will. Bus or train?"

"It's up to you".

"The bus is going to be cheaper. We can go to the bus station ticket office now if you want?"

"What.... you mean you're going to get up and go just like that?" he exclaimed.

Well, what was there to hang around for?

"Alright, let's do it."

I jumped up, grabbed the holdall, then slung it over my shoulder. When the opportunity came, you had to be prepared to get up and go that instant. We marched off down the hill.

"This is bizarre", he said, shaking his head.

Oh, welcome to Greg's mad little world, mate.

We passed the train station.

"That's the spot where I was sleeping", I indicated.

"Oh yeah, what was that like?"

"It sucked. I won't try and glorify it", the reality of how bad it was had finally sunk in.

He ordered me the ticket at the desk. The next bus to Rome would be leaving in about 90 minutes and was an overnight affair.

"And here's 20 euros for the ride", he said, passing me the ticket.

"My name is Ian by the way".

"Greg", I responded.

"Okay, your bus leaves from over there. Well, mate, I wish you all the best. Right, well I'm going back to listen to the cricket and sink a couple of Peroni's".

That was it, out of here tonight. I certainly hadn't seen this one coming. I retired to the café/bar to toast Sicily goodbye.

"Buonasera. Un grande americano, per favore".

A grande Moretti followed that.

Being stuck down here in Sicily, right at the bottom of Europe felt very cut off. But once back in Rome, in a city I already knew didn't seem too daunting a prospect. I went outside by the bus stand and waited. It was due in about the next 20 minutes.

"Hey Greg", I looked around. It was Ian, the Australian again.

"Umm…. I hope you don't mind me doing this, but I got back home and realised that I hadn't helped you enough".

There was a white envelope in his hand.

"This money came into my hands. I don't know why I'm doing this, but something is telling me that you deserve it….and…. you're going to go away and do the right thing with it. Because…. I don't know…. There's just something about you", he said puzzled.

THE WANDERER

He wasn't mad because truly mad people don't question their own decision making.

"That's enough to get you back to England, but spend it however way you think is best".

He passed me the envelope. I looked inside. There was a bunch of notes in there, and the notes were brown. Fifties.

"Wow. I don't know what to say – but thanks".

"No worries, mate. Here's my card. Let me know if you need anything else. I've been where you've been", he added enigmatically, and with that, he was gone.

I thought back to what Julia in Florence had said. *"When you live on the street, you get your saviours – they come out of nowhere"*. She'd been right.

I jumped on the bus feeling like Charlie after he'd been given the golden ticket to Willy Wonkers chocolate factory. The envelope containing 250 euros felt like a hot coal in my pocket as we climbed onto the Italy bound ferry. This may not seem like a lot to you, but when you're living on the street virtually penniless in a foreign land, it's a small fortune.

We went through a long tunnel after long tunnel along the motorway. Most of the other passengers had fallen asleep. But not this one. I was busy making plans. And stuff going back to England. This had happened for a reason, and it wasn't for me to pussy out. There was one last mission left, and that was the return match to Berlin. Ha-hah, just like Steve McQueen – but going in the opposite direction.

The next morning, I dashed straight through Rome and kept on working my way up, only stopping for a hair cut and a shave in Bologna. There was a bit of a wait around in Innsbruck. Yeah, Austria again. Gggrrrr. Even being up close with the Alps wasn't doing it for me. Then not long after I was on another bus which was heading past the landing lights of Schonefeld airport, the main airport of Berlin. The following day I was trotting along the tarmac of Templehof airfield, feeling that calm, happy vibe again.

Well, it had taken a little longer than I expected.

Chapter 7

The setting sun

But again, what to do? The only person I'd kept in contact with from my stay in Berlin last year was Bernardo, the Brazilian law student. But would he even remember me? There was only one way to find out. I paid a visit to the local internet café to send messages to contacts. I also sent Ian a message from the contact info on his card. I wanted him to know how his money had got spent and what I'd got up, rather than just blazing off and him being none the wiser. The following day there were responses from both. I checked the most relevant first.

Bernardo:

"Hey Greg, of course, I remember you! So, you are back in Berlin. And I'm still here too. The good news is that I've been granted permanent stay here. I'm sharing a flat right in the heart of Kreuzberg" He supplied his German cell phone number with a, "give me a ring, it would be cool to hook up sometime."

I tried ringing him a couple of times, but it went straight to voicemail. The message from Ian read:

"Good afternoon, Greg. I appreciate you getting back in contact" He referred to my original e-mail and addressed it point by point:

"Blitzing through Rome":

"I'm glad you did this as I couldn't see how Rome would offer you much more than Messina, other than a change of scene."

"Non-return to the UK:"

"I'm not surprised by this either. I didn't think you looked like you were ready to go back to England – at least not yet, anyway".

"Arrival in Berlin"

"Funnily enough I had you down as German before we spoke. I don't know if it was your purposeful stride or that you seemed quite organised. It just seems that Germany probably paid a big part in your history somewhere. I too believe there was some kind of meaning in our paths crossing that day".

Interesting.

I walked back down towards Friedrichshain. Then I saw it, the Berlin Wall. Or rather what remained of it, now known as the Eastside gallery. There was a stretch around a mile long that they'd kept and turned into an art gallery. They'd invited artists from all over the world to cover it in modern art murals, much of it with a satirical theme. How could have I spent three weeks here last time and not seen it? The first picture that caught my eye was of a girl firing a syringe at her head in a nihilistic fashion as if it were a gun. It reminded me of Selina.

I took a walk back to Kreuzberg. It was like something was guiding me back to the scene of the crime. I passed the entrance to the Backpax hostel where I'd stayed previously. Everything seemed so different. Now it was summer compared to the cold, bitter but beautiful winter of before. There was the "Dawn till Dusk" spat kauf – a 24-hour off-license. They didn't mind it if you sat outside on the benches with your purchased beer. There were a group of people of all nationalities gathered their chatting. But one of their voices sounded familiar. (I never forget a voice.) That dude with the thinning hair on top and a beard. In a city with over 4 million people there, he was sitting right in front of me.

"Bernardo?" I said, 90% sure that target one had been located.

He looked up puzzled as if to say, how does that random bloke off the street know my name?

"Yes?"

There was a pause, then a flash of recognition dashed through his eyes.

"Greg?"

"Yes…I got your e-mail this morning. I didn't recognise you for a second. I thought you might have been that Icelandic guy I met last night. You look so different. You're really tanned. But of course, yes; you've been in Sicily. Sit down. Here let me get you a drink".

Moments later he returned with a bottle of Sternberg export that was so cold it had particles of ice floating it.

"Zum wohl! It's good to see you. So, what have you been up to?"

I was bursting with stuff that I wanted to tell stories about, but I had to remember that this needed careful refining. I wasn't going to disclose that I'd been living rough near enough the entire time since we'd last spoke -

although I'd imagine that he could guess a good part of it. I began by reciting the tale of how I'd been able to leave Sicily.

"Woah! You have a guardian Angel, I think", he commented.

Now it was my turn to get a surprise visit.

"Greg? I don't believe it!"

I turned around to see a bearded fellow. The accent and his eyes I recognised but couldn't place the identity. Wait a minute. It was Marco, the Israeli that I'd been out clubbing with on that first night here. The funny thing was it wasn't until now that I'd learnt his name.

"Yes. I know, it's the beard I've grown since the last time you've seen me. I live in Berlin now", he beamed.

Now I was busy bending his ear about the places I'd been to.

"But how did you get the money?" was the first question he asked.

"Oh, you know, I get by – same as always", I replied with vagueness.

"I've done a fair bit of travelling as well. I went to Frankfurt after here".

I'd remembered him saying that he'd got a job offer down there.

"But I hated it. It's like The Manhattan of Germany. Too sterile for me. So, then I ended up taking a trip to London. But I'll be honest; I didn't like it there either. Yes, it's a beautiful city, but I found it quite…. unwelcoming".

"Yeah, London is never inviting if you're on a limited budget", I replied.

"But I met this busker girl on the street though; she was cool. But there was something about her which made me think she was homeless. It wasn't anything she said; it was just…. this intuition. So, I took her back to my place, and I shagged her", he finished quietly with a grin.

"So, the only place to go back to was Berlin. I've got an apartment in Neukölln and a job as a housemaster (basically, a caretaker).

THE WANDERER

Neukölln was a former rough district here but had become very popular with expats arriving on a wing and a prayer as the rental prices were cheap. It was viewed as the "new Kreuzberg".

"But best of all I can understand what the Germans are saying to me now", he smiled with happiness.

"It's Summertime; the hostel is going to be packed full of teeny bopping teenagers, but I might pop down there later", Bernardo offered.

His female Dutch flatmate came to join us at the table. She appeared to of had a hard day at work.

"I think we are too hardcore for the Japanese guy living with us. The other night, we were up the whole time on speed, and he really didn't like it at all", she pondered.

Bernardo finally relented, and I found myself following him up the staircase to the hostel. The Irish receptionist was still working behind there, looking as put upon as ever.

"Hey", he responded and offered a hand to shake. Although Bernardo had got an apartment a long time ago, this place was still clearly his social hub. It had been his reluctant home for several months while his permanent resident status was to be decided; he'd been caught in international limbo. For he had also been internationally homeless, all be it in a more respectable sense. He'd been sick and tired of not having a proper base, but this establishment still served as a kind of social ambilocal cord.

"……. Oh yeah, so what were you doing for money? Were you working?" the I R said after I'd given him the synopsis of what I'd been up.

I went on to explain how good fortune had come into play.

"Oh Jesus Christ", he said open-mouthed. "He must have been crazy".

I laughed at the response.

"No. Just being nice, I think".

"But what about if he hadn't of given you all that money. *What* would you have done then?" he chastised, like a mother scolding her child.

"I always find a way", I answered nonchalantly and sipped on a rum and coke that had been left behind.

I looked around me. It had been last December that I'd walked out that door, thinking that I'd be back within two weeks after having a couple of beers with the red star lads. Not once had I visualised what was to occur instead. Like I always say if you find yourself stuck in and bored, then pop out for a bit of a wander. You never know who you might bump into or what kind of serendipity might occur.

The deep House pumped out of the speakers, and the excited clubbing tourists turned up. A gaggle of conversation took place in the background. I surveyed the scene. I'd made it back to headquarters. There had been times when I thought I might not make it through the night. Then there was being stuck down in the dungeon in Palermo, feeling so alone and cut off from the world. If it's one lesson I'd take from the experience it's this: even when you're in a dire situation make a plan, even if that plan doesn't seem realistic at the time. Then keep moving towards it and eventually you'll get there.

"I've stayed in hostels all over the city, but there's nowhere else quite like this one. It's the atmosphere of the place. I don't know what it is. It's something unique" Bernardo reflected

"It was my home. The people here were my family", he seemed happier now he'd had a few drinks down him.

As the music played in the background, I brought up the subject of Berghain. Berlin's world-famous club with the notoriously harsh door policy.

"Is it as good as people say it is?" I asked.

"It's un......real!" the IR answered.

I pushed him for more detail.

146

"The atmosphere inside is electric, the sound system is amazing; the party goes on the whole weekend. You feel completely different inside after the first visit there".

"What special tricks have you got to pull to get in?" I asked.

"It's totally random. I'd say they knock back about 60% of the people who try".

He confessed that it took him seven attempts before the bouncers finally admitted him to the hallowed club. Perseverance paid off.

"Ah, they let me in the first time. I did the same as when I walk through customs. I got in the middle of the crowd and quietly glided in so that nobody would take any notice of me", Bernardo stated in an unassuming fashion.

That's how cool Bernardo was. He didn't need to pretend to be anything different.

Outside, it was turning light already. Bernardo finally picked up his coat. I promised the receptionist that I'd be popping back in for a drink sometime.

"You can come back to mine for a bit if you want. I can offer you a bath and some breakfast", but I can't offer you a home", he said quite clearly.

"That's fine. I didn't expect you to. But yeah, jamming around yours for a bit. That would be cool", I replied.

We walked up Orianestrasse. Rote a Rose was still bopping along. His apartment was located in Heinrichplatz, right by a u-Bahn station. It can't have been cheap. We both sat down in the living room. He glanced down at a cluster of paperwork that was written in German, then selected the electric bill to study.

"They've got a funny way of wording things here", he shook his head.

"How long did it take you to learn German?" I asked.

"About a year".

"Where did you learn it?"

"Firstly, I put myself on the government intensive course?"

"What was that like?"

"It starts out quite straight forward, but then it reaches a stage where it gets complicated. Then you have to start thinking in German. But I tell you one thing: if you stay in Berlin then you'll never learn the language as you won't get the chance to practice; everyone speaks English here. What you've got to do is take yourself off to a small town or village where they don't speak English that much. Then that forces you to learn it. When you first start, you walk into a shop, and you don't understand what they're saying to you because it all sounds like one word. You feel so stupid, it's hell", he shook his head.

The Japanese flatmate scuttled in, said the briefest of hellos, then locked himself in his bedroom without a word more.

"You were lucky that you missed the Winter here. It was so long. It went right up until March. I remember being in the Haupt Bahnhof waiting for the train to Hamburg. It was delayed because of the snow. There was no waiting room, and it was so cold".

"What was doing in Hamburg?"

"I had to go there to apply for my indefinite leave to remain. When I went, I wasn't too sure of my chances. There were a lot of people there. But I was one of the lucky ones. I thought the Brazilian bureaucracy was bad. Then English......but German......that's something else".

Emigrating to Germany was a dream for many. And Berlin was deemed to be such a glamorous location. But Bernardo had highlighted the many pitfalls and hoops that you had to jump through. Be that finding accommodation, discovering how everything worked and learning the language. It sure seemed like hard work; a task that not everybody managed to pull off.

I took Bernardo up on his offer of letting me use the bathroom facilities. Never turn down a bath because you don't know when you'll be getting another one. Upon my return, he was busy cutting up slices of salami, then making it into a sandwich for me.

"I'm sorry, but I don't have much to offer you in the way of breakfast".

"Nothing to apologise over, man - this is good".

He passed over his packet of Marlboro seemingly as a way of making up for it. The guy smoked more than I did.

"Uhh. I don't want to be a lawyer", he quietly pondered. It was clearly playing on his mind.

"But you graduated from law school".

"Yes. But studying law and practising it are two completely different things. I thoroughly enjoyed studying it; the philosophy behind law is very interesting. But to argue your points in a court of law, you must be the Alpha male type who loves arguing with people all the time, and I'm quite the opposite of that", he concluded.

"I never liked school, the whole education system. It's for followers", he said while shaking his head thoughtfully.

I bid Bernardo a good day. He was a generous guy, but I didn't want to go infringing on anything. Now feeling exhausted and in need of sleep, I headed straight to the Lust Garten, a green patch by museum island in Mitte and lay on the grass, falling into a deep sleep almost immediately. By now, I could sleep just about anywhere.

Things quickly fell into the same routine almost by default. By now I'd accepted that perhaps this was just how life was. It's the same thing as what happens when you're suddenly made redundant from your job, so out of panic you accept a low-level occupation to keep the wolf from the door. You know, only for a month or so, while you're looking for something else. Then before you know it, five years later….and you're still there……

My nightly sleeping spot was in a cluster of thick bushes by Prinzenstrasse u-Bahn in Kreuzberg. See, I'd got myself a trendy address already. Except that I didn't do that much sleeping at night. I fell into a funny nocturnal pattern, especially at the weekends. They were what I'd look forward to the most as that meant they'd be copious amounts of drink lying around. It being Berlin it was all in bottles. Becks, Carlsberg, Berliner Pills. Though curiously nobody ever left Sternberg export, the cheapest one, lying around.

You went to where the cluster of clubs was, especially around Warschauer Strasse. The kids would group together, having brought their bottles from a spat kauf. Then one of them would yell, "quick, it's time we went off to Watergate before the queue gets too long". Not being allowed to take them in they plonked their near full bottles down on the wall. Bus stops were another good one. You'd find all manner of things left there. Alcohol was one of them as people weren't allowed to take it on board. But folk would often leave entire bags of groceries there. Maybe they'd forgot to take it with them. Oh well, we couldn't let it go to waste now, could we? I quickly figured out what time the bakeries chucked out. This happens daily as they need to sell their produce fresh. I went around the back and carefully selected what appeared to be the freshest selection. I picked out any cheese and egg that was in them as this will give you food poisoning if it's gone off. I made a point of sniffing everything first before it entered my mouth. And if it smelt fine, then it probably was. I got into the habit of sniffing all food first, just like your cat does when you give him his bowl.

Then I got to know which restaurants left their produce neatly in a bag out the front for whoever needed it. People like me, I guess. They do this at around tenish in the evening. Several trays of pasta and pesto or tomato and basil. Delicious. Clothes were relatively easy to find as well. As usual, you ran it through the shit or soap powder test. Sometimes you'd find a whole holdall full of them. The Lustgarten served as daily headquarters. That translated into 'pleasure garden'. It was surrounded by all the museums and cultural places of interest, so it gave the area a very intellectual feel. I liked it here because it was full of families and tourists – not the sort that would give you any bother. I'd grab a snooze first, pretending to be a tourist that had dozed off. You achieved this by always lying down on a towel, then having a bottle of water a paperback book (left halfway open) and a city map by your side.

Then I got on with writing my journal on a pad of paper (a kind of precursor to what you're reading now). It was important to have a cathartic, mental exercise. It helped me make sense of the past events and above all else question my own decision making. I was analysing what I did. It was an exercise in staying sane/being less mad. Then I'd drift into a full, proper deep sleep where I'd dream vividly – really bright and colourful dreams. I had some wicked dreams in that park.

Here in the Summertime of the German capital, life was easy. All the basic needs were met. I knew my way around. The cops never bothered, nor did anyone else. Approximately 10,000 people were living on the streets of Berlin – a whole army. Rather than being viewed as a social outcast, you were seen more a part of everyday life. A curious thing had occurred. Living on the streets like this in Berlin made me feel like I fitted in better. You melted into the throbbing heart of the beating city. I had nothing to worry about.

But then I looked around me at the families: the fathers who were about the same age as me with their wives and playing with their young children. Shouldn't I have been one of them by now? I'd got caught up in a crazy and unconventional life, by-passing all the traditional milestones. And now it was a ride that was difficult to get off. I looked at these guys with envy. They probably worked in reasonably decent jobs, providing for their families and then went to go home and see them. Why couldn't I be one of them? But instead, I'd become an international wanderer, set to wander, the long lonely path all the way to his grave.......

The Summer continued in uneventful fashion. The grey storms clouds gathered above, and the thunderstorms began. It was a frequent occurrence here. Everything went all muggy, humid and grey. Then there'd be a crack of thunder. It gave the place an eerie and moody setting. I woke up one morning and stared at my surroundings, the thick bushes. Was this real? For the first time, I had serious thoughts about going back. The end of Summer was approaching. I still happened to pass by the "Dawn till Dusk" spatkauf from time to time where the clientele sat outside. I got talking to a lady that used to work at the hostel and happened to mention my thoughts about returning to England.

"You should try hitch-hiking", she said suddenly.

"Do you reckon I could get as far as Belgium?" I asked with caution.

"You could get all the way to Dover if you wanted to. With hitch-hiking you can get almost anywhere", she replied with conviction.

Could this be possible? Getting back to the UK with no money?

"Come on; it's not that far", she added.

By now, of course, the council had figured out that I'd vacated the previous premises. Well, it had only taken them six months. So that was the primary source of income gone. I hadn't wanted to leave Berlin as it had become a safe haven. Due in this duration I'd stayed here for three months. There always comes a time in a place where you think you are beginning to overstay your welcome. You need validity at every point, especially when you're in a foreign country – you have to justify your existence there.

I looked up the geography of the roads across Germany to see if this mission was in any way realistic. Nickolassee service station to the South-East of Berlin was where you had to get yourself to. The earlier in the day, the better. Any day of the week was fine, though at weekends you'd be competing with more people. Over 800 miles back. Yes; I was quite sceptical, to say the least. Then what about sustaining myself whilst I was out there?

Still, indecision leads to inaction and inaction leads towards a situation that you don't want. If I stayed here, then things would remain the same. Pleasant, but not going anywhere. So after careful consideration, I allowed myself one final weekend in Berlin - that being our August bank holiday. In true Berlin bohemian, nomadic fashion I got poetically drunk from street procured booze then stood on the bridge at the end of Warschauer Strasse where East meets West. I often stayed out here until the sun came up in the morning. Some places you feel magnetically drawn to, and this was one of them.

The next day it was with something of a heavy heart that I took the S-Bahn all the way down to Nickolassee service station. At that point, I had less than 10 euros left – just enough cash for some provisions. Yes, I should have got there this morning, but procrastination delayed things until gone 3 p.m.

I made the sign up for Hanover. That seemed like a happy medium. Anything further away and it might put people off. This had to be the most stupid idea in the whole history of stupid ideas. I positioned myself in the corner where the cars could see me and would have ample distance for stopping time, making sure that I was on the right side of the road with the traffic heading West. Then I placed a stupid grin on my face to look more personable and stuck my thumb out. An optimistic prediction was that I'd get picked up within a couple of hours by a single male driver. But what I hadn't bargained on was one of the very first cars stopping. Nor had I expected the driver to be a young, attractive stereotypically German blond-haired and blue-eyed female. Least of all, did I expect her to be a young mother with her toddler son in the back. But that's exactly who my first ride was.

"You're going to Hanover?" she motioned for me to get in.

"Sorry, my English not so good. And sorry there's quite a mess in the back". I certainly wasn't complaining about either. She began thundering down the autobahn at near 90mph, spending half her time with her head turned around to me while talking. I didn't ask her about where the father of her child was – though I can't say I wasn't tempted. In less than an hour, I was halfway across Germany.

"Vielen dank, Guten tag, now" I waved goodbye to both her and her young child. Shame. Perhaps she could have taken me on a little bit longer. The place where she'd dropped me off wasn't ideal for getting another ride. So, I'd have to make my way to the next service station on the other side of Hanover. This would involve a total walk of some 16km and would require me to walk into the city itself. Yeah, now I know why they call it hitch-hiking. I was in a village called Lehtre. It was dusk. I looked up to see where the setting sun was. That would indicate the Westerly position and in which direction I needed to be heading.

Come to think of it; it also indicated which way the ultimate destination was, even though that was a long way away. I looked up once again at the setting sun as if it was paving the way to where I wanted to be, and it became my focal point.

"Just keep following that, and you'll end up where you want to be!" I yelled at myself as I marched through the German countryside. In case you might think I'd turned into a bit of a hippie at this point, yes, I did end up sleeping in the woods that night. But only because it was the safest place to be, as there were plenty of woods around Hanover.

Inspired by this success, I got up early the next morning before the dog walkers came along. They might momentarily think that they'd found a dead body dumped in the woods. And let's face it – everyone wants to find a dead body dumped in the woods just like they see on those Crime Watch reconstructions. I walked some way out of the city, then risked jumping the tram up to where the Western service station lay by the A2 autobahn. A good wash was required in the toilets before I presented myself to the passing traffic. Then I sprayed an ample amount of deodorant because of all that sweating.

This time I made the sign up for Dortmund. I scanned the number plates of the cars going past. What I was looking for were Dutch number plates, or even better, Belgium ones. A brand-new silver Audi pulled up. I glanced down at the plates. They were registered to Belgium. Bingo!

"Dortmund?" the driver called out of his window.

I enthusiastically nodded and trotted over.

"Deutsch, Francoise, English, Italiano?"

I stated my preference as English then said that I was heading towards Dortmund but wondered if he was heading any further. I might get out of this one yet. We drove off, once again heading down the autobahn towards Benelux, making progress all the time. He was a middle-aged businessman travelling from a meeting in Braunschweig, going back to his office in Holland and then onwards to his home in Belgium.

I sat there trying to provide good conversation and not say anything controversial. After all, that's the reason why he'd picked me up. He dropped me off somewhere between Koln and Dusseldorf. I didn't want to push my luck by asking for any further. After all, they only want your company so much. Though, this had an unfortunate side to it. I was now in the most densely populated part of Germany where all the highways crisscrossed. The traffic could be going just about anywhere and at this point, people were unlikely to want to stop.

Just like anything else, a tonne more walking was involved. One thing I will say about Germany: they do mighty fine pavements. Even going through the most rural area, there was always a sidewalk. To get beyond the main highway crossroads I ended up walking the whole night, 'cause there was sod all else to stop off for. As long as I followed the sun during dusk then made sure it was behind me in the morning, I knew that I was still on track. You probably think why I didn't just look up on google maps. Well, these were the days before I had a smartphone.

GREG LYNN

As dawn approached, threatening grey clouds were looming. The heavens were about to open, so I sort refuge in the local woods. It's amazing how much these can shelter you from the elements. Then the downpour began. I don't mean that it rained; it proper pissed it down monsoon style. It was moments like these when it felt like I was being punished for past sins. Fortunately, I still had my waterproof jacket on. I crouched down and flung my arms around the pocket where my essential travel documents were, like a mother protecting her new-born baby. Because if they get ruined when you're abroad, you're screwed. I thought about all the people I met along the way: the Greek priest, George, Selina, Julia, Angelo and Austrian Alex. The main characters. They'd snapped into my life, but then snapped out again just as quickly. Each one leaving an unforgettable memory, as if they all had some kind of message for me which needed to be listened to....

Oh, and it rained! It was relentless. There was no let-up. Forget the cold; out here the wet and the rain was well and truly your enemy. When you're soaked, your morale goes, and that's the one thing that will always keep you going. Not to mention that your belongings can get ruined. For the first time on this trip, I felt virtually beaten. Would it ever stop? Yes, of course, it did. And two days later I'd made it as far as Brussels.

Every city has its strong points, and in Brussels, it was finding food. Proper gourmet stuff still neatly packed into its silver tray; a nice bit of chunky sirloin steak with salad and onions to go with it. Plus, there was always bags full of Belgium chocolate. Plenty of calories, still needing calories.

I was now thinking about the journey ahead. The next stage would be down to Lille in Northern France. But that was a place where you didn't want to get stuck in. (A lot of aggressive drunk people roaming around, apparently.) Then I'd have to find somebody willing to give me a lift back through the channel tunnel. Considering how many illegals were trying to get through to Britain at the time, I figured that most people would be cagey about giving randoms a lift. And we all know what a dim view the British take on hitchhikers. For now, it seemed safer to stay put in civilisation.

There's a very fine line between being hardcore and being stupid. Besides, I certainly wasn't in a rush to be getting back. I'd have to do things the old-fashioned way: wait till I got sent the next £50 from family (on the 20th September) then get the Eurolines back to London. You know, like normal people.

The ring road around the centre of Brussels was in a hexagon shape, which made it easy to follow. At every point, there was a metro station, and other people were sleeping there. Sleeping in metro stations is generally something that you do only in the most extreme circumstances, i.e. when it's sub-zero. But sometimes you're so tired you don't care where you end up.

The next morning came with the familiar wake-up call from transit security guards.

"Bonjour, monsieur"

"Bonjour"

"Ca'va?"

"Ca'va bien, merci"

Then came the come on, time to get on moving line. Just how many languages had I been told that in? By now, this was all getting very tedious. It certainly wasn't fun anymore, just a drag. By this point, I was physically and emotionally drained. The days that passed were about as dull and uneventful as you can get. But sometimes a bit of non-activity is nice.

Brussels wasn't the most exciting place I've ever been to but seemed to have its fair amount of social problems: a lot of girls working the streets and plenty of old blokes passed out on the corner through drinking the country's renowned strong beer. No city was complete without one of its random encounters with another intl hobo, and Brussels wasn't about to disappoint. The scruffy bags stuffed with our possessions and slightly lost and bewildered look shared was always our conversation starter. The Tunisian called himself an 'artist'. He fitted the description with his long, dark hair, intellectual way of wording things and enigmatic air. He confessed straight away to not having valid ID papers.

"I'm returning to England soon".

"Please, take me with you!"

"Hmm. I think without papers that could be a problem", I replied.

"I'm trying to get into a night shelter for this evening. There is one here that deals specifically with non-nationals", he stated optimistically.

Me personally, another night out in the wilderness didn't bother me at all.

"But you don't have a sleeping bag, you should be worried".

Hardly. It wasn't cold yet, and as long as you lay down on cardboard and put your jacket over your body, you'd be fine.

He cramped himself into the telephone booth and dialled the free phone number that he'd found off the back of a leaflet. There was a long wait before somebody answered the phone. In the meantime, he had to endure the waiting music.

"Here, listen to this", he laughed dryly then handed me the receiver.

The lyrics sang, "*where you gonna sleep tonight?*" in a maudlin tone. This was someone's idea of a joke.

"You know, I have been all over Europe, living like this and people always ask me the same question: what are you doing here? It's like wherever you go, people don't want you there. So where are you supposed to go?" the young Tunisian said to me as we trudged off towards the shelter. Yeah, I knew the feeling.

Thankfully, by the time we got there, they only had one bed left, and I let him have it. But they were kind enough to give me some blankets. I found a quiet local park somewhere out of the centre and lay camp there until the morning of Friday, 20th September.

THE WANDERER

Sixty euros received.

I ordered a coffee in one of the cafes on the small side streets, now pleased with myself that I'd learnt to order coffee in 3 different languages then headed to the Gare de Nord. There was a bus leaving for London late that evening and I was to be on it.

This wasn't a,' good to be returning home' feeling. The living out of a sleeping bag life would merely be continuing, and I had to come to terms with that fact. The same rules would still apply, and some of the same tricks would have to be applied. I considered this while in the waiting room. Eventually, it was time for the bus to board. I sensed a loud fracas going on behind me, then someone groaning like a wounded animal.

"That's bang out of order, that it; kicking a bloke in the head while he's on the floor", a fellow English passenger tutted as he observed the proceedings.

There was the faintest glow of achievement when the bus departed. But only because I was to be finishing this road trip still in one piece. I slept for most of the way, only awakening to go through immigration at Calais. The bus seemed to hammer it all the way there way quicker than it should have done, and the bus driver seemed suitably impatient with everyone. I was barely aware that we were travelling up the motorway through Kent. We arrived at London Victoria at 04.30 – 2 hours early.

I stepped off and who should make a beeline for me, but a Big Issue seller.

"I've only got one last copy left. Will you *please* buy my last magazine?" he pleaded.

"Sorry, mate; I'm broke as a joke".

It was almost a year since I'd left. Seven different countries and approximately 6,000 miles travelled without the use of a single aircraft. I'd only gone to Kreuzberg for a party. How on earth did that happen?

Chapter 8

Nowhere to run

O ften when I was in a sticky situation abroad, people would ask,
"why don't you just return to your home country?" What they didn't realise
is that life would be just as difficult, if not more so. The situation forces you
to confront your issues: lack of standing in society, low social capital, an
absence of anything substantial. I spent the first fortnight visiting family
and friends all around the South-East of England, drawing on whatever
lifelines wherever I could; a bath here and there, plus the all needed moral
support. Of course, I still had no money, so this would involve quite a bit of
creativity when it came to getting about. Plus, there was the having to stay
somewhere overnight, in transit, in places such as London and Brighton.

The same tricks were pulled, procuring food that tourists had leftover in Leicester Square then finding somewhere discreet to sleep. The trouble was that London was such a compact city, full of people with literally street after street after street. I certainly didn't fancy joining the gang of desperados that took to camping outside Victoria station.

Again, doing this means that you'll probably get your head kicked in at some point, not to mention the sheer public humiliation. So, I was forced into the outer parts of town and spent two days sleeping underneath a flyover in Hendon out of sheer exhaustion.

On my travels, it was always the adventurous, never say die spirit that had kept me going. In places like Sicily, I had been something of a novelty; being the token man can often work in your favour. But here I was no different from the thousands of other street dwellers.

The other big problem was having no clear target. Across Europe, there had always been a clear objective, a point A to point B. Even though it was a little insane, it had kept me motivated and focused. By now, I couldn't decide where the permeant base was going to be because there was nowhere solid to go. In short, I was a plane without a runway to land on, so was left circling in a perpetual holding stack.

I'd had the vague notion of starting over again in London, the city where I'd prospered as a young man. But this was quickly proven to be an absurd idea. In London, if you don't have money or any form of social standing then you're royally screwed; you're a little ant scampering about trying not to get crushed. I'd passed through Brighton on route to see a family member, but that was an even worse place to set down. At that time Brighton had a very acute and concentrated smack problem, especially around the London road area. It had a dark and deeply disturbing vibe which, to this day, I've never experienced anywhere else. I had a bag stolen while in my sleep. That was a good reason enough not to stick around. After all social engagements were fulfilled, I had to make the firm decision of where to settle. I guess back to Bristol it was. But this was with reluctance as it just seemed like going back on one's self. After all, it's human nature to strive forward, probably inbuilt within our DNA as part of our evolution.

I took a seat on the last InterCity train out of Paddington that evening and quietly arrived back at Temple Meads station in the dead of night. I was struggling to navigate my way around. It felt unfamiliar after having to find my way through so many different cities in the meantime. Returning to England had seemed like arriving in another foreign country. Everything appeared different, and it was weird hearing people speak English again.

Nothing had changed. With a shrug of my shoulders, I lay down cardboard and sleeping bag in the flyover by the Cumberland basin, right where the city meets the North Somerset countryside. (Less than 200 yards from where I'm writing this now.) The only people you got around here were early morning dog walkers or the graffiti artists graffing up the concrete walls, not the type to cause me any bother. The area had a tranquil feel to it which I liked, plus you got a great view of Clifton suspension bridge illuminated at night.

The next morning, I was awoken by a clip-clop, clip-clop sound. I opened my eyes to see two WPC's mounted on horseback going past.

"Are you alright there, darling?" one of them asked sympathetically.

I responded with a thumbs up.

"Just checking, honey. Take care now".

After getting up, the first thing that needed to be taken care of was stashing my stuff. This necessity is a bit of an art form. You need to leave it in a place where no one will ever find it. A nice thick bush well away from any walkways will do the job. You also don't want it to get wet or corrode. So the essential things like your sleeping bag need to be wrapped up in plastic bags. Make sure that no one sees where you're putting it. Trust me; you've always got something that would be worth a lot to someone else. A proper Winter sleeping bag and suitable clothing and boots, it could be the difference between life and death. Sometimes I'd come back at night and think shit, where did I leave it? Everything looks different in the dark, and a load of bushes will all look the same. So I'd leave an empty packet of red rizla underneath a stone, and that would mark the spot. (The rizla packet is innocuous, so nobody is going to take any notice of it, and the red colour means you can see it in the dark.)

Almost by default, I was back in Bristol's close-knit homeless community. It's been well documented that the city has a substantial homeless/housing problem and a very significant socially excluded underbelly. For the sake of our survival, we quickly formed our own clique's, even though we kinda hated each other at the same time. It was an odd co-dependency. Each day I'd bump into old associates.

"Hey, it's good to see you Greggers; we all thought you were dead!"

It was best not to judge each other as we all had very personal reasons for why we ended up where we did. You had everybody from just about every conceivable walk of life. Though broadly speaking the demographic could be split roughly into two. On the one side, the born wreck heads; they're the ones you see slumped out in shop doorways with no teeth left. I will point out that the story of how they got to be like that is a long and complicated one. On the other side, you had the lot who used to work in well-paid jobs and had led happy and contented lives, but then a train wreck had occurred. More often than not, it was an acrimonious divorce case; the wife had got the house. So former stockbroker came to mix with former crane driver. While former scrap metal worker now played chess down a soup kitchen with former university lecturer. People from totally different backgrounds, yet somehow, we'd all joined each other on the same path. I was known as the bloke who liked travelling. The one who lived out of a rucksack and wherever he lay his head was his home. That made me the hardest one to work out of the lot.

Still, things could have been worse. Anybody who's ever lived it rough here will tell you that it's by far the UK's most homeless friendly city. It came with a myriad of support services on offer. You were sure never to go hungry. The danger lay in gaining about two stone in weight from all that carbohydrate and bakery given out from free food places. "You'll never go hungry in Bristol" was a sentiment that was echoed time and time again. There's an old joke, "the only thing that you have to pay for here is a packet of rizla". Another transient once stopped me to say "you're obviously homeless, do you know…."

"Is it that obvious? Do I look that rough?" I replied, mortified.

"No. It's that bag full of Pret a Manger sandwiches that you've got in your hand. That's what gives it away".

There were plenty of clothes and other amenities from the places on offer as well. Sometimes you could spot other transients from the brand-new North Face or Berghaus jackets that they were wearing. Though, like many other things, this was a double-edged sword. Few can deny that having ample support was a good thing – indeed, vital. Though I called this whole business, 'the free food merry go round' as it was mainly concentrated around the city centre, which is very small. Doing the same thing day in and day out and seeing the same old faces while we wearily looked at each other. It quickly became a habit where you forget that at one time, you were capable of looking after yourself.

So what was a way of becoming more independent? Why don't you get a job? You might say. Well believe it or not, when you live on the street, your employment prospects are severely limited. I'd had a falling out with the dole office that morning. They don't make any provisions if your NFA. You were still fully expected to find a job despite the apparent barriers this created. They'd been busting my balls about not applying for some poxy call centre job. Sleeping out in the cold night after night can make you a tad touchy, so I'd ended up snapping. They could stuff their £67 a week.

Then I cast my mind back to a family day out in London some 6 or 7 years prior. We were in Covent Garden when out of nowhere sprang a Big Issue seller accompanied by a ginger cat that he had on a leash.

"Hello, my name is James, and this is my cat, Bob. He comes with me everywhere".

James began reciting his life story of how he'd grown up in Surrey, been a teenage tearaway and then got involved in drugs etc., etc. There was something that made him different from most of the other Big Issue sellers. For a start, he spoke in a middle-class accent and reminded me of Pete Docherty. (Very talented, likeable, yet tragically self-destructive.)

"Yeah, yeah to be honest mate your teeth tell the whole story (blatant smack habit) How much for a mag?"

"£2.50"

"I've only got a £20 note. Can you change it?"

".... Just about". He dug into his pocket for his stash of pound coins and duly dispensed £17.50.

I'm a bit ashamed to say that I counted it back out in front of him, and yes, it was correct. We wished each other a pleasant day. That was James Bowen and his cat Bob. They both went on to become rich and famous.

From a little research gathered you could forget selling the Issue in Bristol. People didn't want to know. Besides, I knew too many people there. But Bath, on the other hand, was said to be brilliant and Christmas was coming up. So I got myself down to their office, stating that I was keen to become a vendor. I gave the cover story that I was kipping on a mate's sofa in nearby Saltford. As it was another city, another council took care of issuing the badge, so you required a local connection. It was a bit more complicated than I'd imagined. You got interviewed about your background, asked to fill out and sign a load of paperwork and agreed to all the dos and don'ts. You also needed a reference from one of the day centres.

For the first week, I was to be a 'floating vendor'. I had to take whichever spot was free. If you managed to sell more than 20 mags in your first week, then you could start choosing your pitch. First dibs went in order of who'd managed to sell the most the previous week. All mags had to be purchased by the vendor first at 50% of their retail price. Strictly no tick. You could buy as many mags as you wanted and once sold the money was yours to keep. You were regarded as self-employed. They offered support such as help with getting a bank account, plus some initial coaching. I liked the sound of it all. It was enterprising, pulling your self up by your bra straps.

All that was needed was £50 for the start-up, and I was good to go. I came back and brought five mags as a test run. (You got your very first two for free.) Then headed out onto the street. Yeah, I'll be honest, in the beginning, I felt like a complete twat. It was like hitch-hiking in Germany all over again: stood there with your hand out, trying to appear endearing. Would this work?

It took less than 5 minutes for the first sale, and within an hour, the lot went. Could I be on to something? Another memory appeared. It was from Felix Dennis book, *'How to be Rich'*. The only decent book I've ever read on how to make money. The golden rule that he'd repeated, again and again, was the importance of cash flow. Whether you were running a multi-global corporation or a couple of kiddies with a lemonade stall - if you didn't manage your cash flow properly, then your business would be stuffed immediately. I bore this in mind and ensured to keep back £20 to buy more mags.

In many other cities selling the Issue may have been just a 'fags and beer' gig, but in Bath, it was serious business. In one of the UK's most affluent cities, there was the potential to earn decent money, i.e. over £300 a week. Plus, the very compact nature of the city meant that you never had to walk for more than 10 minutes to get to your spot, unlike in London where you might have to go for miles.

I'd started on late Wednesday afternoon and kept on going back every day. It was difficult not having my own pitch yet as about an hour would go buy then another vendor would turn up saying, "I've booked this spot, mate". (They were either apologetic or very territorial.) I wasn't a proper vendor yet. By Saturday, I'd managed to sell 36 copies. The top sellers were achieving well over 100.

Hmm…

Nope, apparently, 36 on the first week was very good. Come Monday, I'd have the right to choose a pitch, and it would be *mine* for the whole morning. It was like trying to get a fire going; you began carefully with the kindling wood, then kept on adding small bits until you had a steady heat base, then added the one big log on in the hope that it would go whoosh.

Life now had a bit of rhythm. I'd set my alarm for 7 in the morning, just like you do when you've got to get up for work. It would still be semi-dark when it awoke me with that irritating, high pitched noise. I'd rub my eyes then feel the cold wind on my face; it was the moment where things felt surreal.

Then I'd take a brisk walk to Temple Meads station with that, off to go and do your bit in the world feeling. I'd grab a copy of the Metro, then dash off for the 08.00 train alongside the lawyers on their way to a meeting in London. Rhythm. Structure. Something constructive to do due in the day. A sense of normality. It was priceless.

That Thursday afternoon, I ended up getting put on a pitch by the Abbey by accident. But it turned out to be a happy one. For this was the first day of the world-renowned Christmas market, which I was right next to. And there were going to be plenty of punters in town with cash in their pockets. (Thank god I did this before contactless cards came out.) Positioning was vital here; you want to be there, but not in their way (unlike chuggers who can literally block your path). A nice bit of subtlety but be very much seen and heard.

"Big Issue to go with your toffee apple, sir?"

"……err…. yeah, go on then".

As it was the Christmas special, they'd upped the price to £3 which made them more expensive to buy. I also thought this would make them harder to sell. But no; I was managing about a 1 in 5 hit rate. They were flying out of my hands. At 1 point, I even had a queue. This was tremendous. In less than an hour, I'd sold my stack of 20. But I'd have to wait until the office reopened after lunch to buy more stock. Now I was hungry.

"I need to buy some more mags, please", I said to the girl behind the counter.

"But you had a load this morning".

"I don't care. More, I want *more*".

"Alright. How many?"

"About another 20 should do it, I reckon".

"Are you sure? That's going to cost you £30".

I considered this for a moment. It was a bit of a gamble.

"Yeah, okay. Give me 30 then".

And on it went. Come at 5 o'clock I only had two left. Then the bloke who should have had that pitch turned up. Forty-eight mags sold in one afternoon. Then I made about the same on drops as I did on sales. A drop is when someone says you can keep the change or gives you a donation. I made a profit of near £150, and I left there walking on air.

Unfortunately, matey ensured that he was never late for that pitch again. By now, the fire had got going, and I was in business. I made outside TK Max on the road up from the train my regular morning pitch. Not too busy, but not too quiet. You'd typically catch the people that were still on their way to work. Then in the afternoon, I'd take whatever I felt was going to be a good one.

It was all about reading people as they approached. If someone was blatantly in a bad mood or clearly in a rush, then you left them well alone.

Or if they were heavily laden down with shopping, then they're not going to want to faff around getting their money out. If you see a couple then always pitch the male. Otherwise, he'll go on the protective shield his girlfriend thing. Don't bother with arty or alternative types 'cause they're always skint. Then I learnt something interesting: there are certain types of people and specific demographics that find you appealing. One example with me would be a 25-year-old female dancer. For some reason, 70 per cent of my customers were female. The core demographic, if you like, were professional women aged between 28 – 40. Other than that, cool, intellectual types, those who were a tad off centre or affable looking blokes in suits who it turned out were entrepreneurs. These were the sorts I looked out for and pitched.

If someone was clearly in a rush and just wanted a quick transaction, that was fine. Serve 'um and let them go. But I liked the chatting and engaging with people because people are fascinating; every person you meet is a potential opportunity.

My target due in the week was around 20 sales a day. In total this could make me about £60, but on Saturday with all the shoppers in town, I could quite easily double that. I was making it into the top 4 sellers' bracket. To get any higher I'd either have to have been doing it for ages, be a cute female or have a cute dog. Hell, I was making more out of this than I could do in a regular job. And for the time being, it was enough to sustain me.

The routine would be thus: by early afternoon I'd generally raised enough for a night in a backpacker's hostel. I'd go in and reserve my spot for the night. That was £17.50 gone. Come between 5-6pm I'd call it a day on business proceedings and check into the hostel, stating my reason for stay as, 'working in the area'. It was a relief to be back in the warmth and secure surroundings. It was almost like I was travelling again, merely carrying on in the same vein. Though there weren't any cooking facilities here, so that meant eating out, which in Bath was an expensive option. There was one place slightly out of town that I found where you could still

169

get a meal for less than a fiver. Being homeless can be a surprisingly expensive game as everything needs taking care of immediately.

When any of the other guests would ask me what I was doing in Bath my reply would be, "I have a free-lance media sales job here, and I'm staying at the hostel until I can afford to get a place of my own". Well, it was true, wasn't it? But then I quickly learnt I wasn't the only one up to the same game. There were at least three other people here who were a variant of what I was: the working homeless. They held jobs such as chefs and call centre operators, and for now, this was their place of residence until they sorted out something permanent, which always takes time. We became the 'live-in crew' and formed our small clique where we were slightly separate from the crowd of coming and going travellers. This subgroup of people is far more common than you might think.

In the mornings I'd grab a shower, then scoff down the inclusive breakfast and head back out on it. That morning a 'lady' who I came to describe later as 'that skanky bitch' approached me and seemed keen to buy a copy. She only had a twenty-pound note, and could I change it?

"Yeah, just about".

It took up all the change I had left. Why didn't I stop to listen to my instinct? When something or someone doesn't feel right, chances are they probably aren't. That twenty-pound note she'd pressed into my hand didn't feel right either; it wasn't crisp enough. By now I'd made friends with a few of the market stall traders that operated there and asked one of them to check it for me.

"Yup, that's a fake alright, mate. You can't see the watermark properly".

'Skanky bitch' had been off like a shot, leaving me twenty pounds down. It was here that I learnt a valuable lesson: check all of your goddamn notes! From then on, every time somebody presented me with one, my line was:

"I've just got to check that a minute because the other day someone gave me a dud twenty. Of course, I know you wouldn't go doing that love", I'd politely reassure.

"Yup, that looks fine and dandy", I said while holding it up to the sunlight.

"What, somebody actually did that to you?"

"Afraid so. Now, I'll get your change. That's s seven pound".

"Oh, no. It's alright; you keep it".

And that is how you turn a bit of bad luck into good fortune. I kept telling that story to the punters for the rest of that week.

That evening I made my usual visit to the takeaway place and ordered another £4.99 shish kebab and chips. By now, my cholesterol level must have been having a party.

"I was thinking about opening up on Christmas Day. But I don't know; it might not be worth it. What do you think? The proprietor asked me as I munched away. I thought about this for a moment.

"What's your normal daily turnover?"

"About £600."

"Okay, so that puts your revenue at about £200 - £300. You don't want to be making any less than that. Timing is everything here. If you end up opening at the wrong time when people don't come, you'll be losing money. Don't open till 18.00. That's when you'll catch everybody returning from their Aunt Beryl's, and they've seen the whole family. They want something quick to eat at a reasonable price after a long and stressful day before they return home. Nowhere else is going to be open, so everyone is going to come to you. Shut at around midnight. You've got that 6-hour window to be providing what people want. I reckon you'll clean up nice!" I answered while slurping down my cola.

Then my own Christmas Day came. It was just me and the 'live-in crew' in the upstairs living room. I'd reserved three nights the previous day at an increased cost of £27 a night.

"Right, I've put you in room 6 with the rest of your little homeless crew. There's the key; you know the drill", the manager was about as enthusiastic as staying here over the yuletide period as I was.

I swigged away from a bottle of Bacardi, in a sardonic mood. I used to enjoy Christmas. But now I fucking hated it! It proved to be a very lonely time of year where I felt flat. At least there was a roof over my head. I retired to bed early with a biography about Pablo Escobar, then lay awake thinking about what to do in January.

There'd be no point in continuing to be a vendor as now all would be quiet. I hadn't wanted it to be anything more than a Christmas job anyway. My brain couldn't come up with anything that sounded like a proper plan, and I let out a heavy sigh. A couple of days later, I returned to the takeaway place for dinner.

"Hey mate, I took your advice and opened on Christmas Day in the evening as you said. I took £1,000! It's on the house".

But my prosperous times couldn't go on forever. So after the twelfth day of Christmas, I returned to the 'flyover Hilton' in Bristol. While being a vendor, I'd managed to sustain myself through independent means, but that had been a costly business, and it didn't take long for the money to run out. The Big Issue has come into some criticism. All I'll say that from my own experience, it undoubtedly played a crucial part in my rehabilitation. Looking back, I should have taken them up on more of the support that they'd offered and not just left. Though it proved that if I could sort myself out once, then I could do it again.

The Winter of 2013/2014 was the wettest one ever recorded. Every day it rained, and it rained….and it rained. When living out the hardest thing that you have to deal with is the rain and wind, and that came in abundance.

The travelling phase had come to an end, and there was no glorifying this situation anymore. It could only be described as rock bottom and on your arse. The area was well sheltered, but moisture was thick in the air. The rain thundered down and leaked through the concrete above me. The gale-force wind howled. And I wished I were dead....

Yeah, I'd been to the Compass centre, run by St. Mungo's; the place that deals with rough sleepers in Bristol. Though the long and short of it was because I didn't have a drug problem, wasn't an alcoholic and had no known severe physical or mental illness, they wouldn't help me. The questionnaire went along the lines of this:

"How often did I manage to get a shower?"

"About three times a week".

"Did I manage to eat properly?"

"Yes. That was easy".

"Was I an ex-con?"

"No".

"Was I a convicted nonce?"

"No".

"Did I like to burn things?"

".... Not yet".

"Well then, you're not showing any signs of chronic homelessness. The door is that way".

Call me disagreeable here, but I've got strong views on the agencies that deal with the homeless. But out of fear of being sued for slander, I'm going to keep those to myself.

Eventually, though, a member of the public grassed me up on one of those, 'shop a bum' lines and St. Mungoes paid me an early morning visit. At the end of their assessment, I was classified as 'low need' and no associated risk. As punishment, I was sentenced to two weeks in the Salvation Army, on the open prison wing. I entered late on Wednesday night. The stench of 93 rotting souls hung thick in the air. Many people say that they'd prefer to go to prison than end up in a hostel. Fortunately, I wasn't to be a proper full-time in-mate but would be staying in their 'crash pad' and allowed out on day release until I was moved on to a room in a shared house. There was to be another assessment and more form filling.

".... And finally, do you like to burn things?"

As I'd answered no, a man was spewing up pink vomit in the corner then promptly passed out. Over the next fortnight, the routine went as follows: I would get in at the latest possible time, around 23.00, then go to the games room where my camper bed was laid out in the corner. The full-time in-mates would be there trying to play snooker. At midnight they'd all go off to tick their vallies. As soon as the last one had exited, I promptly shut the double doors, locked then barricaded them. This was my room now. Greg has control of this room. No one was getting in while I slept. They'd always be one of the inmates incessantly banging on the doors, trying to get in. But he could keep on banging. The following morning I'd have to be out of there by 9 am and would be left to amuse myself in whatever way possible due in the daytime.

"I can't see you settling into a room in a shared house; you're too much of a loose cannon", a fellow transient remarked while we were stuck in one wet Saturday morning.

And he was kinda right. They plonked me right outside the city in South Gloucestershire, the arse end of nowhere. I'd tried to regroup as best as I could, eventually starting work in construction. It was the only job that I could get. But the workflow was irregular and unreliable, which made trying to claim housing benefit a nightmare. So I fell into rent arrears. There was also the small matter of the £1,600 odd that I owed Bristol City council due to a certain housing benefit overpayment.

When you've only got four walls and a bed, and you're on your own, it's not exactly the best scenario for rebuilding your life. I soon became bored, frustrated and depressed. The landlord could evict me if they wanted; I didn't care.

Halfway through one night, something odd happened: I leapt out of bed and threw myself onto the floor, and there I slept. It was as if my mind was going through a psychological preparation before I'd consciously realised what was about to occur. The streets were calling! But it certainly wasn't going to be in Bristol. Now faced with danger, I was seeking refuge in the last place that I'd felt safe and comfortable. It was to be back to European headquarters......

Chapter 9

Berlin's unofficial tour guide

"**E**ntschuldigung haben sie feuer, bitte?" I said while waiting for the bus outside Tegal airport.

Unfortunately, airport security had deprived me of my lighter.

"Vielen dank".

"Bitte".

It was a glorious late summer afternoon. I'd arrived precisely one year after leaving. That resulted in a liberating feeling washing over me. I'd flown in via Copenhagen. Several tourists came up to me, asking for directions as the immediate layout was obscure. Berlin is especially renowned for having user-unfriendly airports.

"Take this bus to Hauptbahnhof, from there you can get the express train to Schoenfeld, and don't forget to validate your ticket".

I thought back to the day when Yogaman and I were fumbling our way down to Kreuzberg. We had to stop and ask people for directions. Now this time I was the one giving them out. Upon departure it had been the same procedure as before: book the ticket at the last minute, scrape together a few hundred quid, then sling a rucksack over my shoulder and say a prayer to whoever was listening. I knew the money wasn't going to last long, about enough for 1 or 2 weeks of fun. But that would have to be worried about later.

As before I spent the first week or so staying in Backpacker hostels. Once again, my companions were the fresh-faced, 'yeah, Berlin; isn't it amazing' crowd. Deja vu had struck. Inevitably, I ended up hitting the clubs. It's nice to feel young again, but in reality, this was something that I'd long since outgrown. You know things aren't going right when at least two of your group get knocked back at the door for not having ID on them. It was an odd situation to be. My youth was over, but I still hadn't found a new spark yet. But on the plus side, I got to hang out with a couple of 18-year-old student girls. I gave them the low down on the club scene here and the city itself. Pass on the knowledge, then move on.

Berlin had changed a fair bit since the last time that I'd been here. The city always seemed like it was in a perpetual state of transformation. There were way more police patrolling the streets. This was possibly in response to the refugee crisis. The first day that I'd arrived getting off at Görlitzer Bahnhof I was greeted by a group of West African refugees desperately trying to sell weed, presumptuously beckoning me over. Just because you were a Westerner with a rucksack, they thought this immediately implied that you were up for buying drugs.

"Nein, nein", I said with impatience.

The city's police often stopped the Africans. For they were undocumented. It was another example of the authorities trying to exert control and keep tabs on people who had no legal standing here. They'd come from failed nations such as Nigeria, Sierra Leone and the Ivory Coast in search of a better life. You can never blame people for doing that. They'd done whatever it took to raise the thousands of dollars that were demanded by unscrupulous people smugglers (though controversial rumours are rife about who and how this is financed.)

Their journey began by jumping onto the back of a severely overcrowded truck which made the perilous journey across the Sahara Desert. The heat would have risen to over 50 degrees Celsius while the infamous dessert wind blew sharp sand grains across their faces. No concessions got made for the poor sods that fell overboard. A truck speeding along at 70mph wasn't going to stop for anyone. Time was money. Once in Libya was where their problems really began. It could go two ways: the first being that they'd be forced to work their passage further by other gangs. Or they might have to endure months living in a Libyan refugee camp, where they were treated to a daily cup of tea and piece of bread. Slowly, they'd have starved almost to death. Plus, living in such unsanitary conditions meant they were much more prone to catching diseases.

Once they'd got out of that lot and made it to Tripoli, they'd have boarded a vessel that was utterly unseaworthy, managed by a skipper and a compass man whom only had the faintest idea of what they were doing. A good many of these vessels sank in the Mediterranean Sea. The lucky ones would have got picked up by the Italian Navy.

For those hardy souls that were still going, they'd have finally made it to the promised land of Europe. Might as well head to the wealthiest and most powerful nation there, Germany. You've got to hand it to these boys; I thought that I was a hardcore traveller. But had it all been worth it? Scratching a living outside the U-Bahn, selling junk on the street, while the government tried to prevent their movement, and they were still in a state of limbo. Was life better over here for them? Probably not. Anyway, fuck-um; I'm glad that the cops were giving them a hard time. That meant they'd be paying the likes of me less attention.

The Syrians seemed to be better received, though. A good many of them were well educated and skilled. They made an effort to learn the language and integrate.

And not all was peace and love with the residents either. Disgruntlement was in the air about a whole host of issues. It had resulted in many protests. But there'd often be more cops than protesters. Housing and gentrification were top of their concerns. As so many people had moved in from all over Europe and beyond, demand for accommodation was high. The rental prices had shot up. That had forced a good many of the locals into the outer parts. When I'd got here, Kreuzberg still had a grimy edge to it. But now the rich kids had moved in, and it had become fully hipsterfied. Yup, vegan cafes everywhere. They'd been a lot of talk in the press about Berlin being no longer being 'cool' anymore, that the party had moved on elsewhere. Not that that bothered me; there was so much history to the place and had such depth to it that it was impossible to be spoilt by hipster pretensions describing it as no longer '*the place*'.

My last few euros got spent down the Eurocan bakery on coffee and borek. Now the 'enhanced travelling experience' was about to kick in. I was bopping down Friedrichshain and being the complete chancer that I am happened to notice the doors open on a suitably graffed up townhouse. It appeared unoccupied alright. Even the walls on the inside were covered in graffiti.

Here's how to stay in a building that doesn't belong to you in a foreign country without arousing suspicion (as far as I knew squatting was illegal in Germany). You walk up perfectly normally as if it's your building and you have perfect right to be there. People only start giving you dodgy looks if you start *acting* dodgy. Here's one crucial thing that I've picked up about human nature: people are only bothered by your behaviour if they are directly affected by it in some way. If they're not, then they couldn't care less about what you get up to.

I travelled to the top of the 5-story building as height is always your friend. At the top was an attic with plenty of floor space. I lay down my belongings and made up my bed for the night. A lovely cosy home in a very convenient district found just like that. Perfect. To celebrate, I drank from a bottle of Vodka that had I'd procured off the street, then fell asleep for the night.

But then I was awoken by the sound of voices coming from downstairs during the night. It sounded like somebody was having a party. Could this place be squatted? No, the voices sounded too civilised. Nobody knew that I was here. The best thing to do was to sit tight and be quiet. Then I heard footsteps continuing up the stairs. Who was this? I turned around to see a man carrying his bicycle approach the landing. Keep calm.

"Guten abend. Alles gut, ja?" I said, trying to put a bit of authority into my voice.

The man looked back at me slightly sheepishly.

"Oh, sorry. Is it alright if I leave my bike here?" The accent was Australian.

"Ja, bitte shone".

"Thanks", then he turned away and walked back down the stairs.

I could already tell that this building had work going on as there was builder's material left scattered about all over the place. That wasn't necessarily a problem. As long as I left no sign that I was there, then that would be fine. I needed not to muck about with anything on-site. I picked up everything. That included all the dog-end cigarettes. If I departed by 7 am before the workmen got here, then they'd be none the wiser of my presence. The next day I quickly walked out of the front door just as their van pulled up. They were busy shifting out plasterboards.

"No. Can you leave the door open", one of them said.

"Bitte", I obliged, then melted away into the hustle and bustle of the streets.

Would the doors still be open in the evening? I went back to find out, and sure enough, they were. Now a base had been secured. I got on with the business of building up a routine. Once I'd left in the morning, the rucksack stashing procedure got executed. Only this time it involved climbing over a 7-foot wall, depositing it in a bush and leaving the waterproof covering over it. Then I'd make my way to the Ost Bahnhof. There was a little place by the side where they made a free breakfast in the morning, the Bahnhaus mission. They were affiliated to the Salvation Army in some way. En-route there I'd collect at least four aluminium cans. Here in Germany you could take these to a supermarket, put them in the recycling machine and then it would print out a ticket. You got that cashed at the counter. They paid 25 cents for each can. With 1 euro in my pocket, I had enough for a shower at the Bahnhause mission.

I'd pass the old buildings of the former East Berlin. The sheer grittiness of the architecture gave the area a very atmospheric feel. Then I'd walk right along the East side gallery, admiring the mile-long stretch of artwork. It always put me in a happy mood. Then it came to the part of the day I loathed: waiting outside the Bahnhaus mission in the queue with a bunch of pissheads as they only allowed a few in at a time. I'd found this place by merely keeping an eye out for the line of bums, and in Germany, they always have one of these places by a major train station in a discreet corner where jo-public would be none the wiser of its presence. Here was a good place to practice my German. They were less likely to ask what you were doing here if you spoke the local dialect.

"Guten morgen. Ich komme hierher zum fruhstuck, bitte".

The food here wasn't bad, plenty of fresh fruit, nutty bread, meat and herbal tea.

"Dusche, bitte", I said, pointing at the shower.

"Ja, eine euro".

That was personal hygiene and breakfast consumed. Then I'd get on with the next project, learning German *properly*. I'd got hold of a few textbooks that were all in Deutsche, then positioned myself down the Bibliothek (local library) and set to work. That's right; I was going to teach myself. God help me. At first, it appeared to be a complex language as the words were so long, and the grammar was alleged to be a nightmare. But no; once you got your head around it, it wasn't too bad at all. It was a very logical and straight forward language. One by one, the series of odd words lit up like a light bulb as soon as I discovered what they meant. By the end of the day I'd learnt to count; as soon as you'd learnt up to 10 everything else was an add on. By the end of the week, I could translate a whole letter. If anything, it was something to do.

"Excuse me, I'm going to the toilet; would you mind keeping an eye on my laptop for me?" a punter sitting next to me would say.

"Ja, kein problem".

This was good news at it meant that I looked respectable enough to be trusted. It's all about keeping up appearances. In addition to that, I'd do a lot of reading. First, reading the Guardian and the New York Times from cover to cover. (They delivered English newspapers there daily.) I'd go for a walk, digesting the world's current affairs and forming my own opinion of it all. The world sure seemed like a volatile place now. Then I'd pour through that day's copy of the financial times. By now, I was developing a keen interest in business, economics and global commercial systems. Without this mental stimulation, it was all too easy to be locked in one's thoughts. Out here, you did a lot of thinking, and if you weren't careful, your thoughts could kill you.

The weekends were what I looked forward to the most in the party capital of Europe. It was Friday night – get pissed for free night! My alcohol consumption had shot up to around 50 units a week. My name's Greg, and I'm rapidly developing a drinking problem.

THE WANDERER

The clubbing tourists had a funny habit of coming up to me and asking where they could get such and such. I guess because I looked worldly enough to know, yet trustworthy enough to give the right advice - an odd niche.

"I can't tell you that myself, but whatever you do, don't go buying from one of the Turks on the street. You'll get ripped off", was my stock answer.

Then they wanted to know where a particular club was. I'd give the directions, but they'd just look at me blankly as the long street names in a funny language didn't mean anything to them.

".... I'll show you. Come with me; I'll take you there", I said after the awkward pause was over".

Well, I hardly had anything else better to do, did I?

Or they'd come up to me and ask where the decent party was that night. I'd look at their demographic then direct them to where I thought they were best suited. If they were a bit more on the hardcore party side but fresh and eager, then Tresor would be a good bet (an all-night Techno party). Or if they were a bit more fresh and funky then one of the underground House clubs by the Spree. I wasn't going to send anybody to Berghain. If they were new and unsure here, then they'd end up getting knocked back at the door. I might as well save them disappointment.

"Excuse me, do you speak *English*?" a group of young Brits asked me in a slow tone the way that Brits do when abroad.

That made me laugh as for some reason; everybody thought that I was German. I guess it was the blue eyes and blonde hair.

"Ja, ich kann der helfen?"

"oh...."

"I am English, yer muppet", I'd joke with an exaggerated accent.

"Mate, stop fucking with us; you're *German*".

183

Now they looked even more confused.

"Definitely not mate. I was born in Slough to English parents. What's up?"

"They wouldn't let us in at Watergate. I wondered if you knew anywhere that was good tonight?"

"Why did they knock you back?"

"It's the male to female ratio. They don't like it".

I looked at the group. Four guys and two girls aged about 18 to 21. The girls were okay looking.

"Don't worry. It's a shit club anyway. There are better parties out there. There's the 'AVA club'. It's just up there. I'll show you".

By now, I knew just about every inch of the streets of Kreuzberg and Friedrichshain.

"Where are *you* going tonight?" he asked.

I was quite tempted to reply with a, 'I live on the streets, I'm not going anywhere', but thought better of it.

"I don't know yet, we'll see. Right, first of all, your group is too big. They don't like big groups in Berlin. Split up into two and put the girls at the front of each group. You might fare better that way. Have a good one, yeah", I said and disappeared off into the night air.

I got back to the 'attic apartment'. The builders knew that I was there by now but didn't seem too bothered. Once every so often I'd oversleep in the morning, only awakening when they were coming up the stairs. I'd have my stuff arranged so that I could get up and out in 45 seconds flat. There was an awkward moment while they gave me funny glances. Then I'd scuttle down the stairs. Their work was progressing nicely, and now they'd installed the insulation. That was going to keep me lovely and warm. Good job, lads! It was Sunday tomorrow, and they wouldn't come here. That meant I could get a lay-in. I settled in with a couple of near full bottles of Becks. The world wasn't too bad a place after all.

It wasn't just the clubbing tourists that asked for my assistance. Due in the daytime the regular ones would be asking for directions. It was usually for 'Checkpoint Charlie', the East side gallery, or museum island. I'd get asked for a light about ten times a day. The Germans loved asking me for a light; perhaps they saw me as the man to ignite things.

"Excuse me, do you know where the Berlin Wall is?" a Turkish couple of ladies asked me one evening.

"That's it right there", I pointed behind me.

"*That's* the wall?" she replied incredulously.

"It's tiny".

"The wall was never that big. It's all the stuff that they had around it like the checkpoints, the floodlights and all the guards", I pointed out.

They wanted to know about the artwork that now graced it, so we went on a walk as I pointed the various murals out.

"I'd also like to find the Turkish quarter. Do you know where that is?"

"Hmm, well if anything I guess that's got to be Kottbusser Tor. It's a bit of a walk, but I can show you".

"What's this area?"

"It's Kreuzberg. Seeing as I was on a roll, I thought I might include a history lesson. I was bored, see.

"It wasn't always like this. Back in the 1960s when the wall got built, nobody wanted to invest around here as it was seen as 'the bad part of town' being so close to something controversial. Thus, the buildings were left empty as nobody wanted to live around here. The area soon fell into decay. By the 1970's it was officially condemned as a slum. What happens when you get a load of vacant buildings due in a housing crisis? You get squatters. It was the immigrants and all the misfits of society. They occupied the premises, but everyone left them well alone; they were left to do their own thing. So, a kind of counter-culture got built up around that. New trends. New ideas. By squatting the old buildings, they prevented them from being demolished. It's often society's off-cuts that are the ones to force change. They created the roots of the cool happenings that you see around you today.

"Make sure you check that 24hour bakery out, by the way; it's wicked. Then the wall came down and in the 1990s when dance music got popular that culture ended up getting co-opted somewhat. That's when all the clubs sprang up", I finished.

"Wow. We're from Frankfurt, and you know more about our countries history than we do".

"I just like this kind of stuff. Now here's Kottbusser Tor, the most Turkish place there is. Have a good night, ladies".

And history continued to fascinate me as 25 jahre mauerfall approached. They were celebrating 25 years of the wall being down. Dotted right along its former existence were boards that told stories of the people who'd dared to cross by ingenious methods. A good many who tried were shot dead. I loved reading these tales of ingenuity, creativity and bravery together with a desire not to accept the status quo, as I believed that they could be applied to everyday life. That's why when I set a goal, I pick one that by rights you shouldn't achieve at that time (think Budapest to Palermo). That's what gets you stimulated to break down boundaries.

The big event came on a freezing and foggy night. We were all crowded together drinking mulled wine (the proper stuff) as they let off hundreds of white balloons along the line where the wall once stood, each one symbolising a future message of hope. It was something that left me speechless.

An old fire truck turned up by the Eastside gallery armed with a couple of DJs'. I'd seen this old fire truck before when they'd played at an impromptu free party. In the end, it had driven merrily off into the distance with the music still playing. People ran after it like kiddies chasing an ice-cream van. It was funny. They played a set consisting mainly of acid house tunes that were in vogue at the time of the fall. I've never heard '*Higher state of consciousness'* sound so cool.

An epic night.

A few nights later, I went back to the attic apartment and hurried up the stairs as always. I was surprised to see a man coming out of the flats. He said something in German, which I didn't understand. He looked puzzled. There was an awkward silence, and then he translated to English.

"Are you with the workers?"

I said nothing as silence is often an admission of guilt.

"Oder....aus der strasse?"

"Ja, aus der strasse", I sighed.

It turned out that this block was fully occupied with legitimate tenants. For the last two months, they'd all thought that I was the site security guard.

"Because you don't look homeless. You are clean. Your bag is clean. It doesn't look like you do alcohol or drugs".

Not one hundred per cent true.

"It's okay; you can tell me your story. I'm a social worker. I am interested to hear your tale of how you ended up here".

So, what was I supposed to tell him? That I got bored of living in a bedsit in Bristol and did a runner. People often asked me about how I ended as I did, but I could never come up with a coherent answer as I didn't even know myself. I replied with some bland one-liner.

"It must be very tough for you here".

Like I've said before in some ways, life like this is difficult. That challenge is stimulating, which leads to gratification. And the easy flipside is the path of least resistance.

He offered me a cigarette, and we both stood on the landing smoking.

"I'm worried about what the owner will do if he finds you here. He may beat you up".

I doubt it, seeing as nine times out of 10 they'll just tell you to piss off.

"I don't mind you staying here. We're all going to move out soon anyway. That's why the house is being renovated. But please, let me know if you need anything".

And with that, he passed me a bag containing fruit and olives. But I'd deemed it no longer a good idea to stay here as the cat was now out of the bag. So what to do when things have taken a dire turn? Jump on the Mein Fern! (The German equivalent of the Mega bus.) I took a side trip down to Leipzig in Saxon as it was said to be the 'New Berlin', so I'd gone down to verify these rumours. It was cool, but I couldn't see anything fantastic about the place.

I hitch-hiked back once again, this time getting picked up by a woman with *three* young children. For Christmas, I fancied a stay in Braunschweig as a change of scene. Yet another Christmas day spent in an outbuilding while it was minus four outside. But it was just another day in the office. By now, I'd learnt how to keep warm in the cold. Get a roof over your head and shelter no matter what rudimentary fashion. Get the floor covered in thick cardboard. Always have a winter sleeping bag. Head feet and hands covered - multiple layers of clothing. I thought back to that first night in Amsterdam when I didn't know my arse from my elbow. I'd progressed in ways that I'd rather not imagine. Once again, I got a ride back straight away off the autobahn exit and made it back in time for New Year's Eve in Berlin. I returned to find the city covered in thick snow.

I'd never seen so many fireworks let off. They didn't just launch them into the air but into the Spree and straight out into the street. It felt like being caught in a war zone at one stage. I swear the temperature got raised by at least 5 degrees. I looked up at the firework spectacle and sensed they'd be something to celebrate in 2015.

What had I done about accommodation issues? I simply found another building. As the city was snowbound, it wasn't a good idea to be sleeping out in that. The cold and damp combo could be a killer. It's funny how necessity can push you into doing things that you wouldn't normally consider. The survival instinct makes you do a split-second calculation: building being worked upon – probably an easy way in – the builders aren't going to be here for a while because it's Christmas. It was calculated in a nanosecond.

I casually walked in through a gap (just like I owned the place) then went in to investigate. All of its essential bare bones had been constructed. Though the roof only consisted of timber covered in tarpaulin. It was going to be freezing up there. So if you can't get as high as you can, get as low as you can! What was downstairs in that basement? I walked down the steps. Part of the hallway had been flooded. The thawing snow on top had turned back into water and leaked right down here. Being around damp water moisture in the cold is never good as it can sink right into you. I made sure that I avoided this area. Then some lighting came on automatically. Electric and light. Luxury.

.   I opened the door and found a habitable room. Though there was lighting inside, there was no natural light, which was a major negative. It would have to do. One major plus point about sleeping on building sites is that you can always find material to make a sleeping base out of, such as insulation boards, polystyrene and tarpaulin. I placed these down on the concrete floor then chucked my sleeping bag on top.

It didn't look like they were working down here, nor had they left any tools or materials around. They had no reason to come to this part of the building. I made sure that the door to the room didn't have a lock on it as I didn't want anybody to lock me inside unwittingly. 'The underground bunker' was to be my new home for the time being, and I bid the world goodnight.

The worst thing about living in a place with no natural light is that when you wake up, you've got no idea of whether its day or still night. I often found myself waking up then realising that it was three o clock in the afternoon and half the day had gone.

It was January, and everything had gone dead quiet. I always hated this time of year as it was so lacklustre. As expected, the construction company turned up a few days later. But as I'd anticipated, they were working in the upper part of the building. I would be able to dip in and out during the daytime, but I'd have to be as quick and as quiet as a goddamn church mouse. It was a full ten days until somebody opened the door to the underground bunker. It was still dark. He didn't see me the first time around. But on the second occurrence, he turned on the light. In situations like this, I played dead, totally still and silent. There was a pause.

"Schlafen mann", he murmured in quiet wonderment then shut the door.

I made sure to clear away any rubbish and empty beer cans lying around. The next morning, I heard a group coming. As soon as I opened the door, I played dead again. I opened one eye to see several pairs of work boots surround me. There was complete silence for what seemed like ages but was probably only a few seconds. A quiet chuckling noise broke the silence, then the four pairs of boots trudged back outside. So, this was funny, huh? But they'd not said anything. I must have done something right.

But now a new plan had to be forged. I was thinking about giving things one last throw of the dice in Hamburg. I remember Bernardo saying to me that I must go there before I left Germany. I waited until I was politely given my marching orders from the bunker. Once they'd begun a project down there, I had to depart.

"Alles klar", I replied.

"Viel gluck" (good luck.) he wished me.

I made my way to the West Bahnhof. I was saying goodbye to Berlin once again. The journey was merely continuing.

"Guten morgen, eine fahrkarte nach Hamburg ab morgen mittag, bitte".

"You speak good German", the guy at the counter said in a pleasantly surprised tone.

"Oh, really?"

I thought back to a couple of years ago hearing all those, '*you're going to be screwed; you don't speak any German*' comments from the doubters. Hah, and they could still barely speak English.

I was to spend the next week in one of Germany's wealthiest cities, and the weather certainly didn't get any milder. The nights averaged about minus two, and the snow kept on coming. I had to make do with cardboard and a sleeping bag in a discreet corner of the park and at night went for adventures down the Reeper Bahn, Hamburg's good time district where prostitution was legal at night. It's also where the Beatles forged their career when they were teenagers, playing every night down the strip clubs. To quote Paul McCartney, '*I was born in Liverpool but grew up in Hamburg*'.

The first weekend when I was bopping through the Haupt Bahnhof, there was a tap on my shoulder.

"Greg, aus Berlin?"

"Heinrich, no way!"

I'd met this chap around three months earlier while I was on weekend duty down Warschauer Strasse. I traced my memories back to that cold December night.

"You look like a man who knows this area", he said.

191

"Ja, das ist richtig".

"Do you know a good bar where I can shoot some kicker......and pick up girls".

"Why, follow me".

From what I'd ascertained he'd done a weekend runner to Berlin while experiencing women trouble. Now back in Hamburg his (currently pregnant) Mrs had temporarily chucked him out, and he was reduced to living out of a suitcase in hotel rooms. We agreed to go to a bar for a drink.

Gotta love the randomness.

"Oh man, will you check out that one over there. She looks *perverted*", Heinrich said, pointing at a fierce blonde German lady in the corner while we downed a bottle of Becks each.

I liked Hamburg. The wealth of the city made my life more comfortable, and they weren't so keen on speaking to you in English like they were in Berlin, which meant that I had more chance to practice. It was the third week of February. I'd been in Germany for nearly six months this time, and I remembered back to what the Jamaican bar lady had said.

'*If, after six months you haven't found work and you don't speak German, then you have to ask yourself what you're doing here.*'

Indeed. I hadn't achieved the first one and only got halfway through the second (up to B2 – lower intermediate level). It wasn't so far back, but the 'hop method' would have to be applied. Undertaking a long-distance overland trip wasn't something that phased me anymore. The next calling point back en-route to the UK was Amsterdam, where it all began. Except they weren't so kind to me this time. I got a police caution for sleeping on the street as it was now illegal to do so here.

"Don't let me catch you again; otherwise it's an 85 euro fine", the officer reprimanded.

Holland is *not* the funky, liberal place that people believe it to be. Its disconcerting being in a country when you know that your very existence there is illegal. Lord knows what they'd done with all the rough sleepers, deported them to Maastricht, maybe.

The Damrak on a Friday night seemed like being caught in the very centre of hell. It was like all the worst parts of a British city centre, 'let's get drunk and have a fight' culture, had been exported there for a weekend. It's the only place where I've seen someone get a proper good kicking while on the floor. You could hear his ribs crack.

"I need a ticket on the first available Eurolines back to London Victoria".

"I've only got one seat left, and it leaves in the next 7 minutes".

"Yeah, whatever, mate. Just get me the hell out of here".

The coach was to board the Dover to Calais ferry instead of the channel tunnel. I was grateful for the chance to stretch my legs out on the deck. There was a cold and gusty wind which made this crossing a bumpy one. The ferry rode steadily along the waves as they crashed against it. The army surplus store gear was keeping me warm. I was dressed in combat trousers and a German air force shirt.

"Where are the white cliffs of Dover? I want to *see* them", I said with determined enthusiasm.

"Mate, it's 4 o'clock in the morning. There's absolutely nothing to see. You might catch a glimpse of them as we turn".

It was time for a bit of subversive mischief back in blighty.

Chapter 10

The warehouse

"I see here that you've been out of the country for a prolonged period.

I'm sorry, but you won't be entitled to any benefits for the next three months. After that, you'll have to undergo a habitual residence test to see if you're eligible", the claims advisor smugly advised.

That was my welcome back to England. The DWP now regarded me as a semi-foreigner. That would make putting a claim in for housing benefit next to impossible, which meant that no housing body would touch me. The Citizens Advice Bureau claimed that they were acting within the law that had just been brought out. My old friends the Compass centre said that even if this wasn't the case, there was very little they could do for me anyway, seeing as very few private landlords accepted people on housing benefit, and there was a severe shortage of properties out there owing to the additional 10,000 students that had moved into the area.

I suppose I should have been annoyed at this point. But no; as far as I was concerned, this was *great* news. So now there was no chance of me being shoved back into a sub-standard bedsit and then sub-existing on the dole. It was solely up to me to sort myself out in the way that I deemed best, not what someone else thought. And that way certainly wasn't going to be through conventional methods. This must be what a company wage slave feels like when he finally decides to take the plunge and start up his own business.

I wasn't alone. The homeless/housing problem in Bristol and indeed right across England had reached an epidemic proportion. That introduced a new phenomenon. Tents had sprung up in just about every green space where you looked. Seeing a cluster of tents pitched in a local park became an accepted norm. You'd see them in the most obscure of places, and the demographic had broadened. It wasn't just the stereotypical 'bottle of meth' crew anymore. Increasingly, more normal folk who'd fallen on recent hard times were finding their way onto the streets. In almost every street corner in the city centre, somebody was there tucked up in their sleeping bag. The official count of rough sleepers here at that time was 57. Though these figures were woefully inaccurate as that was just someone doing the count in the most obvious places. But the majority of people slept out of sight. They could be in a tent up on Leigh Woods, in the caves down by Avon gorge or in sheds and garages. The actual figure was most likely somewhere in the hundreds, though it was near impossible to gain any accuracy on that.

And that in itself was just the tip of the iceberg as homelessness has multiple layers which you can find yourself going up and down in. There were the ones that lived in caravans underneath the M32 flyover or out of vans parked up on street corners. Some would live in obscure abandoned buildings. Then there was the legion that slept on a different sofa every night. Many endured the ambiguity of temporary accommodation. Right at the worse end of the scale were the ones that lived in hostels. In a city that contained half a million people, I'd put the total number at around 4,000. Just for the record, I've near appeared on a rough sleeper register.

I'd almost immediately gone back to a spot in Burrell wood. It had become a default occurrence. Just off the path, there was a tree that had its branches hanging right down, nearly touching the floor. I could see people coming, but they couldn't see me. I always had a dark green or blue sleeping bag as it camouflages better. It's an elementary rule. If people can't see you, then they can't bother you. For those in sight, getting kicked by drunken party-goers can be a regular occurrence. There have even been instances of people being set alight while asleep. Evil, but it happens.

When it rained, I'd slide into my survival bag: a waterproof bivvy bag that only cost 99 pence. Things may suck, but they were exactly what they were. It was preferable to kipping on the floor in a dubious residence in Stokes croft and being awoken by the sound of crack heads getting sucked off as had happened the previous night.

The entire time I was there, only two other people spotted my whereabouts. They were a couple of religious blokes that hung around for some reason. (I assumed they were holy because they profoundly asked me if I believed in god) They had the annoying habit of leaving copies of the Sunday sport all over my 'living room'. Dirty bastards.

"Were you in the army?" they asked.

I shook my head.

"Well, you should have been".

".... Yeah, I should have been a lot of things", I replied wearily.

I'd get up about 7 am, then go through the usual procedure of stashing my rucksack in some bushes by the freight train line, a place that I was sure no one else would go. It was essential to establish a routine and order into your day. I got busy with reuniting myself into the city and catching up with old acquaintances. Every day I'd bump into someone that I hadn't seen in a while.

"You're looking, healthy man".

"It's all that fresh air I get", I'd reply.

If you haven't got any money in your pocket, then social ties are your currency. UK headquarters was where my social network was. A lot of my lucky breaks could come from sheer serendipity. One day I could bump into a contact who swapped me a bit of gossip about things or a juicy bit of information. Take a further walk up the road then I might get a work lead. One chance encounter with a contact could potentially change the course of your life forever.

Just because you were homeless, it didn't mean that your life had to stop right there and then. Whatever happened the show had to go on. Yeah, I still went out to house parties at the weekend and would get chatting to UWE girls. If they asked me where I lived, I'd respond with a, "in a place just out of town with a great view of Clifton suspension bridge". To this moment, I hold the philosophy that you should do at least one thing a day that can take you forward, even if it's only undertaking a bit of research, meeting a new contact or jotting down a new idea. That didn't stop just because I was living out of a sleeping bag in the woods. Owing to the DWP's bureaucracy from now until June I had to survive on zero. Yup, not even a dollar a day. The only job I would have got was casual cash to hand work, which is rare now. (You would also run the risk of being exploited.) In any other location, this would have been challenging. But with Bristol's support facilities, it was possible. I combined this with tricks picked up from international escapades. Now sure, it's possible to *survive* in Western Europe on no money. But let's make one thing clear: I wouldn't recommend it. If you don't pay for something by a financial method, then you end up paying for it in another way, usually in the form of time and energy spent. And this life was an energy-sapping one. The simplest things, such as getting food or getting a shower could take hours.

So, what was the way forward if the conventional route was out of the question? Up until now, you've heard me talk a lot about staying in abandoned/vacant buildings, then stealth it until someone didn't want me there. But this isn't squatting (and I hate that phrase). That was just me being a chancer. There's a reason why I hate that phrase so much. As initially stated, it's probably brought a load of negative connotations to your mind. Clichés such as crusties holding all weekend parties, hardcore drug abuse, trashing buildings, and stripping the place of its copper and lead for it to be weighed in. I won't deny that all this does occur regularly. But the movement's roots may surprise you. It all began after the First World war, when unemployment and rent strikes led to the occupation of municipal buildings. This got repeated on an even bigger scale after the Second World War. There was going to be a lack of social housing for war vets and their families. So groups of soldiers organised mass squatting. Their speciality was army bases. Though the government at the time acted with sympathy. After all, they were just honest people trying to keep a roof over their heads. They were permitted to stay there in the short term. Many received funding from the local councils and National Exchequer. Even the right-wing Daily Mail newspaper commented on *'the squatters robust common sense in taking matters into their own hands'*. The same reason held true for me then – taking care of accommodation issues. Like anything else, there were good squatting crews as well as bad ones.

In 2012 David Cameron's government outlawed the squatting of residential properties. You've probably read the stories in the press about groups of Roma gipsies moving into someone's house while they were away on a two-week holiday. This is, and always has been, totally illegal as the property is still in use by the legal occupier. If that occurs, then its most likely the police will pin a charge of a dwelling burglary on them. And this comes with a substantial prison sentence.

So, in 2015 the law was this: occupying a disused commercial property, was merely a civil matter, providing that no damage had been, or nothing had got taken. If and when the owner turned up, and they didn't want you there, then they had to take you to court. This is a lot more straight forward than it sounds from their point of view. All they need to present to the court is a witness statement and proof of their legal entitlement to the property. The judge will nod her head, grant the possession order, and then the bailiffs will be on their way to kick you out.

So, with that in mind, the world of commercial squatting is your oyster. The first thing that you need to do is assemble a crew of at least two people who are in the same boat as you because you've got no chance of taking a building and holding it down on your own. You'll want your colleagues to be relatively reliable, stable, and dependable with a base line level of practical skill. But here lies your first problem: most homeless people are useless fuckers.

The second fundamental block is finding the right building. But this is vastly harder than you might think as you want your place to be a stayer, i.e. last at least four months and many factors will determine this. Bristol had plenty of unoccupied commercial properties, but most still had an active interest in them. The place might be too near a school or be in an industrial estate where the other companies won't want you around. Anywhere inside the city centre was a definite no-no; it won't last, and there's too much activity around there. Anywhere quite far out of town and you'll be too far away from your much-needed resources.

Nine out of ten crews that attempt this venture don't ever get off the ground. Many squats don't last longer than two weeks (that's roughly how long it takes for the legal process to go through). If you're lucky your place may go on for a few months and if it's a real stayer an entire year. But often by that point, the squat and its squatters will be burnt out and glad that it's over.

Unperturbed, I set about the preparation stage of the project. It was something to fill up my day with, anyway. I'd allied myself to the 'Bristol Housing Action Movement (a support group for squatters in Bristol) and went to their meetings every Monday evening. Almost every day I'd go on the lookout for buildings. Camping in the woods put me in a motivated mood because from here the only way was up. It also clarified my thoughts. There was much research that I had to undertake, as there was a lot that needed to be found out. Who owned these buildings? You could look that up on the land registry.

As it turned out, ownership of buildings wasn't always a straightforward matter. The council-owned many of them but leased them out to other companies which meant they also had a legal right to it. Had these places been squatted before and if so, who by and how long had they lasted? What action had the owner taken? What had these crews done wrong that I could do differently? As I do with everything else, I became obsessed with it all. It was all in the preparation. The real work got done in the days of pounding the streets. Straight afterwards, I'd be down the library at a PC, then back in my little spot in the woods with plenty to think about.

I'd gathered that it could take about three attempts before you managed to secure a building. Attempt one was a slightly fumbling affair.

"I can't possibly fit through that window", I protested.

"Yes, you can! If your head can fit through, then so can your body".

This proved *kinda* correct. Though once in, the motion sensors kicked into action.

"Warning, your presence has been detected. The authorities are on their way", a robotic voice called out.

Was I a punany for scampering back out? Lessons had been learnt. It was all trial and error.

Attempt 2: It was a large church. By now, I had the cracking crew assembled. The lead cracker was me with the assistant cracker by my side and a third man acting as a lookout/tramp liaison officer. Empty buildings often have rough sleepers kipping by them. So, it's the TLO's job to say to them, "yeah broth; we won't be a minute. Remember, we're all in the same

200

boat", then placate him by handing over a big bottle of Frosty Jacks (preferably laced with Temazepam), so they won't cause you any bother.

I spent the best part of a week there mainly on my own. It's funny how members of your crew can suddenly remember that they've got girlfriends beds to stay in. But what a turbulent time this turned out to be. Due in that interval, I had pikeys trying to get in as they wanted to strip the place, the police turning up thinking that it was a burglary in progress and the snooty local residents attempting to lock me in. I aborted the mission. It had been a steep learning curve. Where was all this going? I began to despair. Then I received a phone call from someone else in the squatting community.

"We've got this building that's a bit different. Do you fancy coming down on Thursday to check it out?"

My thoughts of curiosity got the better of me.

It was a late Victorian warehouse just off the city centre but ideally tucked away down a side street. The owners were Harmondsworth pension fund, based in the City of London, estimated value: over £1,000000. The day I hauled my rucksack out of the hedge and moved in was a beautiful warm sunny one.

"Right, muck this up, and you're straight back here", I reminded myself.

It was enough motivation to get going. I looked around the entire floor; there was junk everywhere. What on earth had I got myself into? Along my side, I'd recruited an old friend of mine who was an artist and a caretaker. In turn, he hired a pal of his who was a jobbing carpenter who was living out of a van and needed somewhere safe to park it - a guy with practical professional skills, that could be highly useful.

The shutter doors rolled up, and the carpenter moved himself and his van in. Now we had a three-man crew, enough to get a grip on the situation. I retrieved myself from the back room where I'd made a bed out of pallets and got to work with clearing the entire floor. The site of the mess was doing my head in. I sorted everything out into relevant piles, including stuff that could be useful then got all the rubbish bagged up. In no time I'd filled over 100 black bin sacks. We got a living room made in the corner out of the sofas and other furniture that was there. At the close of business, we watched movies on a laptop *'Fear and loathing in Las Vegas'*, *'24hour Party People'*, Adam Curtis documentaries and feasted on Tesco's finest skipped.

Sanitation was always going to be a problem. The artist had the ingenious idea of plugging an upside-down traffic cone into a drain at the back. What the hell? Well, blow me, it worked! It deposited your urine better than any public toilet urinal. The traffic cone came to symbolise our quirky yet pragmatic ethos.

"I'm thinking of inviting Jumanji in. He's looking for a place", the artist stated the next morning.

Well, where's your squat without an eccentric hippie?

"That's an affirmative", I replied.

Thus, mentioned eccentric hippie promptly moved his trailer in and set up the kitchen area. By that time, I'd had the whole floor cleared and all 100 rubbish sacks quietly squirrelled away in commercial waste bins around the city. A handful at a time, quickly and quietly. The pigeon shit got cleared off the floor, and the mould scrubbed off the walls. Unfortunately, we had to evict the pigeons and block up their entry points. Now I could think straight. Getting a firm grip on the place in the first two weeks is everything. That will dictate your future. The police had turned up at this point with a, "Okay, so you're squatting it, fair enough. Have a good day, lads".

For the time being, I had a place to call home, and that's all I ever wanted. Somewhere to feather your own nest and establish yourself. No more stashing possessions in hedges or peering out of a sleeping bag at the slightest sound. My feet were no longer throbbing in agony due to the relentless street pounding. I could wake up in the morning, make myself a cup of coffee and have breakfast. It was a luxury. They were even calling us the gentleman's squat as we were all aged 30 plus.

One Friday night, we were sat down while not entirely sober. We recalled the conversation with our mad transvestite neighbour, who was squatting the building adjacent. He'd taken exception to the word 'pikey'.

"But what about if we call ourselves pikeys?"

So we took this a step further by writing a caption on a board to be displayed in full view. We felt it summed up our values accurately: *'PIKEY AS FUCK!!!'* with the A inevitably symbolised as the anarchy sign.

The initial stage was complete, and by this point, I knew that we were going to be okay. So now we had the artist, the carpenter, the international drifter and the eccentric hippie. Who was missing from our number?

"I've just bumped into this guy. I kind of know him, and the thing is we need more people here", the artist advised.

"Just as long as he's got some bacci on him", I said while scraping the last remnants out of the pouch.

The door opened.

"Yo, what's happening guys?" a small British Indian bounced in and promptly placed a 50-gram pouch of Old Holborn on the table.

It was Salim. I recognised him from a party in Stokes croft a few weeks earlier.

"This is great, man. Wow, this place is amazing. You've really helped me out. I didn't know what I was going to do tonight".

We entered into an in-depth conversation about Berlin, a place that had played a prominent part in both our lives and immediately struck a chord. Salim was once a resident at the 'Telepathic heights' squat where the infamous 'Tesco riot' had begun. The chap exuded a unique and charismatic air. Even better, he was well into his cleaning. There was plenty of it to be done.

Now a rhythm to the place had been established. I'd walk in on the afternoon, and the artist was busy doing his artwork, painting vigorously on canvasses, then making sculptures out of doles with wires poking out of their heads, which he plunked in a fish tank. Bizarre, but original. Part of the warehouse served as his studio. That was the sort of thing that people paid good to see. Soon his completed pieces came to decorate the squat. Visitors would marvel at it as it wasn't far off professional standard.

The carpenter would be busy in his wood kitchen, constructing and making objects. Salim had his sewing machine out, making colourful hand-made garments from scratch. It was the diligent tailoring that Indians are especially renowned. The hippie would do what eccentric hippies do best: brewing up alcoholic ginger beer or growing his plants. All this was against a soundtrack of acid house tunes and 90's club classics.

"*...Everything starts with an E!*"

"*What planet are you from……planet Ecstasy.*"

We danced around with that weird wavy arm movement. It was the music that we'd grown up with. The place had an old school rave vibe to it.

There was a tune from a local lass that got repeatably played, 'White gal *yardie*' You'll either love or hate that song when you hear it. But it became our unofficial theme tune. I would sing it when I was brushing my teeth in the morning.

"*…. I'm a white girl yardie uh-huh, uh-huh*".

"*Every black man wants to fuck me, uh-huh*".

Creativity and productivity, that's what a squat should be like; a place where you could do the stuff that you wouldn't be able to do while holed up in a miserable bedsit staring at the wall. Inevitably, we'd gather around discussing politics, but there's only so much of that you can do. I've never been into the whole political ideology that some squatters are. They're the irritating ones that you see sat about getting stoned, chatting shite without really a clue of what they're going on about. Then they'll disappear off to their mum and dad's in Surrey when it all goes tits up. The usual route after that is, they'll shave their dreads off then end up getting a job in insurance.

My primary motivation had been finding somewhere to live. Don't forget that I was forced into this route after all. The cultural and social aspect would come after that.

The proceedings around the corner in St.Pauls were an excellent example of how *not* to do it. Decourcy House, the former probation centre was regularly making the headlines. It was a large building with an open-door policy. This method is always a bad idea (particularly in that location). Because then you'll have any dysfunctional munter turning up or people looking for a place to conduct their dodgy business. They had over 60 people at one point. Having a large group of drug addicts, alcoholics and the mentally ill all cramped together in an uncontrolled and unstructured environment means that they'll rub each other up the wrong way – which leads to dangerous violence. People were coming out of there on stretchers. One even ended up in a coma.

Rule number one: your building is only ever as good as the people in it. Be very careful about who you open that door to. Try getting someone undesirable out when they're in your residence. It ain't pretty. People could accuse me of being paranoid about this. Maybe I *was* too concerned about security – but it was for a noble reason.

Throughout my nomadic career, I'd become well versed at finding useful stuff on the street or procuring discarded things, but this was about to be taken on to the next level. 'Skipping' (or 'dumpster diving') the act of gathering produce out of a supermarket skip that they'd placed in there because they couldn't sell it. Just about every squatter or homeless person will have done this at one point. Here's a statistic that you may find hard to believe; back then, a third of the stuff that you saw on supermarket shelves ended up getting binned. Now they'll sell it onto 'Fair share' where it gets donated to a soup kitchen who turn it into mush and serve it up to unhealthy munters who don't get any healthier. I was to devise a more efficient procedure.

My skipping partner at the time was a guy who had his own council flat but still chose to spend most of his existence living on the street. (This isn't uncommon for people who've spent a long time homeless.) We'd meet up at the bottom of Park St at smack on 11 pm because just after closing time was when they chucked out. It was safer with the two of you as that bin lid crashing down on your head is mighty painful.

A professional skipper is never seen without his bottle of hand sanitiser, torch and pair of gloves. Yes, this does involve getting inside the skip and digging right down; if you want to find the buried treasure, then you gotta dig deep. Not just grab the sack full of gack (doughnuts and pastries) like those crusty amateurs. This may sound revolting, but it had just come off the shelf and was all packaged and bagged up. It was no worse than taking your trash out. Curiously, most of it was still in date. (I checked over everything.) The use-by date that they have on products has a two-day safety window on it. So if it was dated the 11th and that day was the 12th, then it would probably still be all right. You got just about every kind of product imaginable. But I only handpicked the best stuff, like that rump steak or packets of chicken Caesar wraps. If ever in doubt you smelt it, just like your cat does. And if it didn't smell right, then it probably wasn't.

The Tesco and Morrison combo got done in 15 minutes flat. Timing and speed were everything because many people were up to the same game as us. We'd walk up the steep hill then stash our securely sealed loot in a grit bin. Why? Because no one ever looks in grit bins. This saved us having to carry it all for the rest of the circuit. By now we'd be in Clifton, the wealthiest part of town. Most other folks were too lazy to do the same. It was here where you'd find the best clothes that hadn't quite made it to the charity shop: woollen sweaters, Armani jeans or a nice pair of safety boots.

One time I found a proper Italian designer suite. That would do for a special occasion.

The Clifton village Tesco skip was especially good for finding booze. They tried to hide it in the bottom underneath the garbage. I kept an eye out for the bits of broken glass. That meant that a bottle out of a multi-pack had got broken. So they had to chuck the entire pack out.

We'd sit down on the bench and tuck into our hot fish and chips that the chipper had just placed out the front, washed down with a nice bottle of white wine. We discussed in detail what we'd do when we finally made it to be millionaires one day. Refreshed we'd take the long walk to Waitrose Henleaze, and this was where you found the crème de la crème. It would also keep for considerably longer. With bags retrieved we'd hit the city centre for one last crack. I'd got back around 3 am for with food for all the family. I liked this feeling; bringing home the bacon, being the provider. I had no qualms about everyone else tucking in. After all, you get more when you're a giver.

I'd repeat this exercise some three times a week, and sometimes I'd be bringing back hundreds of pounds worth of goods. Paradoxically, it was often stuff that I wouldn't usually be able to afford. The jackpot night came when we found a skip full to the brim with booze. Though it presented us with a logistical challenge, if you've never tried lugging several rucksacks full of beer and wine for 3 miles, let me tell you, it's bloody hard work.

But it wasn't just clothes and groceries. Homosapiens of the Western world are a mighty wasteful species, especially students. When they were moving out, they chucked out all manner of things: mundane items such as bedding and crockery to electrical goods like heaters that were still in perfect working order. We'd go to the skips by the blocks of student accommodation. Yes, they'd even throw out working laptops and speakers. But you don't *ever* touch a laptop found on the street; *anything* could be on it. This form of urban treasure hunting became addictive. It resulted in a dopamine rush flooding my brain almost every night – just as potent as any drug. This lifestyle meant that my path became intertwined with the city's army of homeless gambling addicts, or HGA's. For them, finding valuable articles on the street was their living and pass-time. The worse their gambling problem, the better they were at finding stuff. In 2015 Bristol won the award for Europe's greenest city. We were doing our bit for recycling.

Salim had managed to get with an 18-year-old webcam model whom he'd brought back. That was good. A little bit of glamour added to the place. But then their moans of delight kept me up the whole night.

"Salim, hurry up and finish her off, will yuh."

"I can't cum, in it".

I'm proud of the fact that in my entire homeless career, I've only ever broken down in tears *twice*. The first was on a park bench in Hamburg. And the second was on this occasion while staring down at the concrete floor. Yeah, I was lonely.

And things wouldn't continue smoothly. After the Boomtown festival came people that had partied hard but had nowhere else to go. It took our official number up to nine. This new scenario significantly altered the dynamic and put the place under pressure. It wasn't just the full-timers, but the wag crew, friends, and friends of friends would also be in attendance. Sometimes I'd be tripping over bodies on the way out. The gentlemen's squat? We were now the Saturday morning kids club!

"Come on, Greg; it was always your dream to squat a warehouse and be the guiding light", my friend Nicki would remind me every time I complained.

There was work to be done to ensure that the ship didn't capsize. My skipping escapades alone took up 16 hours of my week, then there was all the cleaning and disposing of rubbish. If this isn't taken care of, then the rats will turn up. Now I knew what a site manager felt like when he went around patrolling the place and would take umbrage about something seemingly insignificant. Those cables lying in a puddle of water could cause a problem. That leaky roof would need flash banding. I better buy some rat poison. That revolting green colour on the walls was depressing me, so I whitewashed it all with some thirty litres of cheap white paint. People thought that I was mad for doing this, but it did make the place look better. And when somewhere looks better, its inhabitants are more likely to *act* better. And that front door; I kept an eye on that front door 24/7 – especially while I slept.

A victim of this sudden change of cause was Salim. He ended up having a violent breakdown. If this continued, then it would be profoundly unsettling for everyone involved. The place wasn't doing him any good. The situation required careful and delicate handling.

"Look, everyone's allowed to crack up once, but throwing tables at girls faces? It's not cool, broth" I said.

He was asked to leave, if anything, for his own good. Now, where's webcam girls' number......?

"It was *such* a cool place", she later remarked.

It would be arrogant and pretentious to call my self 'the leader' or 'in charge'. Control is often an illusion. The truth was nobody was in power or leading. They never really are in a squat, despite what some people like to claim. I would instead state that I was the one who took *responsibility*. The true alpha male doesn't go around acting like one because in any group he's the most trusted one who's intentionally or unintentionally selected by the group. To be a good leader, you don't boss people around; you make them want to follow you. Oh yeah, and a control freak controls nothing.

But your place is never going to last forever. Sometime around September, I sensed this. What were those strange motion sounds coming from outside? Eerie. They gave me an odd, uneasy feeling. It was time to do some forward planning. It had long been an ambition of mine to go travelling in South East Asia. Yes, I know that's a great cliché, but it was just something that I had to do. I set the deadline for January. And there was only one way that I was going to achieve this – by going back to work.

Yes, I don't spend all my time whinging about the social's lack of generosity - I do occasionally work. The first job was for some hippie outfit that was prepared to pay me £10 per hour. Their business was converting empty office buildings into social housing. It's quicker, more cost-effective and easier to knock them down and build back up from scratch, but what did I know? I was just the demolition monkey.

They were getting quite a bit of media coverage. *'The One Show'*, the worlds most generic TV programme came into film.

"Look at those two, they're working away like little soldiers", the presenter, Dominic Littlewood commented on our work rate.

"If it weren't for us in here now, then squatters would be here smashing the place up", the site manager claimed in an interview just as I was ripping down a wall.

This was the start of cash flowing its way back to my bank account. The next job was back on a commercial site for a professional building company. My living circumstances dictated that the proof of address would need to be blagged. At the time my C/O address was Bristol Methodist centre 31-33 Midland road. Before I'd had documents sent there stating the address as merely no 31 Midland road to make it look like a residential address, this is what I sent the agency when they requested it.

"Hmm…. that's come up as Bristol Methodist centre", they remarked after keying in the postcode.

"Yes…. I live in the flats *above* there".

I was good to go.

By now I'd climbed my way up the greasy pole to become a *skilled* labourer or monkey with thumbs. Four other agency monkeys and I got tasked with taking the lead roof off Clifton Cathedral, an enormous imposing building. We were dressed in white boiler suits swinging about in safety harnesses, 100 feet up in the air, stripping off tonne after tonne of lead, then getting it all down and loading it up into the led skip. It was gruelling and potentially dangerous work. But we had a good crack between us and joked about our lack of career success.

"Polska labourer, fighting on arrival....... fighting for survival."

"He was a Polska labourer......", we'd sing.

My phone rang. It was the agency.

".... You sent the contract out in the post last week, did you?".

The Methodist centre had moved to an address that I couldn't fudge.

"Well, I've not received it. Is there any chance that you can e-mail it to me? Then I'll get that filled out and sent back in time for this week's payroll".

The day was long. I'd rise at 6 am, then get back around the same time in the evening. But I was getting around £340 a week, after-tax and could make do on £50 a week to live on. Enough for bus fare, bacci and a beer. The rest got saved. Straight after work, I'd shower in the changing rooms at Easton leisure centre to get rid of all those lead flakes. Back at the ranch, the place was turning me into my mother.

"I come back from work, and the place is in a tip. None of you lot appreciates what I do. You think that this place runs on thin air!"

Come the weekends all I wanted to do was get back with a takeaway, snort a gram of speed then quietly lie down in my room and chill-out. The Saturday morning kids club would indulge in the Black Swan/Lakota night club combo then have their after-party here afterwards. Looking back, they were only having fun and doing what young people did. I was showing my age by my grumpiness.

I walked back in on Monday morning feeling a little rough.

"Were you out shagging your mates Mrs at the weekend, then?" the scaffolders bantered.

"You didn't sleep in that changing room last night, did you?" someone said to one of the roofers out of jest.

This made me chuckle inside; I know people who have done that!

"Where do you live, Greg?" our ganger asked me with ominous curiosity later that day.

"I share a flat in Bedminster with another bloke".

"How much rent do you pay?"

"£400 a month, all in".

"Core, that's cheap".

Was there something I was giving off without realising? I aimed to get my head down and be as quiet and non-descript as possible, then get on with the job.

"If they were to make a film about Greg's life, I reckon they'd call it 'The Constant labourer", my colleague joked.

But there were more important things on my mind. There was now enough money in my account to get the operation started. That Friday I booked my ticket to Bangkok. I got my self inoculated against every tropical disease going and took out comprehensive medical insurance.

".... Ahh...ha.... hah, there's nothing like a good Rabies shot; it gives you a well good floaty buzz", I drawled, entering the warehouse after coming back from the clinic.

Now I knew that for every 2 hours worked was another day that I could afford to live in South-East Asia. Back at the Cathedral, the rain lashed down.

"We need that roof covered in protective tarpaulin. This gale could cause the roof some serious damage. Come on, boys, get up there; the lead is worth more than you are".

We scuttled about like actors in a Carry-On movie as the 60mph wind came. If I slipped over the side right now, there wouldn't be a bone left to break. As always happens with labouring crews, everyone either walks or gets fired. I ended up being the last one standing, and as a loyalty bonus, I got tasked with cleaning the gent's toilets. Okay, so maybe my time was up as well. But now there was something else that required my attention.

I looked over at the patch of waste ground next to us. It had been dug up then backfilled. Portacabins had been placed in the far corner. It was about to be turned into a building site. There was going to be activity in this area soon. I was surprised that we'd lasted this long. Surely the owners knew that we were here by now. Then a man approached wearing dark clothing and a bunch of papers. Without saying a word, he flashed his badge. I gave a knowing nod in return. He handed the documents he was carrying.

"Good luck", he said solemnly.

"Fair enough, mate".

It was addressed to *'Persons Unknown', a notice of court hearing, 22nd December.* That was in one week. It had taken until last September to find out we were here. So those weird noises were the sound of a private detective taking pictures of the inside. Now, this was obviously someone trying to get their desk cleared before they broke up for Christmas.

Here's the thing with squat court cases; you almost always lose. It boils down to the straightforward fact that they can prove ownership to the building whereas you can't. The best that you can typically hope for is that they've got a discrepancy in their paperwork, for example, not dating it. This can get the case adjourned and buy you a couple of weeks. Some people will try quoting that 'Blacks law' stuff which they saw on a YouTube video. But they don't know what they're on about and it simply doesn't wash. Once papers are pinned up on your front door, then your place has had it. Your time would be far better spent looking for somewhere else to go. But you should always go to court. It's only a civil matter anyway, and you don't even need to give your name.

I looked around me. The place had had its day. Often when you get kicked out, they're doing you a favour, and everyone can get on with their lives. But the date, right before Christmas, was awkward. I figured that the best thing to do was try and negotiate a two week notice period. That would take us into the New Year. I went and got my suit dry cleaned.

The afternoon that I stood outside Bristol Civil Justice centre was a suitably grey and filthy one. Their barrister was there looking bored. He wasn't up for any conversation beforehand. His client had strictly instructed that there was to be no negotiation. So that one was out of the window. The judge clocked us for what we were straight away. I stood up and gave the, 'we're nice boys, really' speech to her in an attempt to salvage the situation.

"Well, I'm very pleased to hear all that Mr Lynn, but the law is still the law. Possession granted forthwith".

It wasn't all bad news. There was a writ in there that if served meant that High Court bailiffs would be coming that evening. But the judge was adamant that wasn't to be the case. I can only think that the artist had done it for us on the 'Oliver Twist factor'.

"I'd like to thank you for your understanding and sympathy ma'am", I concluded and left the courtroom.

One last trick. I went back the next day with the papers. This time I wanted to negotiate with the bailiff department and request a Christmas amnesty. The security guard at the entrance recognised me.

"Hey, my man", he greeted cheerfully.

"What's happening, broth?" I replied and approached the reception.

"I'm looking for the bailiff section, please".

"They've just shut for Christmas, sir".

"What, so they're not working?"

"No. No evictions are scheduled to take place until 4th January".

4th January. How interesting. That's was the day my flight was booked.

"Thanks for the info".

I walked back in with much higher spirits and informed the others of the good news. Though I also advised them to get their affairs in order for when the big black men came, they were also told that High Court bailiffs *were* permitted to use force. But they'd be no need for belligerence.

Now it was Christmas. Always an awkward time in the drifter's calendar. I spent that duration darting around the country, visiting family and friends which dug into my precious savings. I saw the New Year in at some shite free party in Keynsham. It seemed fitting to meet up with my skipping buddy and sink two cans of strong lager by the Opera House in suitably trampy fashion before I went. I took him back to the warehouse.

"Wow, this is magic!" he exclaimed.

Well, of course, it was; a little bit of my soul had gone into it.

But by now, my thoughts were totally upon the departure. The cost of flights, jabs and insurance came to £900. And Christmas is expensive for everyone. I'd be arriving with £750 to my name. It wasn't much. You simply can't save that much on labouring gigs, even when your outgoings are negligible.

This trip was a far bigger proposition as I was to be on the other side of the world and would only be allowed to stay in each country for a permitted amount of time. But I was buggered if I was spending another Winter out on the street here in England. Winter now took on a completely different meaning. It was a case of following the birds and flying South. The act of slinging a rucksack over my shoulder seemed like a cliché now.

"Stay out of trouble you crazy kids", I sang then took the bus to Heathrow. I was booked on the overnight to Abu-Dhabi with Etihad for a connection with Bangkok. The queue for check-in was over an hour long and gave me plenty of time to develop a bit of disenfranchised paranoia. I glanced at the Arab guy at the check-in desk dressed immaculately in a beige blazer.

He knows. He knows that I've been living in a grimy warehouse for the past seven months and that I spend half my life going through skips. He's not going to let me on the plane, my thoughts raced.

"Evening".

"Good evening Mr Lynn, sir. How are you today?"

"I've put you at the front", he smiled.

He'd put me in the guest seat just one row behind business class. A few yards in front were a load of wealthy Arab's being served with champagne. I could just about smell that champagne and lent forward expectantly. But then the curtain was briskly shut in front of me. One day, one day.....

We taxied and took off. I sipped from a glass of red wine. Ahh.... made it out of there alive. But then I remembered something that Nicki had said to me recently.

"You're precariously balanced on the edge, and it wouldn't take a lot to shove you right over it".

He was right. My day of reckoning was to come deep in the Cambodian jungle....

Chapter 11

24 hours to death

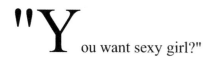"ou want sexy girl?"

"Mai ow, khop koon."

"You want sexy boy?"

"Mai ow, khop koon."

He eventually quit following me down the street. The night air was hot and sticky. The bright and garish neon signs of Silom illuminated the night air. Everything was different – the smells, the noises, the heat. When first arriving in a new place I'll tear my luggage tags off, so it's not apparent that I've just landed and don't have a clue about anything. There are always people looking to prey on newcomers, and you're at your most vulnerable when you're in unchartered territory. But on this occasion, it was dead obvious that I'd just stepped off the plane. I was still pale. A Westerner who'd been here for some length of time would have picked up a suntan.

Being a lone male traveller in my thirties would indicate to anyone that I wasn't married and didn't have kids, so probably had more money than your average sweaty backpacker heading towards Khao-san road. If only this were true. This would also make a lot of people assume that I was a sexpat, hence why I was getting canvassed so much. And why is it that wherever I go, I immediately end up in the good time district?

I checked into the back-packer hostel with a sense of tedious familiarity, then brought a surprisingly expensive beer from a local bar to toast my arrival. Thailand wasn't cheap anymore; a bottle of Chang was about the same price here. I wearily fell asleep afterwards. Maybe things would look better in the morning. I soon got word that the eviction had passed away peacefully and without fuss. The warehouse was eventually knocked down and turned into student flats (what else?) The project was conducted by Midas – my *least* favourite building company.

The next day I'd predictably ended up down an Irish pub with an Australian, a German and a South African guy called Morgen. The deal with Bangkok is that it's a place where people are either starting or finishing their trip. I and the Aussie kiddie were commencing ours. The German and the South African were completing theirs. Morgen took the dominant role at the head of the table and was busy giving his traveller advice.

"You've got to go to Laos; it's beautiful. One of the most beautiful places that I've ever been to. Do the cruise down the Mekong river".

My sort of plan had been to head north to Chang Mai, then into Laos, down to Cambodia and possibly Vietnam. Myanmar was a tempting possibility. But to obtain a visa you had to show them your bank statement, and for me, this definitely wasn't a good idea.

"Cambodia is the craziest country that I've been to; it's where I saw the maddest stuff happen".

Morgen showed us a video of him firing various powerful firearms down at a shooting gallery in Cambodia. He chuckled to himself.

"I like the Cambodians because they're different from everyone else in South-East Asia. They look different. They speak differently. And their language is different. But they're the kindest people out there. I was sitting on a beach one day, and this guy kept on offering me his cans of beer".

I told him about my intention of going to Laos after Northern Thailand.

"Chiang Khong is the border town. You've got to stay at the 'Hub-Pub'. Hey, it only costs 50 Baht a night (£1 at that time). You can't go wrong".

He attracted the attention of the waitress.

"Can we get four more Chang beers, please".

"It's run by this British guy called Alan. You'll recognise him straight away – he's from Liverpool. You know what? He holds a world record for cycling from Chiang-Khong to Bangkok. I can't remember the exact time, but I think he did it in something like 24 hours and he did it to raise a load of money for charity".

He sounded like an interesting ex-pat that had appeared to go a bit off the beaten track. I wanted to meet this guy.

"Alan at the 'Hub-Pub in Chang Kong, is it?" I said while making a note in my diary.

"Yeah, tell him I said hi".

We went to the street food stalls afterwards. A big bowl of sticky rice, of course. 'I'll have some of that, some of that, and a bit of this' - all for 50 Baht. The best and the cheapest food that I've ever tasted has been from one of these street stalls. You looked for a place where the locals went. That meant that they were getting repeat business, so the food must have been of a decent quality.

"We're all off down the Khao-San road this evening. Do you fancy joining us?" my travelling companions asked.

"I'd rather have my bollocks scolded in boiling water than hang out there" was my brutally honest response.

The next day out of Hua Lamphong station, I boarded the bumpiest train ride ever. They'd got the high-speed train but hadn't got around to putting down the high-speed rail track yet. After being disappointed with Chang Mai, I got off the tourist bus in Chiang Khong feeling like I was absconding from a primary school trip. I wanted to create my own adventure. The sign for the Hub-Pub was right in front of me. It was aggressively signposted for the whole 200 yards there. I followed it until the sound of a scouse accent was in earshot.

"Good evening, sir", a stocky man with a bald head waved me over.

He was there with several other middle-aged men sat down.

"You must be Alan?"

"That's me".

"Morgen from Jo'berg says hi".

I ordered a drink from the bar and sat down at their table. I had a feeling this was to be a more interesting conversation than the usual, 'what country are you from? Oh yeah, my second cousin's fiancé once went to a party in Stokes Croft', etc. I explained that I was to be crossing the border to Laos the next morning.

"The border doesn't open till eight, and it's still 12km away, but Alan will give you a lift up there for 50 Baht, he's good like that".

One of the old boys was an old school cockney. His friend spoke with an East Midlands accent. The third in their number was an Australian called

Murray. I wanted to find out what this place was about and more about Alan's world breaking cycling achievement.

"He put this town on the map! Nobody had ever heard of Chiang Khong before then, and everyone just passed through to the border", the Cockney said with conviction.

"He doesn't make any profit out of here. That's why it's so cheap. It's all done to assist people while they're on their way. And I'll tell you something else: he raised a million Baht all for charity with that. But now the locals reckon he's getting too big for his boots. That's why they've been spreading stories about him. Now he's getting the authorities coming around every second night. They want to check up on this that and the other".

I went and ordered another beer from the bar, being served by Alan's wife, who was inevitably half his age. The man himself was busy putting their adopted Thai son to bed.

"I get the feeling that they don't want us Farang's in Thailand anymore. It's not like they need our money now", I commented.

"Back in the 90's they'd have bent down and kissed your arse. Now it's become saturated. This tourism stuff, it's all plastic. Have you seen what's been going on in the Southern Islands and Phuket? They've destroyed the coral reef".

I'd noticed that many expats had figured that Cambodia was now the promised land instead of Thailand. The land of smiles had become developed. Now that the border had been opened with Myanmar, the Burmese migrant workforce had been let in, and they'd got them to do all their grunt work for as little as 100 Baht a day.

"This is the real Thailand", the cockney said, spreading his arms out.

I told him about my target of the Cambodian coast.

"Too much Yaba. Too much partying. Too many Russians", he scoffed.

221

Oh yeah? It sounded great to me.

"20 years ago, on that coast, you'd have had that beach to yourself, but now you couldn't even stick a pin down, it's full of so many sunbeds. Mind you Phnom Penh, the capital, is alright if you can make it there".

"He took another look at me".

"Steer clear of the Yaba, son".

He'd probably noticed my twitchiness.

"You don't want to get caught with that over there. I know this one bloke who got caught sniffing a line of coke. They took him back to the station and gave him a right good hiding. And this bloke could *handle* himself. Then they marched him down to the cash machine and made him withdraw $1,200. And that was all for one line. *One line*!" he exclaimed.

Yes, that sounded horrific, but there's always more to these stories than people first let on.

"You think that Thai prisons are bad? Well, Cambodian ones make them look like a holiday camp. In there you get your prison number tattooed down your forearm".

Now there was me thinking that a Cambodian prison number tattoo might look quite cool, something to show the girlies down a nightclub if you ever made it out of there alive.

"I can tell that you're a good lad, you'll do alright son. Remember, you learn every day. It may seem strange out here first, but once you get the hang of it, give it two…. or maybe three weeks…. you'll be *brand* new. You learn every day", he reiterated.

"I don't know what this travelling business is about anymore. I guess by now I should have been settled down got married and had kids and all that", I sighed while sipping my forth Chang.

"Nah…. grow up and become boring?" do all that when you're 50. Get around as much as you can and enjoy life. I've been married twice and let me tell you that it's the worse thing I ever did. You'll do alright son, trust me".

The next morning Alan was busy cooking breakfast but was interrupted by the sight of a police car turning up.

"Oh Christ, what do they want now?"

The officer stepped out.

"Alan, why you know return my calls?"

"What calls?"

"I left two messages for you".

"Well, I've not got them".

"Okay, let's *talk*."

They put a hand around each other's waist and wandered off towards the road, whispering in a low, hushed tone. He returned, shaking his head.

"I've got to fucking teach them English for free now. I think it's going to go something like this: 'repeat after me, 'I am a dirty immigration officer'. That's good. Now can you say the word cunt? 'I…..am…….a cunt"..

The backpackers were giggling at all this by the table.

"I don't know why you're all laughing. You're not here to *enjoy* yourselves".

"Right, let's get you guys to the border. It's gonna cost you 50 Baht each. Who's got 50 Baht?" he said, sounding like a game show host.

"Have you all got your dollars for the visa fee? If not, we're going to have to stop by a bank".

GREG LYNN

We all piled into the people carrier. En-route Alan was busy making disparaging jokes about Mancunians which none of the mixed nationality passengers got.

"There it is, *the border*".

I spent 10 minutes diligently filling out the visa forms. Only for immigration not to bother looking at them. They were only interested in receiving the $35.

'*Our rules. Our tax. Our money*", the receipt self-righteously claimed.

Now we were in another country. The only thing in front of us was the Mekong River. It flowed all the way down to the Gulf of Thailand. I wanted to go on the fast boat. It was more expensive but would get me to Luang Prabang in a matter of hours. I tried talking other members of the group into doing so.

"No way, man. It's like super unsafe", the spotty American kiddie whinged.

Unfortunately, in a group situation, people will listen to the one who declares the most impending doom. So the packed-out slow boat it was. But it was way too cramped as it was stuffed full of fat tourists. I went and hung out in peasant class at the back. It was much more fun.

We moored up for the night. The local entrepreneurs were canvassing for customers to fill their guest houses the moment we stepped off. I naturally had my defence barrier up, but I took a place that was going for a mere seven dollars a night. My own bedroom. The roof didn't leak. It was warm and dry. I didn't have to worry about who was coming through the front door. Somewhere safe. It was a rare luxury in my life. It's the basic, simple things that matter the most. I drifted off into a deep sleep almost the minute my head hit the pillow. That was helped by the air quality as well – so fresh and pure. Laos reminded me of a tropical version of the highlands of Scotland.

The second day of chugging down the Mekong river saw me stood right at the back. I gazed at the fast boat zooming along at 70mph. I stayed one night in Luang Prabang then continued down to the capital Vientiane. Sitting outside in the sun and watching the world go by over a couple of bottles of Leo beer had become a favourite passtime of mine.

Back in the hotel room whilst up on the balcony, I heard a voice calling up.

"Hel….lloo!" the voice was deep, rough and husky. It came from a…. lady wearing black thigh length boots and a short mini skirt who was standing on the street corner.

"Twenty dollar – I give you good sucky, sucky".

'She' was stocky, tall and broad. I returned an apologetic smile by way of declining then ventured back inside. So that was my first encounter with a 'ladyboy'. Take it from me; they don't always look feminine and sweet.

I thought about the next leg into Cambodia. My bus to Phnom Penh was booked for the following evening. After undertaking research, it seemed like you had to be careful on the border. Doing land border crossings in another country is always an adventure. The bus ride down was scheduled to take 21 hours. We boarded and were allocated our sleeping quarters up on the top deck of the double-decker, sleeping top to toe. When the time came for us to step out, the heat hit me straight away.

The 'local grease ball Mr Fixit' came and explained the procedure. We had to give him $45 each and hand over our passports; then he'd go and deal with the immigration police on our behalf. Anybody who'd bothered to research this immediately kicked up a fuss, stating that the price was $35. Oh, that's how things worked; the ten bucks extra for 'express processing services'. We were literally in the middle of nowhere. The road was just a dirt track surrounded by jungle. The official border crossing consisted of a small wooden hut with a couple of guards idly sitting down eating their lunch. Out here away from the rest of the world, they could do as they wished.

A short little man in uniform who looked like a James Bond villain approached us carrying an electrical device.

"Your passports are with the guy?" he asked before zapping us each on the forehead with infrared light. Presumably, this was to check our temperature to see if we had a fever. He then passed out a leaflet to us each which outlined all the nasty, horrible tropical diseases we might get here.

Mr Fixit sped off into the distance on his motorbike with a cheeky grin plastered across his face.

"There he goes with our passports", a British woman commented.

We'd arranged to meet with him on the other side in ten minutes.

"I'm not leaving here until I get my documents back. He better not have run off with them", an Israeli backpacker said with increasing anxiety.

I didn't foresee a problem. Yeah, if it was just 1 or 2, then it might be cause for concern. But not when it was a whole group of 11. Sure enough, the man eventually reappeared, and I hopped back on the bus. It chugged its way down the potholed road. Immediately I noticed that Cambodia was somewhat different from the rest of South-East Asia. It was the least developed with its own rustic charm. A lot of the buildings by the side of the road were tin shacks. It was rough and ready.

As we neared the capital, the area got more built up. It must have been wedding season. Loud, pumping music played from the huts as people danced away enthusiastically dressed in their party clothes. They clapped in time, encouraging other members of the group to do the same.

As the bus approached the station, I could already see the gaggle of tuk-tuk drivers waiting in anticipation. A bus full of Westerners, they all had somewhere to go. Their canvassing started even before we stepped off the bus.

THE WANDERER

"Hello, hello you. You want tuk-tuk? Where you go?"

I hurried through the scramble and around the corner.

"You looking for somewhere cheap to stay?" Come with me. I take you", a particularly sleazy man said in a low tone.

I shook my head. I don't ever let myself get led anywhere. It's simple, walk down the main drag and you'll soon find a place offering you a single room for 15 dollars a night. The bright neon lights lasered up into the air. Forget Bangkok. This was the place to be. It had way more character and energy. I figured that a couple of days could be spent here before heading down to the coast. The traffic took no notice of pedestrian crossings and even less attention to the red flashing lights. Never mind being attacked or mugged; by far the most significant risk out here was getting run over.

I settled into the China town guesthouse for the night. The sign on the wall read: *'no smoking, drugs or weapons allowed in your room. You want girl, come and ask at reception'*. Well, how very civilised. I spent the next couple of days exploring the city. It had to be the most off the wall place that I'd been to so far. This town deserved to be checked further, and I vowed to return sometime later before getting on another bus to Sihanoukville. The name of the place made it sound awful, and first impressions weren't encouraging. The strip leading down to the sea was like Blackpool's golden mile had been exported to a tropical climate. But there's always something about the sight of the sea for the first time on a road trip. It makes you feel like you've achieved something.

But now there was a problem. The money was due to run out. Same old story. South-East Asia maybe a dam sight cheaper than England, but don't forget as a non-national in another country, you've got to pay for everything. When you wake up in the morning, the first thing that you need is a coffee. That will cost you a dollar down the local stall, then a dollar and a dollar. Staying in tourist accommodation could still cost you as much as renting. Getting a tuk-tuk when you first arrive in a new town and need to get to your desired location asap, another five bucks. It all adds up. Then here's how you really lose money: every time you first get charged $5 for using a farang card, then get charged off your own bank. You could be losing up to £7 on each transaction. I'd arrived in Bangkok with £750 to my name. Yeah sure, that was mad. Then I'd dashed through my itinerary as quickly as possible to reach the intended target before the money ran out. Three countries in the space of 3 weeks, all travelled overland. It had been an intense experience.

Now there was just $30 left. Enough for a couple of nights stay in a cheap hostel, the type frequented by young annoying party types. Sihanoukville was a significant city in Cambodia. Its beach, Serendipity Bay was lined with bar after bar. At the happy hour, the beer got served for just 50 cents a glass. It also served as a transit point for the islands of Koh Rong where trust fund kiddies from all over Western Europe went to party not so hard earnt money away. The famed full moon parties in Southern Thailand had spread East here. Though from what I could gather, they were something of a cheap imitation. Raw, untreated sewage was being pumped directly into the Gulf of Thailand where bathers swam. It produced a revolting smell.

With less than 48 hours to go until the 'enhanced travelling experience' kicked in, I tried to prevent my mind from panicking and stay calm, as panic can lead to all types of distorted thinking. A young British traveller had taken it upon himself to snort a line of ketamine out in the back communal area. I found him particularly annoying, loud-mouthed and obnoxious. Now halfway towards the K-hole, at least he might shut up for a change.

"You're lucky it's my last night here tonight, Danny. If the manager had just seen you do that, you would have been straight out", said one of the hostel workers.

He smirked and gave a cocky retort.

THE WANDERER

"You wanna take a little more care out here, Danny; this is the place that they call the Wild East. All sorts of unsavoury things can take place after dark out here on the coast", he advised further.

Sometimes it seemed as if these kids forgot they were in a foreign country that functioned very differently to their own. They paid for everything in US dollars, were eating Western food and everyone they dealt with spoke English. Some Americans seemed to think that if they got into trouble, then their embassy would bail them out. Of course, it didn't quite work like that.

The hostel worker felt that he needed to make his point clearer.

"If you were unlucky you could get a jail sentence here for doing that. Do you know what the average life expectancy of a Westerner in a Cambodian jail is? It's six months".

"But I know some guy who got locked up and......"

"I'm going to repeat that: the average life expectancy of a Westerner in a Cambodian jail is six months. Goodnight Danny".

I checked out the following morning and spent the last couple of bucks on bottled water. The local tap water was unsafe to drink, so you had to buy the ice-cold bottled stuff from one of the many local stalls. Even the locals had to do the same thing, except that they brought gallons of it in bulk. Here where it was 35 degrees every day, and with an intense piercing heat from the sun, you sweated it out quickly. Now, what I always say to anyone who's going travelling in a hot country is whatever happens *always* make sure that you've got $10 left for water. I was about to find out how important the stuff was. Out on the beach, a well-spoken British man had an animated conversation on his phone.

"I need you to go down to the Bar Zulu in Kampot, see this guy and punch the living daylights out of him. Do you reckon you can do that? Good, I'll pay you $100".

So that was the going rate here.

What to do now then? Simple, go for a nice long walk and think about it. I'd heard that Otres Beach, a few miles up the coast was a funky, laid back place and that's where my feet were headed. There were plenty of scantily clad bikini wearing ladies to admire on the way. Maybe if I kept walking in this direction, then I'd hit the Vietnam border sooner or later. Just keep walking....

Up in front of me, my path was interrupted by a small river flowing into the sea. The deepest point looked about four foot deep. It was just about crossable without having to get my bag wet. I and my main rucksack had become separated in Chiang Khong. Now I was down to my bare essentials bag. That didn't suck quite as much as it sounded. As carrying a large rucksack everywhere with you makes you stick out. And that's precisely what you don't want. It's also less weight to carry around. It was surprising how little you needed: one change of clothes, toiletries, pens, papers, suntan lotion, plus insect spray and a decent book as well as travel documents which were always carried on my person. That was it. If your bag weighed more than 8 kilos, then you were packing too much.

On the other side of that river was a small island. Not many people would bother crossing that river. So it would do nicely for daily headquarters. Yup, it was crossable if you didn't mind getting wet. There was a shaded area by the beach, which I promptly got myself positioned. The next thing to do was calculate the risk assessment. Mosquitoes and the Dengue were the most significant threat as they're the greatest killer of humans. I promptly sprayed myself from head to toe in deet spray. That would keep them at bay. Next, water; there would be plenty of that lying around on Otres Beach and Serendipity Bay. And I'd be doing my bit for the environment by picking up after those lazy tourists who didn't know how to use a bin. Staying out of the scorching sun was vital. That was going to be difficult. Sunburn may not sound that serious but trust me – it can be. I took out the bottle of suntan lotion then applied liberally. There was a wooded area behind me. It looked thick enough to be out of sight. There were only a few locals that would be frequenting this area. The bad boys and the random crazy blokes that came out at night would be hanging out where I'd been previously. So that was that, nothing more to worry about, for I was on holiday on my little private island without any gormless kids to keep me awake at night. I remembered what Nicki had said.

"*Strand Greg on a desert island and two days later……he'd have a dole claim up and running*". Time to sit back, relax and gaze out to sea. Trapped in paradise. Things could be worse.

That evening I retired to bed in the wooded area behind me, but at dawn, I got awoken by something that I hadn't banked on; a herd of Water Buffalo grazing. They looked down at me curiously. The most notable thing about them was their massive horns. I played dead - no sudden moves. Most animals won't attack you unless they deem you to be a threat, especially to their young. Nevertheless, this was still a disconcerting moment.

'*What's that? It moves a little. Doesn't look very edible. Hmm, nothing too interesting*', you could almost hear them saying. They shrugged and casually wandered off. Maybe this wasn't the right place to sleep after all. Besides, it was near a swamp, which meant that the Dengue were flying about everywhere.

The next night the full moon appeared. It was way brighter and bigger than I'd ever seen it before. It lit up the night like a torch in the sky. The sound of blasting music got carried across the sea from Koh-Rong. They used to think that some people went a bit mad on a full moon night. That's where the phrase 'lunacy' is derived. Then I remembered that my return flight from Bangkok would be taking off around now – without me. Oh well, I'd have to worry about that one later. In truth, I'd only got a return ticket for immigration purposes (a lot of airlines won't carry you without a return ticket). I gazed up at the moon again in awe. It had power alright, and right now, I was feeling it.

"I don't think that I was meant to be on that plane back home tonight", I quietly murmured to myself.

But where was home? At the moment, it was on this coastline.

For the next week or so my days were spent wandering up and down the five-mile coast that served as the main tourist drag, scavenging for leftover water. There was no food to be had. Anything that was left out quickly perished in the heat. Here, in the Wild East, the rules were very different compared to Europe. I'd left the UK with just 13% body fat on me and that had been dug into while hurriedly arching through the Golden Triangle. If you don't eat, then your body will burn through its lean muscle mass first. When living like this, you can't afford to lose any of that.

But all wasn't lost. Come Monday I'd have some remaining holiday pay paid from the agency going into my account. It wouldn't be much, maybe $120. But it would be enough to get down to Kampot, spend a few days in civilisation and take it from there.

Before leaving, I stocked up on vital deet spray and suntan lotion, jumped on the bus and checked into Captain Chim's guesthouse in Kampot after eight days of roughing it. Kampot was a lovely, charming town. Quiet and laid back. But with plenty to do around there.

I spent the next few days lying in bed trying to get rid of whatever it was that I'd picked up. From now on I'd only been getting small dribs and drabs of money sent over from the UK, and the next one wouldn't be coming for nearly a month, and that would only be for $70. Vietnam was less than an hour away, but going there would just be digging myself into a deeper hole. It seemed more sensible/ less mad to head back to Thailand, the most developed country here and make my way to the international hub of Bangkok. But in the meantime, survival was going to have to be configured, and that wasn't going to be pretty.

Sleeping out on the street is dangerous and foolish whichever country you find yourself. That's something reserved for the severely mentally ill who don't know what they're doing. For those of us with a little more survival instinct, we head out of town and out of sight. Seriously, a Westerner sleeping on a bench by the river. How would that look? It was guaranteed trouble. In Bristol, I'd always headed to the woods. My brain had become hardwired that way. Out here, it was the same procedure. Except that here it was the far more dangerous jungle.

I was somebody from an affluent country in one of the poorest nations in the world. What would they think of a tourist who'd run out of money? There wouldn't be much sympathy. I was going to have to tough it out on my own. With some trepidation, I trudged off.

The walk out of town involved going past a load of dogs. There were plenty of stray ones here. They ran after me and barked, defending their territory. I saw them off by throwing imaginary stones at them. Thank goodness that I'd had my Rabies shots. Though if a rabid dog ever bites you, the pre-vaccine will only give you enough time to get to a hospital. The disease has a 100% fatality rate; no one has ever survived it. It's a very nasty way to go. You'll flail around like a raving lunatic first and everyone will think you've gone mad. The concept of zombies got inspired by the sight of people experiencing this affliction.

Once out of Kampot, I walked along the dirt track, located a nice thick area in the distance, then walked down the sandy path. Again, Mosquitoes and the Dengue were the biggest concern. I sprayed myself liberally with deet spray before bedding down. Red ants and other creepy crawlies were the next big problem. I tried hard not to think about the cobra's that would undoubtedly be out and about. The thing is a cobra out at night will typically be in the business of hunting mice and other small animals. They'd see me before I saw them and would probably think, '*fuck tha*t' and scraper away. Those that get bitten by cobras' are often asking for it, i.e. snake charmers. When confronted they'll put their hood up first as if to say, '*get the hell out of my face'*. If it came to it, I planned to put my bag in front of me, and hopefully, it would sink its venom into that instead. After it strikes several times, its poison will be spent. Anyway, apparently, cobra's are quite a docile bunch after all. Nothing too much to worry over. But if you do get bitten, you'll be paralysed first. The only thing that can save you is anu-venom stored at a hospital, which they probably won't have. So you'll have to endure an 8-hour long, painful death

At dawn, the Dengue or white tiger moths came out. Then the sun rose high in the sky, and I did my best to stay out of its rays, sheltering underneath some bushes while dripping in sweat. Now I'd love to say that I spent my time there cracking open coconuts and eating tree bark while merrily swinging away in a jungle hammock but Bear Grylls I am not. At this point, my jungle survival skills were a little amateurish. There was only one thing on my mind, and that was getting water.

For most people obtaining the stuff has never been a problem. You simply turned on the tap. To be deprived of it is something unthinkable. As a general rule of thumb, you can go for three days without it before it's fatal. However, while out here sweating buckets and going through a lot more physical activity than usual, that could happen a lot quicker. I figured that I had 24 hours until I passed out and would be needing 4 litres a day. There was a holiday resort about 12km down the road. That didn't seem like a bad bet, but getting there was going to involve energy that I didn't have. It would mean being out in the heat and sweating more, using up the bodies precious fluids that were already in short supply. Stay here and slowly perish or keep moving, and there could be something to gain. I went for it.

Every few hundred yards or so there was a plastic bottle that still had something left in it. Many motorcyclists passed through this route. Whatever was there I gulped it down, even though it had turned warm. Ordinarily, this journey would have taken me less than 3 hours, but every step felt like my feet were tied down with concrete blocks. The sky was cloudless and had a vibrant blue colour. Keep on moving. It's always good to have a target. By the time I'd got to the resort, my feet were throbbing hard. It appeared to be shut as there weren't any customers there. The only sign of life was a maintenance man doing some work in the sun lounge. He'd left his two bottles of water lying on the wall. Oh well, if he didn't want it. Finding that now seemed like coming across rare bottles of whisky, a jackpot find. To celebrate I walked to the shore and took a dip in the sea, the first of this trip. The warm water seemed incredibly soothing. The setting sun appeared in the West again. Only another 6,000 miles back....

At the entrance to the resort, I found some bushes that would keep me hidden from view. There was no point in walking back tonight. Walking down that road alone and in the dark could be dangerous. So I curled up for the night. To my intense relief, it began to rain. I held my mouth open and let the water drip inside. The next day the long walk back began. Every couple of miles I'd stop underneath a concrete bridge to be in the shade. At around the halfway point, I doubted that I was going to make it back. Just then, a motorbike pulled up. The rider was female.

"Where you go?"

"Kampot".

"She handed me two ice-cold bottles of water. I barely managed to utter the words 'arkun tran' before gulping them down in a matter of seconds. Oh, my lord, did that ice-cold water feel good going down my throat.

"I saw you by the side of the road, and I thought, I pity him".

I pity the fool!

"I give you a ride back to your guesthouse, but first I need to go to my farm".

I'd never envisaged my first time on a motorbike to be with a kindly Khmer lady. She was maybe in her late thirties and had a motherly look to her. The sky had turned a gorgeous pink colour as we headed back down the road and around the corner to her place.

"As you can see, I'm very poor; I don't have much land".

Several pigs grazed out in the back, and she went off to feed them. She'd introduced herself as Kylie.

"Do you have wife back in England?"

ı shook my head. I wished that I'd been more engaging in conversation, but the energy was still lacking. We continued the journey with me on the back of her moto going down the dirt track. She chatted away about her husband and kids. I indicated where I wished to be dropped off, and she scribbled her number down on a bit of paper.

Back to the deluxe jungle suite, it was. For the next 12 days and 12 nights, all I could think about was getting water. I was managing to procure about 2 litres a day by the aforementioned method, but it was nowhere near enough. It was sweating out of my body faster than could be consumed. I only needed to piss once every few days and what did come out was a tiny trickle of dark brown liquid. That would indicate severe dehydration.

This may sound like an exotic adventure, but it was just like anything else – unpleasant and mind-numbingly dull. I became faintly aware of my body withering away. It had been two weeks since I'd last eaten anything having been so focused on getting fluid. Even if you're only lying in bed the whole day, your body will still burn through 1,500 calories to maintain itself at 37.5 degrees and to keep your vital organs going, and that's after your metabolism will have gone into starvation mode, slowing right down.

Fat, muscle, nerve endings, whatever protein you've got left on you; it will get burnt through to keep your heart beating and blood pumping through your arteries and up to your brain, which is wondering why on earth you got yourself into this situation. I'd gone into a lethargic state, barely being able to summon the strength to get up and go for water. The only motivation left was the thought of that 24-hour window.

It was the oddest feeling that I've ever experienced, being literally 24 hours from death. How long do you think you're going to live until? Until you're 70.....80? Right now, I only had one day left unless something changed. My tongue had stuck to the side of my mouth as now my body was having trouble generating saliva. There wasn't much point in crying; there was no fluid left for the tears. I'd run out of deet spray, so the mosquitoes and insects were munching away at me – by far the worst thing.

THE WANDERER

I genuinely thought that I might not make it through this one. My life didn't flash before my eyes; I didn't consider who I might be leaving behind. Instead, the deepest, strangest calmness overtook, and I suddenly let go of any childhood born hang-ups that I might still be carrying around – they didn't matter anymore. I lay back and made my peace with the world. The sun was still blistering down. If I died here tonight, it wasn't a good thing or a bad thing – it just was. It *just was*....

I shut my eyes and enjoyed the peaceful blackness. Then all of a sudden, there was the sound of engines. A group of men approached on scooters. They were indicating for me to get up. Perhaps I was on their territory, and they wanted me to clear off. No, they weren't hostile. I staggered to my feet. One man made an eating gesture with his mouth and hands. Perhaps they are going to eat me? No, this seemed to be an offer. I jumped on the back with them, and the next thing I knew, I was sat down on a wooden hut on stilts, sat in a circle with eight pairs of eyes looking at me. None of them spoke a word of English, and I only knew a few words of Khmer. They passed me a large bottle of water with the insistence that I drank it all. I sipped slowly. When you're dehydrated if you quickly gulp down water, it will go straight through you. Next came a bowl of rice. Again, I munched slowly as my stomach would have shrunk. But best of all, the chap next to me offered out a handful of cigarettes. Due to the language barrier, verbal communication was critical here, plenty of smiles, be humble. Bit by bit, I chugged back on the bottle of water. Whenever they did talk to me, I tried to read the tone.

"No. No America, *English*".

It always helps to make this clear.

At dusk, they served me up chicken, rice, fish and vegetables. By now, I felt like eating, but how did you get this coconut open. A little boy who can't have been older than six ran up eagerly. He was about to show me how it was done. He expertly cracked it open with a meat cleaver, then looked at me with his big brown eyes while he was eagerly chatting away in Khmer.

237

The sky had turned its lovely pink colour once again. It was one of those moments that made me feel quite privileged - being saved by the local tribe. They never advertised that in the tourist brochures.

They passed around a plastic container bag full of home-brewed rice whisky and offered me a small glass.

"To Cambodia!" I said jovially, raising the glass then downed it. It was potent stuff.

I ended up staying with them for the next couple of days and could have got used to it. But by now they had decided it was time for me to go back to the 'man village'. I thanked them for their kind hospitality. They gave me one last handful of cigarettes, and I returned to the 'man village', otherwise known as Kampot.

I'd only been sat by the river for a few minutes when a man with a radio strapped to his side approached me.

"We're looking for a Westerner who's been sleeping in the jungle, have you seen him?"

I shook my head like a 3-year-old who'd been caught nicking sweeties.

"Are you sure?"

I nodded eagerly.

"Come on; we know it was you. Can you come down to the station with me, please? I'll give you a ride. We per-ray for you".

Were they going to start praying for me? This was worrying. I jumped on the back of his moto, and we whizzed the short distance to the local cop-shop.

"Okay, that guy over there, he's our boss. He's going to talk to you".

I sat down on one of the wooden chairs and mentally prepared my story. The Colonel came over. He was the only one who was dressed in an official uniform. The first thing that they were going to ask me for was my documents: name and nationality. I handed my passport then showed him the visa sticker, highlighting that it was still in date. That's what they wanted to know, that I was a real person and was here legitimately. Now nice open body language and a polite smile. I read him; he seemed like an affable sort of chap.

"Colonel please, I do not wish to cause you any trouble. I unfortunately had some problems with my bank account that meant I couldn't access funds. That's why I came into......a small amount of......bother".

He looked at me and jotted down notes. Everything was checked and photocopied.

"You were in a very bad place to sleep. Many Dengue".

I nodded.

"Next time you have a problem, you come to us. You understand?"

I nodded once again.

"Where you stay before?"

"Captain Chim's guesthouse".

"Do you need some food? Some water?"

"Yes, arkun".

He dispatched one of his subordinates down to the shop and not long afterwards he returned with a bag full of bread, rice and sauce, plus several litres of water.

"Now he take you to guesthouse".

I was about to turn around and go when he reached inside his pocket and produced his wallet, then handed me a fistful of riel. It equated to approximately $20 - pocket money to keep me out of mischief.

"Gentlemen, it's been a pleasure", I said then hopped onto the back of the moto.

At the guesthouse, the situation got explained to the manager while I stood there sheepishly. From what I could gather, they were agreeing to tick me until the end of the week. I was then discreetly ushered to my room. I took one look at the bed and promptly flopped into it. The sand and dirt rubbed onto the sheets. The manager knocked on the door; he addressed me like he was visiting a sick relative.

"Would you like something to eat? I can make you something. Some noodles maybe?"

This was an awkward situation. I was supposed to be contributing to their tourism economy, not becoming a burden.

The next morning, I trotted downstairs.

"Mr Lynn, I have your embassy on the phone for you, sir", the receptionist said.

Oh Christ, what did *they* want?

"Hello, Mr", the accent was Cambodian.

"Why you sleep in the jungle?" he asked incredulously.

I shot him the standard story, which basically just said that I was skint.

"We wery, wery worried about you Mr Lynn, sleeping in the jungle wery dangerous. You could get bitten by a snake; you could be killed!"

His young child was crying in the background, which meant that he'd been contacted at home. I must have been talking to the emergency out of hours consulate in Phnom Penh. This was serious.

"Is there anybody that you'd like us to contact in UK. Your wife, perhaps?"

"Nope. I'm not married. There's no one that you need to contact".

"So what do you want us to do for you?"

"Well, you can't lend me any money......so I guess.... nothing".

"The guesthouse has been kind enough to say that they will give you food until the end of the week and you can pay your bill then. What do you intend to do after that?"

"I'm going to head back into Thailand, so then I won't be any of your concern".

"But the police, they are wery worried about you".

"Then tell them thank you *very* much for their kind assistance, but they needn't concern themselves any longer.

I wasn't giving much away, and he knew this conversation wasn't going anywhere.

"Okay.... uh......but don't sleep in the jungle again. Wery dangerous!" he concluded.

I stepped outside to get some breakfast and went up to the local food stall for a bowl of beef noodles. I reached into my pocket to pay her the 4,000 Riel.

"He pay for you already", she smiled.

"Who did?" I asked puzzled.

She pointed to a man zooming off on his moto. He turned around, grinned and waived. It would appear that local tongues had been wagging.

The next day I trotted down for breakfast once again.

"Today is our special day, please have some soup and noodles", the receptionist offered.

It was Chinese New Year – the year of the Monkey. I wondered how much more monkeying around this year was going to have to offer.

An American biker was having a conversation with some retirees on the table opposite.

"It's cobra mating season out there right now, so they're particularly active. They're quite protective of their young, and a baby cobra can be just as dangerous – they have no control over their venom".

Well, that was good to know.

The best strategy from now on was to keep my head down and be as innocuous as possible. I spent most of the time lying down in bed still recovering, watching business news and following the US presidential election campaign. I must have watched more live Premiership football here than I ever did in England. I decided on Pattaya as the next target. Sure, I was probably going to hate the place, but when in a tight situation it's best to head to the most touristy place that you can think of for reasons that I've already stated. The end of the week came. $100 or so received. I went to reception to settle my bill.

"How much do I owe you?"

"You had a fan room which would normally be $7, but we'll call it $3. So the total is $21".

"Okay, but what about the food?"

"I didn't write that down", she said, waving her hand.

I smiled a thanks then bunged 20 bucks in the tip jar and booked a seat on the bus for the border.

"No, no – middle finger first, then the left", the guard said as he took my prints.

Then followed the reassuring sound of the exit stamp, making a double thud. Another country that I'd made it out of alive.

The Cambodians may have suffered devastatingly at the hands of the Pol-Pot regime. The country had a well-documented troubled history. Yet its citizens were the kindest people that I've ever known. Without their assistance, I probably wouldn't have survived. It's often the most impoverished people that are willing to give you the most. Another nomadic friend of mine explained it to me like this: *'there's something about the lone man trying to find his way.......'*

Chapter 12

The land of sin

I appeared to be going up in the world. This time my place of residence was in a beautiful forest in Thailand where every tree was in a single straight line. For a place to sleep, I'd found someone's treehouse. It was a carefully constructed wooden structure, and they'd even left a mat for me to sleep on. Apparently, if you're in a tight spot here, then you can knock up the local monks at the Temple who might be willing to put you up for the night. But I didn't fancy doing that. A foreigner with nowhere to stay and with no means of supporting himself was going to provoke a load of questions immediately.

I was in the settlement of Trat, the first town after the border. All money had been used up on getting this far. It was 146 miles to Pattaya. If I got my act together, then I could be able to make it there by hitch-hiking and arrive that evening. There was only one way to find out. I stood by the side of the road this, time doing the pat-down as opposed to the thumbs up. The journey would have to be broken down into a series of chunks again. The geography all the way there looked dense enough for it not to be too much of a problem.

It wasn't long before I was in the back of a pick-up truck after telling the driver that I was going as far as Chonburi. It may have been uncomfortable, but the wind rushing down my face as we sped along the highway was refreshing. It felt life-affirming, and I was happy to be making steady progress. Whatever happens, keep on moving because you'll only end up sinking if you standstill.

According to the scales when I weighed myself that morning, I was a mere 63 kilos - the lowest it had been due in my adult life. I'd lost 9 kilos in the space of 7 weeks. Forget the expensive diet plans; if you want to lose weight quickly, then head off to South-East Asia without enough money.

On the next ride, I was sharing space with a couple of guys who were doing chicken deliveries, and then on the final one, I was sitting in the passenger seat of a Toyota. The guy even brought me a meal as we stopped at a roadside café. As darkness fell, the illuminated neon sign of Pattaya came into view in big red lettering. I'd arrived in the land of sin.

Yup, every stereotype was true: middle-aged Germans and Austrians walking hand in hand with young pretty Thai girls half their age. Ladyboys lined up along the seafront touting for custom. Go-go bars galore. High rise hotel after high rise hotel lined the whole stretch. Every other building was either a bar, guesthouse or restaurant. This entire city *was* the good time district. Its very existence depended upon people coming down here from across the globe and wishing to spunk their money.

Though there were plenty of reports of men having their drinks spiked by so-called ladies then being robbed of all their valuables while they were in a drug-induced stupor. Of course, that was hardly a concern to me. Here's one of the few other good things about having no money: nobody can con or rob you. Anybody who doesn't have genuine intentions won't want to know you. So that might allow more honourable people into your life. I thought that I was going to hate this place, but I actually liked it. There was a certain vibrancy and energy, yet it still retained a laid-back feel. Just about anything went. That's why nobody was paying any notice to little old me.

Following the usual procedure, I picked up the seafront and walked past the many marinas having to negotiate my way past all those goddam territorial dogs once again. Once past them, I was out of the built-up area and could sea woodland in the distance. Though this time, I managed to find an abandoned hut. It took all my remaining strength to climb into it. Anything to get away from those biting insects. It was there that I stayed for the next two days, lying on the floor while I thought about adapting to the new environment. The euphoria I'd felt about making it this far soon faded away and in its place was sinking morale: different country, same old bullshit.

The next day I was trying to find my way back to the coastline, but lack of food meant that there wasn't enough energy to fire up the brain's neurons, so my thought process was going around in circles. This meant that physically, I was quite literally walking around in circles with my head bowed low.

"Hey", a female voice cried out.

"Where you go?"

I didn't know how to answer that question anymore.

The voice had come from a lady who was running a roadside stall. She was there with a man about the same age who I assumed was her husband.

"You looking for somewhere to stay?"

I nodded.

"Did lady steal your money?"

I gave a non-committal answer which didn't give much away.

"Don't go sleeping outside – snakes!" she advised.

She almost seemed to gauge what was going on with me without having to ask too many questions.

"Here, I show you somewhere to stay".

Oh, really, I was intrigued.

She led the way across the road then through a gap in a boarded-up fence and across a patch of overgrown wasteland. At the end of that, she opened a glass slide door and showed me into a bare room. The place appeared to be a derelict hotel building. Though what connection she had with it, I don't quite know.

"You stay here tonight", she said then handed me a roll-up mat to lie on.

I followed her back out to her stall. She was busy cooking dinner. Never turn down a meal when it's offered to you while you're out on the road. I gratefully tucked into the meat and rice.

"You wanna beer?"

Result! I'd landed on my feet with this one. She handed over a bottle of Singha beer. The sun was starting to set again, and I felt more relaxed now. She then handed me some burning incense which was meant to ward off the mosquitoes.

"You come and see me tomorrow. I make you breakfast".

I merely nodded.

When unexpected things like this happen, you barely have enough time to process what's going on. But my instincts told me that this was a safe environment. I headed back across the road to the abandoned building and lit the incense. It appeared to be working. This place had certainly seen better days, but at least I was out of the elements.

I obeyed her request of going to see her the following morning. In between cooking up rice and a fried egg, she served the passing motorcyclists by pouring petrol into their tanks from disused glass Pepsi bottles. A tall ladyboy wearing a helmet was one of her customers that morning. They chatted together in Thai. You can always tell when somebody is talking about you, even when it's in a foreign language. The ladyboy turned around and handed me a 100 Baht note.

"Now you give her the Wai", said my new landlady.

I gave the Wai for the first time, putting my hands together and bowing (Westerners aren't supposed to do it). Then feeling somewhat rejuvenated, I settled into the routine of becoming a beach bum, lying on the sand in the shade and gazing out at the Gulf of Thailand. There wasn't much else to do. Simply lying around all day in the sun - it wasn't such a bad life after all.

While sitting down by the benches, I'd end up having random conversations with people. One of them occurred with a well-built West African guy who now lived in Korea and was here on holiday. He was talking to me about getting caught short 'down the 'Walking Street'. I'd wandered along there my self quite a few times. It was amusing just seeing all the various forms of life that hung around there. I was kind of glad that I didn't have any cash to burn as going down that stretch seemed to be how it got sucked out of them.

"You must be very careful down the go-go bars. You make one mistake in there and then that's it, they'll fleece you. Especially the Russian places, they are the worst", he said gravely.

I looked up at the line of corporate hotels and wondered where the finance had come from to build those.

"Though it's much better if you bring the girl back to your room. Then she must leave her ID at the reception. When she leaves and has to go to collect it, they'll call you first to make sure that nothing untoward has happened before they give it back to her".

Prostitution was still illegal here. Though, as long as the girl was over 18 it had become the most overlooked law on the planet.

I'd generally head back to the 'hotel' around 9 pm and enjoy my bare-bones existence of lying on the ceramic floor.

"Why you no come and see me this morning?" my landlady scolded, wagging her finger.

"But I thought you'd be busy; I didn't want to bother you too much, see".

The truth was that I hadn't got out of bed until 11 that day.

"You come and see me tomorrow. Your clothes, they dirty. No one talk to you when you have dirty clothes. Give them to mamma; she wash them for you".

The next day I was reunited with clean clothes. And then that strange phenomenon kicked in again. I'd be walking back into town when a local would smile and pass me a 100 Baht note.

"Koopkhun", was all I could say then offer a brief wai.

This was starting to happen on a regular basis. On the one hand, I must have looked wholly screwed for them to do this. But on the other, I was still managing to endear them in some way. Back on the beach at least once a day, one of the women who ran the drink and snack stalls would come over offering me some fish, rice and a drink. I guess I stuck out being a little different (or maybe I wasn't too dissimilar from those skinny stray cats wondering about that they gave titbits to). Being the token man can often work in your favour....

And now there was something to look forward. My landlady's younger sister was in town that evening, and she was to be there with her American husband. She'd cooked up a real feast and kept the Bamboo Whisky and cola flowing. Her brother-in-law was an Alaskan which, after all, is America. It was good to be conversing with an English speaker once again as this meant that I could delve into proper conversations. I have an accent that's very difficult for foreigners to understand so need to concentrate on talking slowly and trying to pronounce everything correctly, which meant that the conversation never got beyond anything superficial.

Frank, the Alaskan talked about time on his farm, which also involved a weed grow (legal in that state). This was the first time that I'd ever met an Alaskan, so I was keen to hear what the place was all about. Having your own land, being able to run your own business from it and live the life you wanted. That sounded great to me. For some reason, Frank and his Thai wife still lived in separate countries and didn't see each other very often. I decided it was best not to ask any questions about that arrangement.

We continued having the pick-nick by the side of the road. Every so often, a customer would want their tank filling up, and my landlady would chuck in a bottle full of petrol while puffing away on a cigarette.

Frank would be departing for Alaska the next day, and I was off on the next hop. 2,300 Baht received (those annoying ATM charges when you've only got small amounts) I gave 1,000 Baht to my landlady as a token of goodwill. You remember your favours while out on the road. Then I hopped on the bus for the short ride to Bangkok. There was enough left for a night's stay in a backpacker's hostel, a meal from a stall and a can of Chang. Then I was back on the street along with the cockroaches and giant rats.

It didn't take long for me to wander back to Silom, the place where I'd first arrived. You always end up being right back where you started, but under different circumstances.

"You want sexy girl?......hey; it's 'no money' from England! You still, no money?"

"Yup, no money, no honey".

You know you're doing all right when the local hustlers award you a nickname. I'd hang out here until 1 am, then walk back down to a much quieter area by a park and sit at a bus stop, pretending that I was just waiting for a night bus while reading a Patricia Cornwell novel. To be seen reading is good because it's an innocuous activity and makes you look conscientious enough to know what you are doing. I'd judged to be sleeping out on the street here way, *way* too dangerous. Even I've got my limits. This was a city where severe naughty business could occur. Plus, with all the trash, dirt and pollution it would be decidedly unhealthy. When you live like this, you don't just see and hear a city, you get to feel its energy physically, and it doesn't always feel pleasant.

When the sun rose, I'd mooch around for a little longer then go and lie in the shade in Lumphini park, definitely the nicest daily headquarters that I've had. Finally, here I could sleep in safety and peace while pretending to be a tourist who'd fallen asleep sunbathing. These little luxuries were priceless. Though the act can't have worked that well; by day six, the local bums were giving me friendly grins and waves.

I was sharing this place with all manner of lizards. There was a monitor lizard who was at least 8-foot-long. He swaggered through the park as if to say, *'this is my manner, it doesn't belong to you poxy tourists'*. They even had a shower in the gents' toilets which I made use of every morning, and someone had been kind enough to leave out citrus shower gel. Being in a developed and international city that was full of shoppers and tourists meant that I could apply the same old tricks for procuring food and drink.

But there was something else that was bothering me. My visa would be expiring soon, and I didn't have the funds to extend it or get a flight back. So, I was going to have to leave the country somehow and aim for one of their neighbouring ones. Laos and Cambodia were both done with, and Myanmar definitely wasn't an option. That left Malaysia, a country that I knew very little about. The train fare down to Penang was £19. With a couple of begging e-mails that was taken care of and once again I was boarding a train out of Hualamphong station, just popping South. When you're an international hobo distances cease to matter that much. So what if it was a 19-hour train ride down. It meant that I had a home for the next day and a half an even a bed to sleep in at night. I crossed the border with just 12 hours to spare and arrived in a country that was very different from what

I was expecting. For a start there were the skull and bones warning signs: *'being caught in possession of narcotics and or illegal firearms will result in the death penalty'*.

For this was a hardcore Islamic nation that had a profoundly austere feel. Then there were the people. I'd expected them to be like the Thais. But no, they were Southern Indian in appearance with an entirely different culture. They looked at me as if I was from a different planet (I guess that wasn't surprising).

That was all the more reason to get off the street at night. As usual, I walked out of town. Here's one good thing about Asia; there are always plenty of abandoned cars lying about. You can spot one by how dirty it is. I tried the lock on the passenger side. It was open, and I snuck in. It was a bit cramped in the back and pretty filthy. Clearly, they weren't down with towing away cars here. I laid a load of newspaper down and whatever else I could find then lay down for the night. Once down and settled, I could start making firmer plans.

My stay here was permitted for 90 days. That was plenty of time to play with. There was no point in going back to Thailand. Penang wasn't going to serve me with that much. It was feasible that I could get down to the capital of Kuala Lumpur, once again a big international city. The benefits there being more resources, greater anonymity, and best of all, it was a major air hub, which meant that I could get a cheap flight back. But that could take a while.

It was often sheer stubbiness that kept me going. Returning too soon felt like admitting defeat. After another night sleeping in the cramped seats of the car, I was on the bus South going through the Cameron Highlands. What was there to be in KL? I was about to discover the oddest city that I've ever been in. In the distance were the Petronas twin towers. At one point they had been the tallest buildings in the world. At the bus station, they had the odd practice of screening everyone's bags before they boarded a domestic bus. Controlling seemed to be the ethos.

Once again, the first two days that you spend in a place are always the worst when you don't know the area. Naturally, I spent that time looking for abandoned buildings. I used the skyscrapers as my visual landmark to map my way around. Roughly 2 miles North of them, give or take 2 miles South of them, and I knew where I was.

I thought I'd come across the perfect place and was about to gain entry when a voice muttered a 'hi' from the right-hand side. It was from a security guard sat down on a plastic chair.

"Hi", I returned and played the tourist who'd happened to lose his way for a bit then bid a hasty retreat.

In a country where they gave you the death penalty for being caught with a spliff, this could be quite a risky business. But when you've got nothing to lose your animal instincts take over. Think you're not an animal? When you're in a 'do or die' situation, you realise that you're are not that far evolved from the Apes after all.

The sight of blue hoardings caught my eye. That indicated a sealed-off building. The gap underneath those hoardings was at least a foot. Plenty of space for me to roll underneath when there was no one watching. Yup, a vacant building on two floors. Upstairs was uninhabitable, so I went right to the back and found a room that was just about liveable. By the look of this place, it used to be a police station (the raised flag in the front garden gave it away).

What was around my immediate vicinity that could be made use of? Some sofas that weren't in bad shape and some leather chairs with cushions. I stripped those off and made up a sleeping quarter, then positioned myself away from the entry point. If I could get in that easily, then so could other people. There weren't any signs of work going on, so I should get left in peace for a bit. Accommodation sorted. There would be plenty of left-over water lying around across the city. Then I guess I just had to starve a little bit more.

The next day such missions were in progress when a local stopped and curiously enquired why I was picking up a half-full cup of Pepsi off the street.

"I did not want to come to Malaysia", I replied almost in protest, then explained the logistical reasons behind me being here.

"So you have no money and no return ticket?"

I nodded.

He looked like he'd just received word of a major disaster.

"Only God can save you now", he said gravely then walked off.

Well, that wasn't very encouraging. I thought I was doing alright given the circumstances. And anyway, it was my birthday tomorrow. But on that day, I woke up suddenly gripped by panic. Aged 35. No longer a young man. Another grey hair, another wrinkle. I glanced at the tiles hanging down from the ceilings and mould on the walls. If I was fortunate, then this was the halfway point in life, and *this* is how I'd ended up: living in a derelict building on the other side of the world with no money and no prospects. How had it all come to this? This was beyond madness! I celebrated by going out and blagging as many free samples of milk chocolate drink that were humanly possible. All the sugar consumed was making me hyperactive.

Then the storm came. Being so close to the equator meant that the weather was quite extreme. The loud cracks of thunder were enough to make my bones vibrate. The noise sounded like a bomb going off. Then the bolts of lightning lit up the whole sky. It was a dramatic yet serene event. I looked up at the majestic Petronas Towers lit up in the distance. Could there be any answers to life's great questions while I continued to wander the streets, not sure of what I was looking for anymore? What was to be the evolution of an international drifter who was homeless in his 11th country?

THE WANDERER

An international crusade? Bollocks. I might as well be in Northampton. Except that it was a little warmer here (and the dog ends were a bit longer). It doesn't matter where you are in the world; your problems will always follow you. Why? Because you're still the same person acting with the same behaviours that manifests the same physical reality. And it had taken me to be this far away to realise that.

On that cheery note, I returned to base camp to discover that my piss was still a disconcerting dark brown colour. Though with this place, I knew that sooner or later, the owner, contractors or the estate agent were going to turn up. Sometime later, I got awoken by the sound of a vehicle coming through the front gate. Blast. I might be able to sneak out without being seen. Too late, he spotted me.

"Have you got the keys to the gate?" the guy called out.

Good. He clearly thought that I was someone official. No Asian would believe that a Westerner would bother squatting a random building here. So let's live up to that estimation. I trotted out briskly trying to look like I was someone important and patted down my pockets.

"I must have left them in the office".

"Where are the boys?" he asked impatiently.

"The boys?"

"Yeah, they were supposed to be here at 9."

"They're out having breakfast. You know what these chippies are like", I tutted.

"Well, can you ring them?"

I patted my pockets down again.

"Darn. I left my phone in the office too".

"Can you go back and get it?"

255

"Maybe. You'll have to excuse me, I'm a very busy man", and with that, I rolled out underneath the fence while he looked on perplexed.

Greg's international property guardian services continued unabated. The actual workmen *did* pay a couple of further visits. But they smiled and waved as I trotted out in the morning. Kuala Lumpur was funny in the sense that by day, the streets were deserted.

"Where is everyone?" I murmured to myself.

"Hey, do you remember me?" a voice asked.

"I was the security guard at Jalan Ampang."

"You like Ampang?"

"It's alright".

"Did you find what you were looking for?" he half grinned.

I nodded, then walked off.

That day the rain came down. It would start all of a sudden, bucket it down for a couple of hours, then go back to being sunny and warm.

'You can't get much purer water than when it's come straight from the clouds', I thought and placed a cup out in the yard. The thick droplets of water splashed into it. I tried it. It tasted dubious. Perhaps rain clouds and air pollution don't mix. There was no doubt about it; I was physically unhealthy now. Every day my veins seemed to pop out more. My bones stuck out. There was no flesh left on my arse. I could feel my pelvis when I sat down. My skin was beginning to flake, a classic sign of malnutrition. Most of what I could forage was let over sugary drink and those calories were quickly burnt off through the amount of walking I did daily. Though one guy had randomly given me 100 ringgits (about £20) and I'd found a whole rucksack full of fresh, clean clothes.

I'd procrastinated about asking to borrow the money for a flight back. The cheapest would be £300. Communication was a problem. Then I remembered something - the Apple stores. The ones in the UK would let you browse their products, and from there you could access your e-mail. Surely the ones in KL wouldn't be that different. This is why I had chosen to base myself in a major city, even though it wasn't interesting – more significant resources. I found the shiniest, glitziest shopping mall and scoped out the electronic gadget shops.

"Can I help you, sir?" the assistant asked as I was fingering a £1,200 mac.

"Yes, I was thinking of purchasing this one. But I'm a little unsure of the connectivity quality in Malay at the moment. Would you mind if I tried that out? On my e-mail account maybe".

There were a couple of e-mails on there asking why I'd dropped out of contact. My fingers dashed through the necessary. Begging for a loan for the flight back is always a humiliating experience, but what choice did I have? The next few days involved alternating between the Apple, Samsung and Huawei stores, getting into unnecessary technical conversations with sales assistants while I blagged a few minutes internet time. Being eight hours ahead, here made things more awkward. Mission accomplished, but it wouldn't be happening until the end of the month. I was going to have to tough it out....

When that day came, after 6 pm, my bank account was a little more substantial. Right on cue, the thunder and lightning struck, and the heavens opened. I ran for shelter, down at Chinatown the most colourful part of town where I'd decided to base up. There was a sort of 'hotel' opposite that offered international telephone and internet services. I say sort of because it seemed to have a lot of homeless people sleeping on its floors. And quite frankly my derelict building provided better accommodation (fewer loonies and rodents running around).

Booking a flight back may seem incredibly easy to you. Just click on 'Flight Scanner' and get your visa card out, right? Well yes, but understand that these were the days before I had an Android and a laptop, was living off my wits with just the clothes on my back and little to no money. It made the most straightforward things far more difficult. You had to be spot on with your planning and timing when executing an operation like this. One little mistake, bit of mismanagement or poor judgement could throw the whole thing off-kilter. For a start, I wasn't exactly supported by the worlds best financial products, just a poxy Co-operative bank card that only worked in a few ATM's. Using an English card in Malaysia on an American website - it wasn't having it. Its international links weren't strong enough. Calls to the Credit Union and the card provider at 30 pence a minute - it was adding up. Nope, the card worked fine.

"There must be a technical problem with Expedia's website", they advised.

This needed doing today! I was going to have to call their head office in Seattle and cut a deal over the phone. Another 30 pence a minute enduring the waiting music on a dodgy handset while rats ran over my feet.

"I'm looking for a single back to London Heathrow. I'm guessing the cheapest routing is with Sri-Lankan airlines".

"Yes, I can sell you a seat for $397, but that's not leaving for another couple of weeks".

"$397? That's about £270, yeah, go for it".

"I'll e-mail you the flight itinerary right away, sir. Your name as it appears on the passport, please".

It's difficult to get a cheap deal right at the last minute, so that would have to do. But a massive wave of relief washed over me. To mark the occasion, I went and brought a cheap fake Rolex watch. I hate not knowing what the time is.

"You're like a stick. Don't you eat?" the man said as he applied it to my wrist.

Unfortunately, these days it was rare, though I did manage an ice cream and a coffee sometimes down the local 7-Eleven store some mornings.

THE WANDERER

"Terima kasih", I thanked.

"Sama-sama"

Fifteen days until departure and every one of those dragged. A minute seemed like an hour. An hour would seem like a day. It was a very lonely business. I vowed to change. For the last night, I checked into some cheap digs down Chinatown to get showered. I rose early at 4 am then caught the bus down to KLIA. The long flight back via Sri-Lanka was a pleasantly mundane experience.

"Would you like one Whisky and coke or two, sir?" the stewardess asked amiably.

Did that question even need asking?

Back in England, it was late Spring, but I wasn't feeling the warmth seeing as there was hardly any body fat left on me. I'd lost over two stone. Like always, I went full circle and bumped into members of the HGA crew immediately after arriving back in Bristol. They recited the tale of when two of them had a recent lucky find. They'd found an abandoned rucksack mysteriously dumped in a shop doorway at the top of Park Street. It just so happened to contain £4,500 in '20s and '50s. A fortune to a couple of homeless blokes obtained in a spontaneous act. They got on the first train to London and went on a jolly. A new record had been set with that find, and that story became part of Bristol street folklore.

You find the best things when you're not looking for them…

Chapter 13

Working-class tramps

The ground was hit running once back in England. I commenced things by doing cash in hand painting and decorating jobs to get the loan for the flight back paid off. It took a month or so. In the meantime, I'd drifted back into Bristol's transient cycle by first sleeping rough (what you do when you've got nowhere else to go) then inevitably ending up back in squat land. I'd once chosen this life, but now it was choosing me.

The South-East Asian trip had taken my personal hardcorenes off the scale, and I was feeling it. People kept on commenting on how much weight I'd lost. It took the rest of the year to get back to full strength again. In truth, various parts of that episode had scared me, and it wasn't something that I'd like to repeat. Interesting times as the Chinese would say. Though I wholeheartedly believe that we grow through adversity. You always learn more through the tough times.

Besides I'd come back with plenty of amusing tales to tell. I'd only been gone for a few months though it felt more like years. And now I'd become very intolerant of people who whinged about how hard they had it. Perhaps that was a harsh judgment. But the way I saw it if you were packing a few extra pounds, had a roof over your head, access to running water and weren't in any sign of physical danger, then you weren't doing too badly at all. Over there the line of bums were all skin and bones, and that's nearly what I'd become. I got annoyed at the sight of seeing food wasted and got infuriated seeing the same thing happen to water. There were plenty of things that I didn't take for granted now.

Things never changed much back here. After all that I was right back to where I'd started. But by now I'd joined the ranks of the 'old-timers', the 'Dad's Army' of squatters. Before, I'd been one of the eldest now I was the youngest as they were in their 40's and 50's. Then I allied myself with a squatting crew of musicians, who'd come down from Norfolk the year before they merged with the Spanish contingent. They played at pub gigs around the city, bringing new and fresh energy to the scene. Their building also served as the place where they put on gigs at least once a week and held one part as their practice studio, soundproofing the walls with carpet.

They say that you can judge a man by the company he keeps, so that indicated me as a cross between a bohemian rebel and somebody who'd been doing this for just a little bit too long. Though in truth, I was never part of anyone's crew except my own. When it all went belly up, which it inevitably did, I was back to enduring intermittent periods of sleeping rough.

There was one place that I reserved for such occasions, and that was underneath a bridge right at the start of Burwell Wood. I'd walk up the footpath then squeeze through a gap in the fence and down an Embankment. That led to a freight railway line. It only had 1 or 2 trains running along it per day, one in the evening and perhaps one in the morning. Being in a valley meant that I was very well sheltered from the elements and no one ever came down here. The bridge and its walls were constructed from stone, which ticked the physiological box of being in firm surroundings. I called this place 'the bolt hole' as it's where I'd duck into for a night's sleep whenever the situation proved to be adverse.

When the seemingly never-ending freight, train clanked its way through at night I'd roll to the other side to be several metres away from the track. Surely the driver would have seen me, then radioed through and reported this to his depot manager – if anything for my own safety. But no, this never happened. If I'd been a bit late with getting up in the morning, then I'd see a gang of track workers coming down dressed brightly in orange. We'd play a game of pretending not to notice each other. In all fairness, they could have told me to clear off as I was trespassing on Network Rail property. A month went past until the foreman of the track workers finally approached.

"How you doing mate, you alright? Just to give you the heads up that we're going to be working here over the weekend and our project manager will be down, so if you wouldn't mind excusing yourself and finding somewhere else. Because I don't want you to get into trouble", he said emphatically.

"Yeah, no worries, mate", I replied.

Back in the city centre, another curious phenomenon had occurred. Bristol had long been a city that attracted wealthy students and that year they'd started blowing coke up their noses like there was no tomorrow. But inevitably not all of it made it up their nostrils and baggies would regularly get dropped while they were in an inebriated state. The packages would get spotted and picked up by the HGA crew who were out on patrol on a Friday and Saturday night before the street cleaners turned up. After a frustrating night of not finding much money, they'd be back off to their tents to go and chop up lines. Funding their gambling addictions had inadvertently led to developing cocaine habits for free.

"I've just found this on the floor on Park street. What is it?" one of them asked me excitably one evening.

"I'd stop flashing that about if I were you; it's enough to get you a prison sentence", I cautioned.

For in his hand was half an ounce of Cocaine that some unlucky punter had dropped. It had a street value of £1,100. We had a good time that weekend.

It wasn't all fun and games, however. Up until now, you've probably thought of most rough sleepers as people slugging away on a can of Special Brew slumped out in a doorway who nobody would employ. And you'd be right! However, there was a small but significant minority who were still able to work. And I became one of them. Claiming dole money just wasn't worth the hassle when you were sleeping out. They'd try to make you do stupid courses that you had no interest in, and the low amount of money wasn't going to make a change to your situation. Free food places and finding stuff on the street is all well and good, but it's a dead-end existence.

When in this situation, I could only manage to work part-time, but when in a stable squat that could easily turn into full time with the added incentives that my outgoings were very low. I didn't qualify for housing assistance or ESA due to my apparent 'low need' status. So work would have to be undertaken if I wanted any shot at a better future.

I'd ring round the agencies on a Monday morning – always the best time to get a job as half the people they'll have sent down won't have turned up. So, they'll be looking for a replacement quick. 'Did I have the experience, a CSCS card and PPE?' Yes, of course, I did.

"Just text me through the details, and I'll be down there at 07.30 the following morning".

These days you didn't even need to go and see the agency, it was all done on-line, which worked massively in my favour. Everything would be e-mailed through for me to fill out, e-sign and return, not posted to an address where I didn't live. By now, I'd managed to acquire a laptop and an Android, which meant that this could be done from the comfort of the Café Nero while using their wi-fi connection. ID docs, sending all the gump off to their umbrella company, was done in the same fashion.

Then you needed to take care of hygiene. This is what 24-hour gym membership is for. I'd always have my work clothing stashed separately wrapped in several bags, so it kept clean and dry. As a litmus test, I'd purposely walk past one of the chuggers. If she pitched me, then that meant I looked respectable enough.

".… Hello, you look like a kind man".

"I'm a complete cunt when you get to know me. What's up?"

"We're trying to raise funds for Shelter. Every year thousands of people in the UK are forced to sleep rough. Can you imagine, even for one second, how awful that must be?"

Excellent.

The next morning I'd be outside a construction site, glugging down a can of energy drink before heading to the site office for the induction.

"You're the labourer, are you?" the site agent grunted with disdain.

"Alright, I've got two deliveries coming this morning, and I need all that yard cleared out".

There could be up to 200 workers on-site, and as an agency labourer, I was the lowest of the low. But here's why this occupation had to suffice given the lifestyle that I'd been caught up in; on-site I could get away with looking a bit rough or not shaving for a few days, which was always going to happen. If anything, you fitted in better. You were anonymous – just another numpty in a high vis. Nobody paid that much attention to you. There'd always be work going which could be picked up quickly without too many questions asked. Given the circumstances getting a £30,000 a year job in an office was simply out of the question.

After rising, I'd put my work boots on, thinking this must be what a prostitute feels like when she puts *her* boots on.

"Come on, suck it up, suck it up", I'd try and encourage myself.

Like a lot of people, I positively loathed my job. You shovelled shit, shifted plasterboards upstairs or pushed along a barrow full of bricks. Then I was the designated specialist in loading up the skips. Just what was it with me and fucking skips? But wherever you were whether it be sleeping underneath a bridge or living in a derelict building, the show had to go on......

"Alright mate, how are things in the plastering business?" that's about as far as the conversation would get with my colleagues. Then at break time while sitting in the canteen, I'd have my copy of the Financial Times carefully concealed inside the Daily Sport, preying that the pink pages didn't poke out.

"Hometime now, boys", I'd hear at 5 o'clock.

But where was that?

Never mind. Come the following Friday I'd be back to the group of people that the government liked to describe as 'the hard-working taxpayer'. That's after I'd been paid my wages via some mysterious umbrella company that decided I was self-employed, so I had to pay both class 2 and class 4 contributions. Then they'd take their £18 cut for the privilege. This was no different from foraging stuff off the street or going through supermarket skips for food. You did what you had to do for survival. Except this method came with a lot less dignity. To quote Bear Grylls, *'survival is rarely pretty'*.

If you were working, then why couldn't you afford to go and rent a place? I hear you cry. Simple. The workflow was inconsistent; it was rare that it was full-time work. The longest time that I stayed on a single site was six weeks. Such was life in the gig economy where you didn't know if you were working from one day to the next. The cost of a standard one-bedroom flat in that area was £800 a month, with bills on top you could be looking at close on to a grand. So that's over £2,000 you're going to have to upfront to a landlord and do you think he's going to accept you when you're on a zero-hours contract getting paid not far off the minimum wage. It was my circumstances that had led me into low grade, precarious work, and now it was that that kept me there. Besides, it takes more than money to dig yourself out of a hole; you're so disenfranchised from mainstream society that it's a long way back.

I looked at my counterparts around me. Builders labourers are the second most likely group by occupation to commit suicide. (Farmers who have access to firearms beat them.) Yes, you guessed it; I could tell from the other labourer's teeth that they had substance abuse issues. Sometimes they'd just let something slip. For example, one guy innocently mentioned the words 'dry-house'. That's a place where they put recovering homeless alcoholics. Few other people would have taken notice of that comment, but it told me a whole story.

Or one assignment when we were doing a rip out the supervisor was gossiping about my colleague (who I'd worked with before) who clearly had mental health problems.

"I saw him walking down Whiteladies road at 8 o'clock last evening. He was still in his work stuff, so he can't have gone home like he said he did. I reckon he was up Clifton Downs perving".

He then went on to mention that he wore the same clothes every day and sprayed himself liberally with deodorant.

Straightaway this indicated to me that he was homeless, probably living in a tent.

One day I was sat outside the Arnolfini, an arty place where we went to charge our electrical devices and use their wi-fi. I was there with one of my former squatting colleagues, Nick. We called him 'the Silver Fox'. We were discussing the merits of what I'd just mentioned. When his squatting days had been over, he'd first gone back to living on the street but managed to get a full-time job as a truck driver.

"How challenging was that?" I asked.

"Not a problem".

I knew this feeling. Once you got into doing your job, you began to forget about your circumstances and were just a guy at work.

Nick had then made his camp in a carefully concealed location up on Clifton Downs and stayed in that job for over a year, only leaving when the company switched depots. That duration included the Winter from when the 'Beast from the East came'.

"One of the other bloke's tents collapsed because there was so much snow on it."

"What was your cover story?" I asked.

"I told them that I was house-sitting for a friend while he was away. But really, I wanted them to know what a hero I was for living in a tent and still managing to do the job. If they found out the truth, then I'd probably have been fired on the spot".

The thing is having a job won't necessarily save you.

"The reason why we choose to live like this is that it's easy, well at least for blokes like us who don't have habits".

He was right; sometimes, this life was just a little bit too easy – that's why I'd become trapped in it.

"Have they got sockets free in there yet?" he asked one of the HGA crew.

"It's looking pretty full".

"Let's go in anyway – maybe they'll all fuck off when they see that the working class are coming" he scoffed.

GREG LYNN

On those homeless charity fundraising posters, they'll always use the stereotypical image of a sad, dishevelled bloke, sat down on a pavement with his dog. (If you ask me, its people like that that give us all a bad name!) But this is what they don't tell you: the nations rough sleepers could be the person you ring up in a call centre, the one carrying a load of plasterboards on a construction site, or the man delivering your bathroom furniture. It might just be the guy sat next to you at work.

When I didn't have to undertake any of that business, and with time on my hands, I did a lot of reading and self-education: politics, economics, business, international and current affairs. I gobbled up book after book, whether they'd be brought from the library or sat in Waterstones for a couple of hours. I was then watching tonnes of documentaries on YouTube. I developed something of an obsession with the global financial system. Psychology was another one of my big interests: why we do the things that we do.

Growing up, I never had much of an education. School taught me how to read and write, but that was about it. I left when I was 16. Couldn't wait to get out of there. So learning about stuff that was important and how the world really worked became something of an addiction for me. Wanting to research how we were heading towards a cashless society or how a third of jobs were due to be done by robots in the future became a compelling need.

Back in squat land, I'd been caught up in a tedious cycle of going from one building to the other. Court papers being pinned on the door were a regular feature. Worryingly, Bristol Civil Justice centre was becoming my second home.

I'd sit down in court looking bemused while someone was there chatting shit to the judge.

"Mr Lynn, do you have anything to add to this?"

"Nothing further, ma'am", I'd sigh.

268

The thing about squatting is that even with the most favourable circumstances, it's always going to go wrong in the end because of factors that are outside of your control. It's always a case of square 1 to square 2, square 1 to square 2. A glamorous, alternative lifestyle? Bollocks. It's only slightly better than sleeping rough and can come with a colossal amount of hassle.

Matters came to a head in May of 2017. We got served with an IPO (intern possession order) on the pub that we were occupying. That meant that we had to be out in 24 hours otherwise we'd be committing a criminal offence even though we'd been there for nine months. This always leads to a chaotic ending while the place gets ransacked out of everything you need. This is often why a squat looks like a bomb has hit it after it's vacated. It was all featured on that programme *'nightmare tenants and slum landlords'* I'd got the business of packing up down to a fine art and could get it done in under half an hour with depressing efficiency.

Somebody had the bright idea of moving to a warehouse on the Fishponds road. I wasn't keen on the idea. For a start, it was right on one of the busiest artery routes out of Bristol, not the quiet, tucked away location that I preferred. There was a tonne of controversy over the site as McDonald's wanted to knock it down and turn it into a drive-thru against strong local opposition. It was officially owned by one of the companies in the McDonalds franchise.

Straight away, the omens weren't right. The locals were very twitchy about this building, right from the start. Our presence didn't endear them as they feared that having a bunch of squatters in could undermine their campaign process. Having the police turn up because they think it's a burglary in progress isn't uncommon, but as paranoia was high, they *kept* on calling the cops on us. We'd walked right into a hornet's nest with this one. In the kitchen, I'd stumbled across some papers which indicated that a builder's merchant had a legal right to the property. I didn't know anything about this lot. Who were they? That dark sense of foreboding engulfed me once again, and I went off to bed, feeling decidedly uneasy.

GREG LYNN

****

I was suddenly awoken by a loud, thumping noise coming from outside. Agitated cries were ringing through the warehouse.

"Smack.....smack", a big black man was attempting to smash his way through the double-glazed glass at the front door. It cracked but wouldn't budge. In total there were eight bulky men stood outside, brandishing batons and cans of CS spray, their faces covered with balaclavas. They lined up as if this was a military operation. Things were about to get nasty. Were we going to get beaten to a pulp just like that front door? It was 4 am. Everybody's immediate thought was that this was a group of vigilantes. I had a different suspicion. Recently, there had been a dodgy bailiff firm (who shall remain nameless) that were going around doing aggressive evictions without a court order. This is illegal. By actioning ambush attacks like this, you can put both parties in danger and even members of the public.

"Greg, call the police!"

I fumbled for my phone then gave Avon and Somerset constabulary a running commentary of what was going on. Now they were having a go at forcing up the shutter doors. Could they be coming through the skylight? Nope. There was a flimsy gate at the back which we never got around to securing. They'd found the weak spot and would be in within a matter of minutes. That sinking, vulnerable feeling hit the pit of my stomach.

"The most important thing is that you keep yourself safe", said the WPC on the line.

He finally squeezed through. It was like watching a pantomime when the villain suddenly springs from behind the curtain.

"Identify yourselves!" I demanded.

"Get out, get the fuck out!" he bellowed.

The warehouse filled with body armoured men in dark clothing. Yup, it was indeed who I suspected. This eviction wasn't going to be as easy as they thought, so they menacingly aimed their batons and CS cans at people's faces. A sharp atmosphere of danger rippled across the place. This was worse than the jungle!

One of our group had picked up a shovel and was brandishing it at them out of fear more than aggression.

"Don't you hurt me!" he cried.

He ran off and locked himself in the kitchen. I hoped he didn't manage to find the sharp knives draw. It's in situations like these when you find out what people are truly made of. Someone else was crying. Stefan was whinging.

"Son, you need to calm…. down. That's it, start taking deep breaths", Nick, 'the silver fox' said soothingly to one of the bailiffs who was clearly out of his depth.

The scene was hilarious as it was frightening.

"Alright mate, can I see your court order please?", I said to the one who appeared to be in charge.

"It must have fallen out of my pocket when I was on my way inside. I'll show you outside".

"Make sure you do", I replied firmly.

He never did, of course, because it didn't exist.

The 'Dad's Army' of squatters admitted defeat, collected their belongings and hobbled out through the shutter doors. We went and decamped at a nearby associates house to de-brief.

"It was our stupid fault for not securing the back properly", the silver fox said shaking his head.

He got up and played Grandad by making everyone a cup of hot sweet tea. The adrenalin was still pumping through my fingertips as I clutched the mug

"That's it, I'm through!" we collectively grunted in turn.

"He has a good perspective on this", Stefan said, pointing at me.

"We stay in squats and go down free-food places; the whole time our lives go nowhere".

Yeah, it was time to get out. I lodged a complaint against the bailiff company via my solicitor. Yes, I even had my own solicitor at this point. His secretary always remembered how I took my coffee. A friend of mine jokingly referred to me as 'Bristol's chief' squatter.

"No, I'm not; I just sweep up and make the tea", I insisted.

"Oh, come on, Greg, of course, you are".

But some battles aren't worth fighting. In truth, the bailiff company had done me a huge favour. I turned my back on squat land. I just wanted to get on with my life. It's at this age that you realise you're not going to live forever.

I became a lodger down in upmarket North Somerset and went back to work full time. Now I was located out of the bullshit, but only a 20-minute bus ride away from the action. But living a life of quiet mediocrity was never going to be for me. I needed more exciting prospects to aspire. And who should I bump into at this point but Salim. He had a nice little hustle going on. A landlord that he knew had asked him to manage one of his properties in return for a free room. That meant he could claim benefits while he conducted his other enterprises. Being the shrewd businessman that he was he'd saved up quite nicely. He'd taken the idea of a squat into a legitimate residential building. We shared the same ethos: keep it a fun place where people can hang out, meet and express themselves, but keep the dodgy cunts out (there were plenty of them out there) and run a tight ship.

I walked in there one afternoon to catch him having a heated discussion with one of his housemates.

".... As much as I love you, Salim, you talk about my girlfriend's vagina again I *will* hit you!"

We built a bonfire in the back garden out of all the left-over wood. There's something about the sight of a bonfire which makes everybody turn up. All sat around the fire, telling stories until 4 am. It was this natural community feel that I liked. Salim and I reminisced about our travelling adventures. I was getting itchy feet again. Intrepid travelling is addictive – once you've started, you don't want to stop. But it had to be different. I didn't want it to be just another international pikey mission.

Qualifying as a TEFL teacher was, of course, the obvious choice. I'd heard you could make up to $24 an hour in Vietnam. Well, that sounded a dam sight better than being a £9 an hour labourer. If I didn't do something proactive, then I was going to stay where I was. With that in mind, I enrolled in the course. Most of the other people on it had just graduated from Bristol University (the archetypal posh kids) and didn't know what to do with themselves. They asked me what I did.

"I work on a building site, love. I shift stuff around and shovel shit".

It was this determination for self-improvement that meant I nailed the course in 4 weeks and got an 87% pass with distinction. Perhaps I was destined for better things, after all. Salim offered a cautionary tale.

"Greg, I can see you doing everything else, but I can't see you doing that".

But for the first time, a genuine feeling of optimism and the sign of making real progress was motivating me. These days I vowed to become a better person. I could go on about how things were the fault of the Tory government and their austerity program or my upbringing. But this is something that every homeless person should come to realise:

You're……. the……fucking……. problem!

A member of the HGA crew who'd by now been housed said that I could come and stay with him rent-free while I saved money. I was back to kipping on someone's sofa. But my mind had gone into complete tunnel focus, as ever with a relentless obsession. I couldn't decide on the itinerary though.

"You should go to India", Salim advised.

Never thought about that one.

The flight to Mumbai got duly booked. Maybe I could fit in Nepal as well. Like always I wasn't going to have enough money to be going with. But that's just the way it was. There was only one more thing to do.

Over 12 years previously I'd sat on the steps of St. Pauls Cathedral clutching court documents in my hand while I waited to get adjudged bankrupt. Since then I'd never had a proper bank account, just a Post Office one or with Bristol Credit Union. But even they had shut down their current accounts, so I had to go in there and physically draw out money. It was like something out of the 1970s, a complete pain in the arse when you were working as they were open for a few hours a day and even worse when I was working away.

I needed a proper bank account to conduct international operations. But would they give me one? It was the one thing I'd never managed to blag before as they were so hot on the proof of address, but now I had official tax documents. I was sat at their branch in the poshest part of town – Clifton. A good omen, surely. I held my breath while she did the credit check, thinking what about this? What about that?

"Yes, you've scored the highest you can. So no problem at all, we'll get everything sent out to you".

What? How was that possible? If only you knew, love! Finally, back to the world of on-line banking, credit card offers and 24-hour ATM access. I was becoming a *real* person. This is probably something you've taken for granted. But trust me; if you don't have a bank account in today's society, you become a non-human.

Salim had also embarked on his travel adventures, and we wished him well. I was pleased for him until the next day I got a text.

"Just been chucked off the plane, innit".

He'd got as far as Oslo when his fiery temper had got the better of him. Naturally, he was whinging and thinking about turning back, but managed to rebook a seat at high cost.

"*Now calm the fuck down, do your seat belt up and be a good boy for the stewardess*", I texted back.

He was despatched to Bangkok.

I said my goodbyes.

"This is the most organised that I've seen you by a mile", said Nicki.

My flight left for Bahrain to connect to Mumbai, the GF006. It was that very same flight that I'd send my air freight on to the middle east when I was an upwardly mobile 19-year-old working for an Import-Export co. Then I remembered what my boss had said.

"*I know you're going to leave here, go off and make millions*".

Chapter 14

The life of a millionaire

"*W*hen you get there, your eyes are going to pop out. It's going to be like nothing you've ever seen before in your life*"*, somebody had advised me about India before I went.

And then there I was at Lokmanya Tilak station in Bombay (everybody still called it Bombay) staring at the multitude of people in front of me. Yes, it was like watching a movie that had been directed in the 1800s. Vast crowds of passengers were stood around the pillars, but didn't look like they were going anywhere soon. The others were sprawled out on mats. They'd set up a semi-permanent base. Many didn't believe in using the overhead walkways, so leapt across the track to save time.

The plane had descended through a thick cloud of smog. Then landing at the airport, the massive inequality that existed within the country became apparent: a cluster of skyscrapers to the left, an enormous shantytown to the right. The smell of rotting garbage was overpowering. On every street corner, skinny kids would approach, begging with their hands out. It was a genuinely disturbing sight. I'd woken up at 3 am in the hot and sticky hotel thinking, *'Where am I? What am I doing here? Who am I?'*

I thought that buying a ticket would be a straightforward business. You went up to the information centre, asked when the next train to Gorakhpur was, then purchased a ticket. But no. I first had to fill in forms declaring that I wasn't pregnant. They didn't believe in queuing. When speaking to the guy at the counter, it was common practice for people to barge in front of me. The sleeper carriages were full for that train. The furthest I could get was Jabalpur. Where was that?

The trains were enormously long. It was never clear which platform you had to be on. Eventually, it creaked its way out. Usually, I liked to travel by public transport in a foreign city to get a feel for it, but on this occasion, I'd opted for a taxi, feeling like I'd pussied out. Then it became apparent why. The suburban line trains that passed us had people hanging off the door handles they were so full. If I'd attempted to board with my rucksack, then I would have been shoved onto the track.

My fellow passengers were a chatty bunch. We sat cramped together and played cards. People came along the aisle selling just about every type of refreshment imaginable: samosas, popcorn and Chai tea.

"Chai.......chai......chai", a seller would chime every time the train stopped.

I tried a cup. It tasted sweet and gingery. I looked out of the window as the countryside dashed past us. It wasn't until the early hours of the morning that the train pulled into Jabalpur. This was a nervy moment as I didn't have any accommodation booked. Would there be anything in the immediate vicinity and would there even be a cash machine here? I didn't even know which part of India I was in. As expected, there were plenty of dodgy people lurking around the station. Being a lone traveller always makes you stick out, which is something that I don't like. There was an old guy in a white robe and a walking stick muttering at me.

"I take you to a cheap guesthouse. Only 200 Rupees".

"How far is it?" I asked.

"2 maybe 3 kilometres".

There was no way I was letting some random person lead me off into the dark no matter how cheap it was.

"I'm going there", I replied, relieved to see the site of a hotel straight ahead of me.

"That one very expensive, 2,000 Rupees."

"I don't care", I marched ahead with the stupid old git following me.

Whenever you're in a situation that feels threatening, head to wherever you see immediate safety, fortunately, the reception was still entertaining custom. Even better, I could have the place for a full 24 hours with breakfast included. 2,400 Rupees, not cheap, but didn't break the bank either.

"Very good, sir. We show you to your room".

As he opened the door, my eyes lit up. It was massive, more like your own apartment. My private bathroom. A flat-screen telly in the corner. A king-size bed. Do you know when the last time was that I slept in a proper bed? It was years ago. I leapt onto it, and the calm sensation washed over me. It's incredible how much these differences make. Now I could think straight. Okay, I was in Central India, about halfway to the Nepal border.

The next day I did a little more research. According to the website, the border crossing was thwarted with problems. If you attempted to cross at night, there was the risk of being confronted by gangs of local thugs who made you buy expensive transport packages against threats of violence. And yes – the threats could be carried out. Okay, so don't do it at night. Head straight through it asap.

I was still to get my head around the complex Indian railway ticketing system. You had first to place your reservation at the desk, go on to some sort of waiting list, then had to find another desk which was right on the other side of the station where you eventually collected your ticket. The next departure wasn't until midnight, and the trains never ran on time.

Some people might consider a night in a sleeper car to be an exotic adventure. But not me. It was like a more colourful version of the night shelter on wheels – and it stank worse. Getting off the three-tier bunk bed was too much hassle, so I stayed in it for the whole duration. I was the only Westerner in sight.

"You are English, why don't you just get on a plane?"

Oh yeah, like that would be fun.

The weather turned decidedly cooler on our approach to Gorakhpur. I was confronted by dense fog as soon as I alighted. This was Northern mountainous air.

"Sunauli, Sunauli!" the bus conductor cried.

Onwards to what travel literature described as one of the craziest border crossings on the planet. It was still another kilometre to the Nepal side.

"Yo broth, I'll give you 100 Rupee to take me up there", I said to a passing rickshaw driver.

GREG LYNN

He peddled as we passed the hundreds of people going about their daily business. Danger over. These paranoid travel blogs, they didn't know what danger was. The violent touts had turned out to be quite friendly and helpful. There was a half an hour wait in the little shed while the immigration officers finished their lunch and then I was in Nepal. The fresh mountain air blew across my face. It had that distinct earthy smell to it. Right, that minute Nepal became my favourite country to date. There was one last extraordinarily bumpy and uncomfortable bus ride to Pokhara. I arrived in the dead of night and awoke the proprietor of the Sunflower guesthouse.

It was a beautifully warm sunny Saturday morning when I awoke. After a mad dash right across India, there was one whole week to do whatever the hell I liked in far more peaceful surroundings. And that involved lounging about by lake Phewa. And then I saw them. Snow-capped in the distance – the Himalayas!

The local Nepalese were a tough bunch. They were one of the few countries never to get invaded and would repeatably tell me so. They smoked their spliffs with rolled-up newspaper instead of Rizla, that's how tough they were. They were very friendly, polite and humble people.

"Namaste", they'd call out, and I'd sit down and have a Gurkha beer with them.

The pennies had to be watched, but there was so much to do here. I couldn't come to Nepal and not go on a mountain treck. If you were gone for any longer than a day or were entering one of the conservation areas, then you needed a permit off the government. It was tempting to head off with a bottle of water and a compass. But I didn't want to get myself lost up there. So, for the first time, I figured it would be best to employ the services of a guide.

"I want the toughest one-day trek that you've got", I insisted.

"We've got this one going to Australia Camp in the Annapurna range. But you might not be able to do it in one day".

"Come on. Let's go. Chali-chali, chali-chali!" I said to the guide as we commenced the climb and headed up into the clouds. If there's one thing that I love, it's mountain trekking - that moment when you look down and see clouds. I wanted to come back here and do the whole 15-day hike to base camp. Fuck it; maybe I'd even reach the summit of Everest itself. Any old Tom, Dick and Harry seemed to be doing it these days. Right now, just about anything seemed possible.

"Okay, but next time quit the smoking", my guide advised.

By the way, smokers tend to fare better at high altitude because their brains are used to be oxygen-deprived. It was a shame to be leaving Nepal. Why hadn't I come here first? But Delhi was where my flight to Cambodia left, and there was a schedule to keep. So I headed back down there.

India wasn't high up on my list; it was dirty, crowded and chaotic. I looked out at the shanty towns as the train rumbled its way to Jaipur with a sense of shock then suddenly remembered that they were better than some of the places that I'd squatted.

"You see how the poorest people in India live", said one of my fellow passengers.

"Yes, but some people live like this in England too", I murmured.

He didn't believe me. Their only experience of the Western world was through watching American movies. So they thought we all lived in big houses, drove around in Ferraris and opened up suitcases stuffed full of cash.

This was Jaipur, the capital of Rajasthan – the nation's most colourful and flamboyant state. I readied myself when stepping off at the station, knowing that I was about to get flanked by the local hustlers.

"Hello, my friend. Where are you from?"

Now they were going to ask me if I was looking for a hotel (always pretend that you've got a reservation if you don't) then they'll try and get you on the whole guided tour of the city thing.

"You come with me on my tuk-tuk, I take you to cheap hotel".

I was polite at first as I could emphasise what living a hand to mouth existence was like; you had to hustle by whatever means necessary to survive. But really, I just wanted this chancer to fuck off. The place that looked the most inviting jumped out.

"No. That one very expensive – two maybe 3 thousand Rupee".

"Bargain, I'll see you later".

Here was a paradox. Living a fly by the seat of your pants existence meant that when it felt too sketchy, I got pushed into a semi flash hotel.

"Very good, sir. I'll take you to your room".

I could get used to this. Spread out on the soft sheets, raiding the complimentary coffee, flicking the remote through the numerous channels. Going on-line to conduct my on-line banking. Could the road ahead finally become more opulent after years of living life as a member of the Lumpen Precariat (the lowest social demographic possible).

A couple of days later, when I was outside puffing away, a young lad wandered past.

"Hey, it's James Bond!" he continued with some further smoozing then asked:

"I'd like to invite you for a Chai tea".

I've always got my defence guard up when travelling alone, but he seemed innocuous enough.

"Yeah, why not".

A moment after sitting down at the table, two other guys suddenly looked up in surprise.

"You were the one at the station the other day; you were very paranoid".

His mates were the railway station hustlers. Was this all some elaborate scam?

"Well, you know, can't be too careful when you're travelling in a foreign land".

I feigned complete nonchalance while munching the samosas and gulping the Chai tea that they'd laid on while amusing them with tales. This was the thing: Indians were naturally very extrovert and gregarious people. They always wanted a picture taken with you as if you were a Rockstar, and I was happy to oblige. (It was a definite step up from being handed a cash donation because you looked so dishevelled.) I always deemed it proper etiquette to get to know the locals – you were in their country after all. In South-East Asia, you often got approached by somebody purporting to be your new best friend. But they were blatantly trying to scam you. Were these guys hustlers or just being friendly? Or more likely, an odd mix of the two.

The plot thickened the next day.

"Hey, I know you, you stayed at the Polo Inn for three nights, and now you're staying in Arya Niwas", said a tuk-tuk driver who I'd never seen before in my life.

He'd correctly recited my whereabouts. The only other time this had happened was on my first day in Barbados when I'd turned up alone in a Ted Baker suit. My newfound friends were sat down, having a fag break outside the station entrance.

"Hey, safe Allie, safe Janjid".

I'd grown up in a very multicultural area and had gone to school with plenty of Indians, so mixing with them felt like nothing new even if it was in a strange country.

"How's business?"

"Slow. The trains carrying Western tourists hadn't arrived yet".

These kids were sharp. They knew what time the punters would arrive by flights from Europe and North America. They'd stopover in Jaipur first before heading to Agra where one of the most popular tourist sites in the world was located – The Taj Mahal.

"Oh, come on fellas, remember, there's one born every minute".

The next day was to be my final one in India.

"Where are you going?" a Tuk-Tuk driver asked me at the station entrance.

"Hell, I'll see you there".

"You want a general ticket?" the guy at the counter said, astounded".

"Yeah, it's the cheapest one, isn't it?"

A general ticket means that you don't have a reserved seat, so you're going to be packed in with every man and his goat. Westerners aren't supposed to do this. Even Michael Palin had travelled in first going across the sub-continent.

"Just take a seat up there", another passenger said, pointing to the luggage rack while I looked around for a place to stand.

So, I joined the ranks of luggage rack class where there was a certain etiquette to be obeyed. Firstly, you had to take your shoes off and converse to whoever was sat next to you while sipping your Chai tea. The 7-hour journey would be just about bearable.

"And what is your good name, sir?".

"Gregory, from England?.

"And yours".

"Ravinder".

"Good to meet you, Ravinder".

"Tell me, how does one get to leave his own country?" he asked with fascination.

For 98% of Indians will never get to fly on an aircraft. I looked down at the now dangerously overcrowded carriage and thanked my lucky stars that I was up here.

With a few hours to kill, I mooched around Delhi, beginning to feel apprehensive about arriving back in Cambodia. Would they let me back in after last time? In a bid to appear respectable I went to a roadside, open-aired barber for a cutthroat shave. He embedded my face with layer after layer of grey gunk. I looked at the reflection in the mirror and figured that's what I'd look like in the morgue. He rounded things off with an aggressive shoulder massage. Now I was ready to face the business end of the trip.

"Thud, thud", the magic sound of the exit stamp at the airport. That was two countries I'd made it out of without having to sleep rough in them. I was on a roll!

India was the most challenging country that I'd ever been to, a test for any traveller. It was so vast and complicated with so many defined cultures that I'd often had difficulty in getting my head around it. Now I was heading to more familiar territory. But there was a problem: I'd be arriving in the 'Kingdom of Wonder' with just 100 bucks. Enough to take care of immediate arrival, but then what? Far from being freaked out by this, I put my thinking cap on. Take notice of what's around you. Flashes of inspiration can come from anywhere.

I was in transit in Kuala Lumpur with a few hours to kill. So was browsing through the web looking at nothing in particular when someone's

Facebook profile suddenly popped up. The pictures showed a girl I used to live with. It depicted her on a beach in Koh-Rong, a group of islands off the Cambodian coast known for its partying. That's it, Koh Rong; a place full of trust fund kiddies blowing their not so hard earnt money on partying. Surely, they'd have a job for some hard-up chancer selling them the tickets to the events?

As we descended into Phnom Penh, the rusty tin roofs of houses came into view, and the reverse thrust whooshed as we took our final approach. A sudden burst of adrenalin overtook my sleepy mood. I wasn't going to lay down and almost die this time. It was time to hustle, even if that meant getting my hands a bit dirty. The Indian 'never say die' entrepreneurial spirit witnessed had been an inspiration. The flight/fight response triggered was on the fight side. If you fret and panic, you'll only create your own screwed up existence.

There was to be no hanging around. I bombed straight for the coast. At Sihanoukville, I boarded the fast ferry. A policeman came on board. That was strange.

"Listen up, everyone. Very important. You all need to put your life jackets on…. now! You understand?" he said firmly then stepped off.

The engines revved up, and we zoomed off into the clear blue sea. It began as a fun ride at an amusement park. First, the passengers squealed in delight. There was another zoom of acceleration, and the ferry bounced along the water, hitting the sea with a colossal thud every time. The vessel shook and vibrated. People were getting covered in salty water at every crash. It roared along at over 40 knots. A Frenchman demanded the skipper to slow down. He retorted with something in Khmer. A Cambodian lady's face crumpled into fear as she overheard.

"He say…. he say, if he does not drive this boat fast then we're going to capsize".

A ripple of panic spread across the boat. If we did capsize then over half the passengers could be knocked unconscious. Yes, there are sharks in the Gulf of Thailand. Folk at the front were vomiting. Me? I was quite enjoying the ride. At the first stop, most of the punters prematurely departed. Welcome to the 'Wild East' folks.

****

"Are you a little bit crazy? Lyndsey the American woman I was talking to said with a sultry look in her eyes.

"Why do you ask?"

"Because almost everybody who comes down here wanting to work has to be a little bit crazy".

"If I say yes, will you give me a job?"

"Here's a question for you: If you opened your fridge/freezer door one day and found a baby penguin in there, what would you do?"

"Is this a test to see if I'm mad?"

"No. But your answer will tell me what sort of person you are?"

"I'd say, look little penguin it's no good you being in here. You need to find food, water and shelter, and other Penguins to hang out with. Be free".

"Yay", she high-fived.

"How cute. That means you're a carer".

Trapped in paradise. I'd done a whole sweep of the island approaching every outlet that had a sign saying, *'Western staff required'*. From what I could gather the deal was you could get a job with them selling tickets to the events that took place on the island on a commission-only basis. Also, in return, you'd receive basic accommodation, food and a few drinks thrown in. That would be the perfect gig for some guy or gal in their early twenties, but for someone my age that was going to look just plain weird. Seriously, would you buy a ticket to a happening beach party off someone who almost looked old enough to be your dad?

From the exchange mentioned above, you can guess that I was finding these lot a little too flaky and airy-fairy to be dealing with. Anyway, I'd conducted my own due diligence because I was genuinely curious about how the island functioned. 90% of it had got leased to the Chinese government. China had reached its claws right into this country and had started pumping serious money into it. Much had changed in the last two years since I'd first been. Sihanoukville had gotten transformed into a Las Vegas of the East. The Chinese gambling obsession had become evident. Major construction was going on in Phnom Penh. Everywhere you looked cranes were lifting LTJ's. The once potholed roads had brand new Toyotas driving along their smooth surfaces. It was rapidly becoming developed. But at what cost? Many of the restaurants and bars here were financed and run by the Turkish Mafia.

By now I'd had to resort back to being 'Jungle Jim' (I couldn't help myself!) and stuffed my rucksack in the thick bushes, marking the spot with an 'X' and leaving a pile of stones there. The only difference being that I had to check the bushes for snakes first.

I was going to have to make money the old-fashioned way – by getting into debt. I waited till sunset (so the sun wouldn't reflect off my lap-top screen) skanked the wi-fi code off one of the bars, sat close enough to be in range, then undertook the unfortunate necessary. After a painful wait, I headed back up to the capital. Phnom Penh – I loved this town. If Bristol had become my UK base, Berlin European headquarters then Phnom Penh served as my Asian headquarters. An international drifter always needs a place where he's got an affinity to, where it's safe and familiar. The fluorescent pink and blue lights illuminated the pavement as I sat eating fried noodles with a dodgy fried egg on top. If only they could sort out the food here, then it would be a utopia.

My days of staying in backpackers' hostels were thankfully becoming a fading memory. For just a few bucks more a night, I could have my own guesthouse room, and that made a whole world of difference. Now I could pace up and down in peace while plotting things through.

I scanned the websites and job boards for TEFL jobs and made half-hearted job applications. In theory, you needed a degree which had always been a cause for concern. But I'd been assured by contacts that this wouldn't be a problem. I wasn't convinced. But to my surprise about half the companies wanted to interview me via Skype. This is why I'd chosen to do it here – you were on the same time zone which made things easier. It was the same as any other interview. I fluttered my big blue eyes and chatted a load of spurious bullshit. Glory be, the next day, there was a job offer in my inbox. I was to be in Hanoi in two weeks. What? This wasn't supposed to happen so quickly. Something must be amiss.

She was outlining everything I had to do to get the working visa and work permit. It looked complicated – and costly. For a start, all my documents had to be sent off to the Foreign Office back in Milton Keynes to get legalised (proven that they were real) then sent back over here. Even by airmail, they might not make it in time. There were just a few hours before the Post Office shut. I got my arse in gear. Then out of nowhere, an attractive young Chinese girl approached me on the street.

"Umm....... I have been here for Chinese New Year, but this evening I fly back to Beijing. I see you are a lone traveller and I was looking for someone to hang out with. Do you want to maybe....... go for a beer?"

This was something very unusual for a Chinese girl to do. It was the year of the Dog. Every dog has their day.......and even labourers get laid.......

"Listen, love, I'm well up for hanging out, but first I need to get to the Post Office to send these documents back to my home country. You're welcome to come with me, but be warned, I walk real fast. Then after that, I can give you all the time in the world. How does that sound?"

"Umm……. okay".

She was a 26-year-old PhD student. Obviously very bright and probably from a wealthy family. But it didn't take her long to realise she'd been caught up in Greg's mad crazy little world.

"Umm…. maybe you are too busy……so……I see you later".

Blast.

Once I'd got back, I propped up the bar at the guesthouse and recited that tale to the barman over a cold one. He looked back at me with a deadly stern expression.

"Let me tell you something", he said, leaning forward and pointing.

"……. You *always* hang out with Chinese girl. She make you lucky", he half scorned.

I had to wait around for the Ming Quan Corporation to send the job offer letter to the immigration department and then they'd send me the visa approval letter. This didn't appear until 3 hours before my flight was due to leave. They couldn't have left it any later. I grabbed it off the printer picked up my bag then flagged down the nearest tuk-tuk.

"The airport!" I stated, jumping in and running a hand through my hair.

"How much you wanna pay?"

"…….10 dollar".

We screeched through the streets of Phnom Penh as the sky turned pink, past the markets and flashing neon lights. I examined my thoughts and mood towards this venture. So, I was going to see an unknown company based on a supposed job offer to a country on the other side of the world that I'd never been to before. This all felt about as solid as a ride on a paper aeroplane. It was like when you could sense a storm before it occurs. An aircraft roared above us overhead.

"Give my love to Phnom Penh!" I shouted to the driver, slapping a hand on my chest then hopped off.

"Oh, you've only got a single ticket. I cannot let you on the plane", the guy said at the check-in counter.

"I've got one of these", I said pushing the letter over, suddenly feeling more important, elevated from tourist to business traveller.

"Ooohh", he cooed studying it.

"That's fine. Your flight boards in 1 hour".

As we took off, it felt like the scene from an aeroplane disaster movie – you know that something is going to go wrong – I was filled with a foreboding sense. The flight itinerary was impractical. It involved an all-night layover in Bangkok. There was a fierce storm all the way there. The plane skidded and slid to a halt on the runway as lightning flashed.

"Sá wátdii – kráp," I said, stepping off after trying to remember what language to speak.

Airport transit lounges and hotel rooms were my home now. This may seem a bit glamorous, but there was still the feeling of not having routes anywhere. Sleep was impossible. Instead, I was running on constant adrenalin. I busied my self tapping away on my lap-top. Before I looked at people who did this as being idiotic, now I was one of them. Not having a wi-fi connection got me clucking. Before, I'd navigated my way around a foreign city purely on instinct and taking note of the visual cues that were around. Now I slung my phone onto google directions and let my self be led up a blind alley by a robotic voice. In the past, I'd gotten a kick out of getting by with no money. Now I was positively obsessed with the stuff.

291

'Who cares if you're not going to like the job, it's all about not being poor anymore', I'd say to myself. Was this any proper progress?

There was a thick mist as we landed in Hanoi, a decidedly gloomy morning. After gaining my 3-month work visa at the airport, a driver was there to pick me up. The next thing I knew, I was stuck in front of a class of forty 7-year olds having to flail my arms around like some likeable retard.

"Hey kids, what did we all have for breakfast this morning?"

"You're too serious; you need to smile more!"

That's because I've never felt like such a bell-end in all my life. Why hadn't I remembered my own mantra? Never work with kids, animals.....or hippies! As it turned out, this was a trial lesson, and if I didn't perform, they wouldn't be offering me a contract. Of course, I didn't have a clue what I was doing, and things bombed. This was a mistake of epic proportion

"Come back tomorrow and try again. Then we'll let you know", she said after giving me a scathing critique. This wasn't a genuine job offer, but a trial shift I'd obviously failed, and this company were nothing more than a dodgy recruitment agency. I'd got sent on an international wild goose chase.

"Fuck um – I don't want anything more to do with them". I grumbled, then headed towards the nearest ATM.

I checked the balance first and struggled to make sense of the numbers blinking at me on the screen. 17,000000 VMD.

Well blow me, the gaffer was right. I *had* become a millionaire. Unfortunately, he'd never stipulated in which currency (it's 32,000 Vietnamese Dong to the pound by the way). I slid the great wad of notes in my wallet, then to celebrate this achievement marched off to a 3-star hotel. They even gave me a free upgrade. A good long sleep was called for, and the food in Vietnam was fantastic.

Armed with a clearer head, I did a little research. There was a quote from the philosopher Alain De Botton that stuck out.

THE WANDERER

'You decide to become a TEFL teacher when your life has gone wrong'.

This was a job viewed only slightly higher than flipping burgers in McDonald's. A train wreck of a career in a dubious industry. Broadly speaking, there are three types of people who do this job: those that were teachers already, graduates who didn't know what to do with themselves, then 30-somethings washed-up losers. That day I discovered that my documents had been knocked back by the Foreign Office because they didn't contain a wet ink signature. Defeated by bureaucracy.

(Yes, I could have gone off with that Chinese girl after all). Not having a degree was also a problem (You need this to get a work permit if you want to work longer than three months.) But I was here now, and this was a sticky situation.

So I did what I always did - did a runner. Yup, jumped on that train down to Ho-Chi-Minh-City as if there was a nuclear rocket up my arse. Unbeknown to me then, Salim was also in Hanoi. The journey down was going to take 44 hours, and they didn't have a sleeper carriage. But what did that matter? I was having a gay old-time downing Vodka shot with the locals. This is what travelling is all about, right?

Unfortunately, the Ming Quan Corporation didn't quite share the same view. By the time I'd got to Saigon several e-mails were informing me of what a cunt I was and reminding me that their employment guaranteed my visa here.

"If we do not hear from you within seven days, then we will be on the phone to immigration".

I e-mailed my side of the story, stating that after their somewhat critical review, I was too demoralised to go back, or even talk to them. (I'm a sensitive soul, see.) I mulled the situation over in a Saigon hotel room and attempted to think straight. So, I had no business being in Vietnam then. That was easy to resolve. Phnom-Penh was only up the road, a mere $10 bus ride away. I hopped on. But now respectability needed to be salvaged once more.

"Do you reckon you can get me a business visa?" I said to the Mr Fixit at the border.

"Hmm…. I'll try, but I can't promise anything. You'll have to come with me and state your business to the police".

"Okay, I know the crack. $45 for them and a tens for you".

He led me over.

"This is the one that wanted a business visa", he said to the Colonel in military camouflage.

He took one look at me and gave a definite nod.

"……What? Aren't you even going to take his prints?" Mr Fixit asked, dumbfounded.

He gave a single shake of his head.

"Arkun, Colonel".

They knew me by now.

Back in Phnom-Penh, I was on home territory, but it had been the most bizarre five days.

"Eh, eh my friend. What's happened this time?" a tuk-tuk driver said as he rode past.

That matter had got resolved. But now I was back to what I knew best: being a street bum in an exotic location. When it all goes wrong you deviate to what you know with alarming speed, and that saw me wandering the streets picking up every water bottle and stray cigarette that I could find. Then, of course, going to locate an abandoned truck to sleep in. The difference this time being that my associates back in England were getting a virtual running commentary of it all by e-mail. They were finding it utterly hilarious.

"It's not funny!" I protested back.

"You're living on the streets in Phnom Penh? That's hardcore!"

"So what? It's what I do".

Yup, within two days it felt like a completely normal existence. By day I hung out on the banks of the Mekong, drinking home-brewed Whiskey with the local bums and off duty hookers. By the third day, I was even getting something of a free-be off one of them. There's nothing like integrating with the locals. I was to join the ranks of the failed ex-pat crew. We sat down on the wall swapping out tails of woe. Americans were the most common nationality, and yes, they'd worked as TEFL teachers at some point or another.

One day I happened to be in conversation with a middle-aged Swede. He was sat down singing merrily, clearly a little worse for wear. He noticed I didn't share his upbeat sense of mood.

"And what is up with you. What is it with all this brooding?"

"No money", I grunted.

I gave a very rough outline of my circumstances but stated I wasn't too worried.

"Hmm, well, I think you should be, at least a little bit".

He went on to explain about his crazy young days travelling through Thailand, chasing girls and doing too many drugs.

"Drugs and sex; two things that can seriously drain your bank balance. But always I had the return ticket. If I were you, I'd think about returning and coming back when you are of…. better means. If you stay out here too long like this, then you can sink to the level of a dog when no one wants to talk to you", he cautioned.

I knew he was right.

"Come on; you are still young enough. You can go back to your country and rebuild, for you are clearly capable. Look at me; I'm the crazy one".

"I'm not sure what to do when I get back", I answered.

"Well to me it feels like you should be working in creative design, or perhaps you have some musical abilities", he encouraged.

"Really?"

"Well put it this way. I don't see you as the man digging up the ground with his drill", he said while mimicking the action.

"That was my job in England", I laughed.

"Did you enjoy it?"

"No, I hated it".

"So why did you stay in it? Did they pay you good money? Or didn't you know what else to do?"

"Because I didn't know what else to do", I confessed.

"Maybe that's not the problem. But to me, it seems as if you are walking through your life without purpose. Find your purpose", he said sincerely, returned to his alcoholic babbling then wandered off.

That night I walked over the Japanese Friendship bridge and stared at the high-rise buildings that were quickly rising. I walked right out of town. A Westerner being this far out at night looked unusual.

"Where you go?" everyone I passed asked.

"That way, to see a friend", I replied.

"I worry about you", one guy said, then rode off.

It was okay; no one was praying for me yet. Eventually, I found a derelict bit of waste ground, went right to the back and ripped all the large leaves off several shrub bushes. With enough of them, this would make a bed of leaves. As always, the two golden rules: never lay directly on the ground or in public view wherever you are. I may be crazy, but I'm not stupid. The night air was warm, and I stared up at the moon. It was a moment of contentment. Part of me didn't want to become wealthy and successful; part of me wanted to stay down here doing crazy shit like this because it *liked* it. Why do you do it? Because you like it! Success is what I feared. Failure was all I knew, and now that felt strangely safe. With great change always comes great resistance.

The next day I woke up and suddenly remembered something. It was my birthday. Thirty-seven years old. I was getting a little too old for all this.

"Fuck this shit", I grunted then sprang up.

I got myself into yet deeper debt, then immediately booked the flight back for the next day. Good old Malaysian, still doing cheap deals at the last minute. But that meant going through Kuala Lumpur once again. What was it with me and this place?

"Terima kasih"

"Sama, sama".

"Welcome to London Heathrow. The current temperature is minus 1".

Oh dear.

"I got offered a job in Vietnam, but it didn't work out", I said to UK border Force, feeling that I had to explain myself.

"Oh, no. What are you going to do now?" the officer (a pretty young blonde woman) asked sympathetically.

'Go back to right where I started", I shrugged.

I stepped out into the biting cold, still wearing shorts and t-shirt.

297

"Jesus!" it was supposed to be Spring.

I hadn't bargained for how accustomed I'd become to the baking heat. I placed my coffee on the bench, not seeing it had a slight curve. In slow motion, it slid off and spectacularly splattered over the ground.

Yup, that summed it up perfectly.

Chapter 15

Same as it ever was……

"**R**ight, I want this hole one metre deep as we're going to backfill it in afterwards".

My hands vibrated as the quango drill hammered through the concrete floor. The room quickly filled with thick dust that Friday afternoon. But another £300 in the bank.

"Yo! There's a pipe down here", I yelled to the supervisor after endless shovelling.

"I think it's dead. Just work around it but go steady".

My colleague was stood there, supervising.

"Bones! Your mate has been there grafting like fuck all afternoon. All you can do is stand there and watch. Can you go and help him? Come on; we're all done in".

Thank you, Bones. But it was more manageable when you were just giving moral support.

"Jamie, any chance you can cut out these steel girders because I keeps scraping on um and they 'urts like fuck", Bones complained.

"You're gay, you are", he scorned shaking his head and grabbed the petrol disc cutter, deliberately firing the sparks into his direction.

"Argh, you almost set my pants on fire!".

"No golden broom award for you this week".

It's a dog eat dog existence on-site sometimes and, on this occasion, Bones had to be the poodle.

This building that we were in the process of turning into luxury student apartments used to be a squat, or rather was an 'art exhibition' for one week. In other words, it had a load of crusties sat around getting munted while they daubed weird graffiti all over the wall and expressed themselves with their slogans. My path had crossed with many of these kids at one point or another. I'd been contracted in to do the rip out, so had taken great delight in taking a wrecking bar to it all. The plaster walls came crashing down, smashing into a thousand little pieces. It was a cathartic exercise that made me feel like I was ripping out my old past.

"Have a good weekend. See you Monday", I said to the site manager.

This was a question disguised as a pleasantry because I was never sure if he needed us back or not.

"See you Monday, mate. Try and get in early because we've got two skips delivered. We'll need 'em filled up asap."

I went off to Easton to meet up with my old cronies from the musician crew who were building an art studio.

Now after all that here I still am living in the concrete shed underneath a flyover, remembering that I must get my voters registration up to date.

"Oh, good for you!", was the councils' response when I told them that I was occupying one of their buildings.

That may contradict to what I said earlier, but it's just me here on my tod disconnected from what remains of 'the scene'. There's no chance of me tripping over bodies on the way out or having the door smashed in by bailiffs at 4 o'clock in the morning. In some ways, it's more stable than some places that I've rented. These days I live a very solitary existence and quietly get on with my affairs devoid of drama. Still, a man walking alone, who travelled the world in a bid to improve his lot, yet despite his best efforts always ended up right back where he started.

I'd love to say that this story has a happy ending, me walking off into the sunset with the woman of my dreams. But no. In the end – it just is......

My future looks uncertain. For the best part of this decade, I've been homeless. To give you a precise rundown, that included three years sleeping rough or living in derelict buildings across the globe, being down and out from Bristol to Phnom Penh. Around the same time was spent living in squats of varying degrees of quality. The rest of that duration was in temporary or basic accommodation. And do you know what? I'm still none the wiser why any of this happened. If someone had predicted that future beforehand, then I'd have looked at them very strangely and quickly ran off (in tears).

Do I regret any of it? Funnily enough, no. What it did provide was a set of unique experiences which wouldn't have got gained anywhere else, and that can get transferred to many other aspects. Parts of that experience were very, very grim, sometimes getting pushed to the limits of human endurance. I guess we all have a masochistic element to us. But it's still life experience; the only thing that you take with you to your grave. And let's not forget, it was also a lot of fun. This brings me back to a conversation that I had with a homeless worker. He recited his tale to me:

"I lived on the streets in London for seven years. Do you know what?..... I loved it! It's the ultimate freedom. You ain't got nobody telling you what to do. It was living life right on the edge. But then I got too old for it. I eventually got a council flat. I couldn't hack living there at first. Had to force myself to stay in for at least three nights a week. Then I'd go back out on the streets to be with my mates and the action. But I always kept that key in my pocket.......and I'm glad I kept that key".

I gave him a brief synopsis of my circumstances.

"Woah, you've been around, you should write a book", he answered enthusiastically.

So I did. This entire account got written while still being one of those homeless folks that you hear of in the media. Intermittently doing low-grade jobs, bumming free food, foraging off the street for whatever was necessary and educating tramps about the global financial system. That all took place in between me huddled over a lamp scribbling and tapping away until the early hours of the morning every day for the past six months – you know, to give it that authentic feel.

My journey sometimes meant that I saw the darker side of life. That made me battle-hardened and darkly cynical. To this day, I find it very difficult to trust people. I look over my shoulder wherever I go and always make sure the door gets locked behind me. Though, out on the road, my faith in humanity was restored. Whenever in a tight jam help would come from the least expected sources. The kindness of strangers is another curious phenomenon. We live in an age where we've become very paranoid and distrusting of those who don't look or act like us. But many strangers and passers-by chose to assist me when I didn't even speak their language.

THE WANDERER

They owed me nothing, nor would they be seeing me again. But they decided to act because they knew that helping your fellow man is what keeps a civilised society going. For this, I thank you all.

In the beginning, I promised that this wasn't all going to be about me, and I hope it wasn't. Had I been on a more comfortable ride, then the many colourful characters that came into this story would never have been met. That would have been a great privilege missed out. The sharp end of your account got told too. I've no idea where you all are now but may the magic of the road be with you.

Being homeless changes you forever. You're never the same person again. Am I a better or worse individual than I was at the start of all this? I still don't know. But one thing it did teach me is that many things aren't worth worrying about but what *is* important. Few things genuinely bother me now. But one thing that does is running out of time. Time, the most precious commodity that you have. These days I try not to waste any of it, but spend it in the most productive way possible, whether that be learning something new, keeping in shape or forging new relationships.

One motivator for all of this is because a good many people in my community who were around me at the start are no longer with us or won't have long left. Fortunately, I never developed a substance abuse habit, gained any severe physical ailments or got a criminal record which is unusual. Most surprisingly, I've still been issued with a clean bill of mental health. It's all about moving on now and arriving at a completely different sphere.

The other day when I was strolling along with the three wise tramps, one of them suddenly said,

'you do realise that by rights, none of us should be alive anymore. I don't know what it is, whether it's god, your guardian angel, whatever, but something. Something out there looks after you".

GREG LYNN

I hope so too because there's still a whole world out there and a life left to be lived. And I'm still standing. But don't try this at home, kids. Hopefully, next time I'll be sipping champagne in Business class. I'll see you down the Copacabana!

Epilogue

"**W**hat have you got to say to all those people out there still lighting barbecues and working on construction sites?" Channel 4 News asked Professor Hugh Montgomery, the professor for intensive care medicine at the UCL.

"Do you know, I've lost my temper now. This isn't about *you*. This is criminal……"

He then went through the mathematical explanation of how we were potentially doing a mighty fine job of spreading Covid-19 and ultimately crippling the NHS.

"Stop doing this. It's wrong", he sternly concluded.

And there was me thinking I was just a hard-working hobo trying to earn some pocket money. I mulled this over for a second, feeling a sting of guilt, then texted my agency with the news that I wouldn't be returning to site tomorrow.

"This isn't just about me…." I rounded it off.

"Yeah, I completely respect your decision, mate", he replied.

But the recent events had put pay to all that. The big housebuilders had been the first to announce that they were shutting up shop, whilst many other firms proudly announced that they'd be continuing to work whilst adhering to 'safe working practices'. But that didn't tell the full story as most of their sub-contractors had hastily pulled off-site, whilst nearly all the agency staff were promptly binned. They, like me, were now busy jamming up the Universal Credit website.

This past week had changed *everything*. Now the streets were eerily quiet. Before, the Broadmead shopping district had been virtually taken over by slobbering bums. But the dramatic decline in footfall meant that they had no one to beg to and no shops from which to shoplift from as they were all closed. And there was little for them to beg for seeing as their drug supply had been severely disrupted. So their rattling bodies had swiftly scurried off.

The shop doorways had been miraculously cleared of rough sleepers and put god only knows where. The hostels and night shelters had been deemed unfit for purpose due in the crisis. So their inhabitants were marched off to 4-star hotels to be fed 3 times a day, comfortably tucked up in en-suite rooms. The free-food-merry-go-round (the vast collection of soup kitchens and soup runs where the homeless community congregated) had finally been smashed. Many have suggested that the aforementioned merely perpetuated the cycle of homelessness. Now it appeared the virus was killing that too.

But not every rough sleeper had been scooped up. Some of them just didn't want to be found whilst camping up in the woods, continuing to work cash -to-hand in the shadow economy. For the HGA crew, their game was at last up. Now that the nigh-time economy was finished, the streets were no longer paved with coke. And now that the betting shops were closed and all sporting events were cancelled, their most harmful of addictions was brought to an abrupt halt.

And then there's this vagrant who doesn't fit into any of those categories, who's still being left to his own devices. The weekend before the lockdown I put together my battle plan. One of the most pressing questions? Where to get a shower? Before, I'd showered daily after a solid workout down the 24-hour gym. But that too was closed.

"Is that going to be your hot-tub for outside, mate?" they joked as I collected the polythene plasterers' bath from the hardware store.

"Yeah, necessity is the mother of all invention", I replied then bid a hasty retreat to go and do a double run from the harbourside tap. After making up my own bathroom cubicle, I chucked 30 litres of semi boiling water into something that is normally only reserved for mixing up plaster. To my amazement, it worked a treat. Probably the best £33 I've ever spent.

The skies above were cleared of chemtrails as airlines grounded fleets and faced imminent bankruptcy, reminding me that cheap foreign travel was now a thing of the past. Going out for a walk is just depressing these days as you attempt the 2-metre distance from anybody who crosses your path, then give an apologetic smile as you walk into the road to keep your distance.

Most probably like you; I now spend most of my time stuck in and bored stiff, watching endless YouTube videos predicting the biggest economic depression ever. Well, if we do, that will once again be entirely of our own making. The inevitable global recession brought on by the health crisis will have had many 'underlying health conditions'. But that's enough of me being melancholy for the moment.

Throughout this book, my most stringent point has been that great opportunity comes out of every crisis and the battle, not just for surviving but thriving must always continue. Though this may indeed be tragic many good things have come out of this already. After all, aren't you enjoying all that cleaner, fresher air at the moment? And now we're finally reminded that we are *not* the most dominant species on the planet. For in the end, everything has a natural balance.

Printed in Great Britain
by Amazon

23689130R00179